# GROWING UP WITH THE NATION

GROWING UP WITH THE

# NATION

*To My Dear Grandnephew*
*Haris,*
*with my Very Best*
*Wishes*

*[signature]*
26.09.20

AHMAD KAMIL JAAFAR

**Marshall Cavendish**
Editions

Photographs courtesy of Ahmad Kamil Jaafar
Endpaper (front): photograph courtesy of High School Bukit Mertajam
Endpaper (back): photograph of Malay College Kuala Kangsar from http://en.wikipedia.org/
    wiki/File:Overfloor_and_Big_Tree,_Malay_ College.jpg

Published by Marshall Cavendish Editions
An imprint of Marshall Cavendish International
1 New Industrial Road, Singapore 536196

Other Marshall Cavendish Offices
Marshall Cavendish Corporation. 99 White Plains Road, Tarrytown NY 10591-9001, USA •
Marshall Cavendish International (Thailand) Co Ltd. 253 Asoke, 12th Flr, Sukhumvit 21 Road,
Klongtoey Nua, Wattana, Bangkok 10110, Thailand • Marshall Cavendish (Malaysia) Sdn Bhd,
Times Subang, Lot 46, Subang Hi-Tech Industrial Park, Batu Tiga, 40000 Shah Alam, Selangor
Darul Ehsan, Malaysia

Marshall Cavendish is a trademark of Times Publishing Limited

National Library Board, Singapore Cataloguing-in-Publication Data
Ahmad Kamil Jaafar.
Growing up with the nation / Ahmad Kamil Jaafar. – Singapore : Marshall Cavendish Eds., 2013.
p. cm.
ISBN : 978-981-4408-42-4 (cased)

1. Ahmad Kamil Jaafar. 2. Diplomats – Malaysia – Biography. 3. Malaysia – Foreign relations.
I. Title.

DS597.2
327.5950092 -- dc23      OCN827759813

Printed in Malaysia by Percetakan Jiwabaru Sdn. Bhd., No. 2, Jalan P/8, Kawasan Miel Fasa 2,
43650 Bandar Baru Bangi, Selangor, Darul Ehsan, Malaysia

*Dedicated to my father,*
*Mohamad Jaafar bin Haji Shamsuddin*
*and my mother,*
*Hajah Satariah binte Haji Abaid*
*who suffered for me and my siblings and stood by us*
*through the many lean and struggling years.*

# Contents

# Foreword

When Kamil approached me to write a short foreword for his book, I was touched and honoured to accept the challenge of writing a brief introduction for a colleague and friend whom I have long known and admired. Kamil and I went through many years of working closely together in the diplomatic world and this relationship has grown into a very close personal friendship.

It was throughout these years of working together on the bilateral, regional and international stage that Kamil displayed his many admirable traits, which have stood well through the test of time and, I would say, are the foundations of international relations. Our official and personal engagement began in 1989 when Kamil was appointed as Secretary-General of Wisma Putra, the Malaysian Ministry of Foreign Affairs, and I was the Permanent Secretary in the Ministry of Foreign Affairs of Brunei Darussalam.

Bilaterally, we collaborated to develop close and friendly Brunei Darussalam-Malaysia ties, which continue today. Regionally, we worked together in the evolution and, in some cases, creation of ASEAN institutions including the ASEAN Secretariat and the ASEAN Regional Forum (ARF), and the various ASEAN dialogue partner relations such as with Australia and New Zealand, Canada, China, the European Union, the Gulf Cooperation Council, India, Japan, the Republic of Korea, Russia and the United States.

Kamil's hard work and active efforts within ASEAN and in the wider regional and international framework should not go unnoticed. In particular, I will never forget working closely with him in our efforts to help Bosnia-Herzegovina in its time of need, where Kamil showed his humanity and care for people and his commitment to the universal principles of justice and the right to self-defence.

Throughout his career, Kamil showed a personal commitment to truth, understanding and a sense of fair play. If there was a way to describe his modus operandi in diplomacy, it would be the motto 'my word is my bond'; a phrase which he practised consistently, and a trait which is sadly missing in today's world. Kamil was indeed the epitome of a true gentleman.

This book, covering the whole span of his distinguished career and the challenges of his early childhood, has evidently been painstakingly undertaken for the narrative details of events and issues it treaded through and the clarity of thought in the way they are presented. It is not only readable, but is in fact a must for anyone seeking to be informed of the art and practice of diplomacy in a developing country (particularly in Southeast Asia). It is not just a record of memories past but also an evolving reference for the future. Indeed by the publication of this book Kamil will be leaving behind an invaluable legacy.

With best wishes to Kamil and the many fond memories of our journey in the diplomatic world and the world at large.

**Pehin Dato' Lim Jock Seng**
*Second Minister of Foreign Affairs and Trade, Brunei Darussalam*

# Preface

The life of a diplomat and foreign policy maker can be pretty much routine and humdrum during the best of times. However, there is no lack of excitements and thrills. The ever changing political world makes sure of this.

Malaysia was a relatively unknown and somewhat insignificant country apart from possessing certain strategic natural resources. But Malaysia has always been a strangely unique case among the newly independent countries partly as a result of the uneventful manner in which it joined the family of nations and also to some extent due to its heterogeneous character. It might be said, too, that, in addition to these unusual features, Malaysia stood out as something of an exception in the so-called Third World by being a former British dependency that has retained a fair amount of the colonial value system in terms of its institutions and its work ethics. Thus, for much of the period of direct confrontation between the Eastern and Western blocs, Malaysia was firmly anti-Communist as it fought the 12-year communist insurgency in the country, which strongly influenced the foreign policy in the early years. The first Prime Minister Tunku Abdul Rahman's "we will sink or swim with the West" summed up our pro-western stance in the early years after independence. Yet we were able to be as independent as possible in keeping out of entangling alliances such as the American-inspired Southeast Asia Treaty Organization (SEATO).

It must be stressed that the propensity for bucking the trend and standing on principles was evident from the early stages when people like the first Prime Minister and his cohorts deliberately chose to avoid being labelled as staunchly allied to either side in the Cold War. It was to the credit of Tun Abdul Razak, the second Prime Minister, who was responsible for the shift in our policy. Non-alignment and neutrality became important cornerstones of foreign policy. However, these hallmarks of Malaysian foreign policy were to reach their full realisation at a later date with the coming into office of Dr. Mahathir Mohamad and the sea change that was to take place in world affairs as the Cold War came to an abrupt end.

The subject of this book will be a personal, subjective account of my life and career as a diplomat. It is my intention to try to explain the decision-making process preceding the policy formulations of Malaysia's approach to a number of specific international issues as well as Malaysia's understanding of regional priorities. On several occasions, it being part of my professional responsibility, I fully participated in these processes, and was in a position to interact with and observe other personalities in their role in formulating our foreign policy.

However, it has taken a lot of learning, a lot of practice, and a lot of mistakes for me to reach the highest professional leadership of the service. In order to get an idea of my 'journey', unchartered as it were, along the path of Malaysia's foreign policy formulation and implementation, I will, in this account, start by telling about my family background, my childhood, and my schooling years, living through the period of Malay political awakening and the dark years of communist insurgency, which were as defining for me and for who I am today as they would be for anybody else.

In each of the following chapters, I will deal with, and limit myself to, matters or problems which have been either of importance to Malaysia in its foreign relations or which I have felt particularly interested in or passionate about. The chapters will follow a chronological order but will not be an exhaustive account of my life and career. Instead I hope to be able to shed more light on the events I will be focusing.

Here and there in my account there are bound to be allusions to my private life such as marriage, children, pets, hobbies, good and bad habits, health and illness, happiness and despair. I have, however, chosen not to dwell on that equally important part of my life in this story.

Being a practitioner of diplomacy, used to writing cold and dry diplomatic reports, writing this book did not come easily to me. It was about five years ago that the idea of putting on paper the story about my life and the 34-over years in the Foreign Ministry as a career diplomat came to me.

I had talked to the late Dr. Chandran Jeshurun, my childhood friend, about him helping me write my memoir. I needed his help. Being a historian, one of the finest Malaysia has had, writing someone else's memoir was of no interest to him. He was hesitant about the *doability* of such a project. But after the publication of his book *Malaysia: 50 Years of Diplomacy, 1957–2007*, he received encouraging words from Professor Ian H. Nish, of the London School of Economics and Political Science, who earlier had supervised his Ph.D. work in LSE in the late 1960s, and who then said that it would be interesting to read an account, told by one of the so-called veteran diplomats, which would show more in detail the goings-on behind the scenes. So I was told by Chandran. We decided it would be worth a try, and we agreed to work together again. Not long after having decided this Chandran died after a short illness. It was Dato' Tan Koon San, who was from the same High School as I and for many years a colleague at Wisma Putra, who pushed me to write despite the loss of Chandran and inspired me to stay the course.

My task at writing was made more difficult as I had to rely heavily on my recollections, and recollections of colleagues, and available published works and material. My own papers and speeches also became useful material. As such there may be instances of oversight as to the dates and personalities involved. For this I offer my apologies. But on the whole I have tried to tell my story as honestly and as accurately as I could.

As this book reveals, I grew up with the Ministry moving in and out of its doors for all my working life.

My early postings served as a step-by-step process of learning the ropes and provided, at the same time, a crash course for me in diplomacy. I went through a tumultuous period of our region that drove us, after the Vietnam War, to seek peaceful coexistence and to begin reconstructing peace in the region. The chapters about the region being riven by conflicts and the saga of the boat people would have relevance to shed light on the tumultuous period at the time. My involvement in setting up the Islamic Secretariat with Tunku Abdul Rahman as its first Secretary-General, the establishment of ZOPFAN (Zone of Peace Feedom and Neutrality), the birth of G-15 in Kuala Lumpur were defining moments in my career.

My involvement with Somalia, Sudan, Bosnia-Herzegovina and Kosovo where Malaysia stood up for the rights of and natural justice for the people in these countries torn apart by internal conflicts, and with Bosnia-Herzegovina and Kosovo, countries bullied by powerful forces, will be reflected in the chapters dealing with these countries.

These involvements I would term as issues beyond the bounds of normal diplomatic practice. But these stories must be told as I strongly feel that they should be part of our national memory.

By the time I returned home to assume the post of Secretary-General, having gone through, besides my early postings, ambassadorial postings in Vietnam, China and Japan, and at the UN, I was well salted and seasoned. I returned at a period of assertive and proactive Malaysian foreign policy under Prime Minister Dr. Mahathir Mohamad. As Chandran Jeshurun said in the Preface to his book *Malaysia: 50 Years of Diplomacy 1957–2007*, "No-one can question his personal integrity and high sense of patriotism in pursuing Malaysia's international goals …." It was a period during which peaceful resolutions of territorial disputes had to be found and other issues that were sensitive needed to be handled with the greatest care.

It was also a time of the strengthening and expansion of ASEAN, the establishment of the ARF (ASEAN Regional Forum), and the putting in place of ASEAN linkages with the other important organisations like ASEM and APEC. I was fortunate to have been involved in and been part of this process of fulfilling the ASEAN vision.

By the time I left the service in August 1996 I had served four prime ministers beginning with Tunku Abdul Rahman, followed by Tun Abdul Razak, Tun Hussein Onn and Tun Dr. Mahathir Mohamad. Malaysia was fortunate to have constructive, assertive and proactive leaderships that had led the country to become an important player in the business of international relations.

That is why I am saddened when I now hear, at the time of writing, disturbing stories of our diplomats' lack of professional direction. And worse, I also hear stories of a hiatus between political and professional leadership. It is, however, not for me to verify the truth of these stories.

In the past we were able to overcome some of the most intractable issues and battle demons. I am now reminded of some lines of my old school song :

> *Famous sons have sailed forth*
> *Borne their honour far and near*
> *Some have fought and conquered "dragons"*

Can our diplomats of today continue to be professionally equipped and intellectually prepared to fight and conquer 'dragons'?

It is my hope that this book will be of some use to young practitioners of diplomacy and students of international relations. My personal involvement on issues that are considered within the meaning of conventional and unconventional diplomacy will, I hope, stir the young minds in Wisma Putra to think outside the box and open themselves to the many thrills of diplomacy. I hope I have managed to capture the general essence and thrust of our foreign policy during the years I was in the Ministry. But above all I hope it will serve as a useful reference.

As mentioned earlier it was Koon San who pushed me to write and inspired me to stay the course. He was most supportive throughout and undertook editing of the manuscript and assisted in the proofreading. For this I cannot thank him enough.

I must also thank Raja Balkish bt. Raja Dato' Amir (Kay to many of us) who was with me in Wisma Putra, and was for a while my Personal Assistant when I was Secretary-General, and still assists me to this day. She has on many occasions spent long hours typing the manuscript particularly in the days when my own knowledge of how to use a PC was non-existent. I owe her a debt of gratitude. My thanks to Sharifah Shifa al-Atas for assisting me in the early stages of drafting and Helen Todd for editing the manuscript at the final stages of the project, and to Christine Chong, of Marshall Cavendish, in seeing it through successfully.

In writing this book I was greatly helped by my wife, Lena, who stood by me these many years to see the completion of the book. The many hours we spent together going through the manuscript, in as detailed a manner as possible, contributed to the fulfilment of the project. My daughter Anis and my son Tariq have made valuable comments, which I have included in the book. They have been a great help to me.

While those whom I have mentioned have given invaluable contribution towards the preparation and completion of the book the final responsibility for any omissions or inadvertent errors are mine and I take full responsibility for them.

I must thank Ambassador Paramjit S Sahai for his 'Introduction'. He was most generous in his review of the book. Last but certainly not least I must thank my good friend Pehin Dato' Lim Jock Seng, Second Minister of Foreign Affairs and Trade of Brunei Darussalam, for having readily agreed to write the Foreword. I thank him for his kind gesture. He remains a true friend.

Ahmad Kamil Jaafar
*Kuala Lumpur, 2013*

# Introduction

*Growing Up with the Nation* is both a treatise and a treat on Malaysian foreign policy as seen through the eyes of its distinguished diplomat, Tan Sri Kamil. It is a fascinating and readable book, full of depth and insight, as the author traces the formulation and implementation of Malaysia's foreign policy over a period of four decades, since its independence in 1957. True to its title, it is a story of an individual who grows personally and professionally along with the maturing process of his nation. It is equally about Malaysia attaining a high place in the world arena through successful pursuit of its foreign policy. The author notes how in Dr. Mahathir's hands 'our nation's diplomatic profile and confidence grew and mine grew with it'. His baptism through the successful holding of the Commonwealth Heads of Government Meeting (CHOGM) and the Group 15 (G-15) Summit in 1990 justified Prime Minister Mahathir's trust in his leadership of the Foreign Office.

*Growing Up with the Nation* is divided into 17 chapters, with each chapter dealing with a specific phase of the author's assignment or with a topic of importance. It is like a string of pearls, each shining on its own. It is about his formative years from childhood till he joined the Foreign Service, which in itself was a chance opening. It is about childhood spent in a multinational setting, imbibing pluralist ethos and receiving a well-rounded education through English medium. All this led to the development of his personality, 'free from religious or ethnic prejudices or divisions'. For Malaysia also, it was a tough and complex journey, meeting internal and external challenges, from the Japanese invasion in World War II, to the racial riots after the Japanese surrender, the Malay political awakening, Konfrontasi with Indonesia, the formation of Malaysia, the split of Singapore and the racial riots in 1969. Ultimately, Malaysia 'came out stronger, more self-assured, and confident of its ability to meet external challenges'.

Covering a vast canvas, the book touches not only on Malaysia's role in regional bodies like ASEAN and OIC, in whose shaping the country played an important role, but also on the intricacies of its bilateral relations with its neighbours and their common search for a way ahead. It provides a glimpse into the foreign policy agenda of its Prime Ministers, in particular of Dr. Mahathir who, with his hands-on approach, steered the country's destiny through a complex web of international relations by responding through a dynamic foreign policy and moving away from 'a knee jerk pro-western position' to a non-aligned and pro-development policy. Throughout, Malaysia espoused 'peaceful existence and the strengthening of regional ties'. It followed a policy of 'constructive diplomacy in a give and take fashion'.

On the question of the complex issue of identity, be it national or Asian, Malaysia played a role in making Asian identity become a more respectable and acceptable concept. Identity politics occupies an important place in international relations. For Malaysia, ASEAN was 'not just for regional cooperation', but also 'for regional identity'. Malaysia is now wrestling with the definition of East Asian and Asia

Pacific identity. For the author, the search for regional strategy becomes even more tightly woven into the search for regional identity'.

The roles played by Tan Sri Kamil in the 'formation' of the Organisation of Islamic Cooperation (OIC) and the strengthening of ASEAN were, according to him, defining moments in his career. He played a major part in the election of Tunku Abdul Rahman as the first Secretary-General of OIC. He worked tirelessly in building confidence within ASEAN as he laid the groundwork as it emerged from its modest beginning. He also played a delicate role in its expansion when Myanmar, Vietnam, Laos and Cambodia were admitted into ASEAN. Similarly, the handling of the boat people from Vietnam, 'became a central issue in my diplomatic career' as the author puts it. This issue is a study in itself, as a way was found between national and humanitarian interests to handle the fate of around a quarter of a million refugees. A significant stage in his diplomatic career was the opening of diplomatic relations with China and Malaysia, as it embraced the philosophy of peaceful coexistence with and equidistance to major powers.

Malaysia's involvement in Bosnia and Kosovo, which had not been in the public domain, is a riveting account of its role, in which the author, as an active participant, was taken to war zones with great risks to his personal life. It was a case of national interest getting priority over personal interest and safety.

The author, in the course of his writing makes certain private observations on the personality traits of nations and socio-economic milieus of those times. He observes that the Chinese remain beholden as they, in the words of Premier Wen Jiabao, 'do not forget what favours others have done....' The Japanese, on the other hand, displayed strong cultural traits, which bound individuals to the nation. He recounts how Dr. Mahathir wanted Malaysians to imbibe

Japanese values of 'work ethics, discipline, dedication and loyalty'. The author himself was affected by their character traits of 'respectfulness, politeness, kindness and helpfulness'. A silver lining was also attributed to the Japanese occupation as it 'destroyed for ever the myth of colonial invincibility'.

The book is about 'Diplomacy', as practised in real life, shorn of the clichés often used when discussing international relations theories. It also enriches our knowledge on various instruments of diplomatic armoury such as 'trade offs, aid strings, economic sanctions, give and take, gentleman's agreements, quiet prior leg work, tough posture, veiled threats,' etc., which were effectively used by the author on different occasions. A diplomat has to have the skills to use these selectively and in the right proportion, as the situation demands.

It throws light on the working and management of the foreign service. How ad hoc-ism prevails in postings abroad. How diplomats can be unprepared for their duties in the absence of adequate briefing and training. Tan Sri Kamil notes that 'young officers just went along with whatever was decided without further ado'. It was a case of learning the ropes on the job as the author received a 'crash course on diplomacy' at his initial posting in Bangkok. It is also about communication gaps between diplomats and others and likely conflicts of approach between career and non-career ambassadors. (Ad hoc-ism prevails in other foreign services also, as I got posted to Lusaka, as my predecessor's tooth got broken when he was hit by miscreants.) Diplomats have to learn to make the best of what comes their way, as Tan Sri Kamil did.

Throughout the book, an important issue that emerges is the need for the grooming of diplomats even though it is accepted that there is no substitute for learning on the job, as it comes through in Tan Sri

Kamil's own career. To meet this need for training of diplomats, he called for the setting up of a training institute. In 1991, the Institute of Diplomacy and Foreign Relations (IDFR) was established under the control of the Ministry of Foreign Affairs. As High Commissioner I worked closely with IDFR and we organised two seminars, one in 1997 on 'India and ASEAN' and the other on 'Nuclear Non-Proliferation' in 2000. One of these resulted in the publication of a book titled *India and ASEAN: The Growing Partnership of the 21st Century*. IDFR is doing a splendid job and can be reckoned as one of the top training establishments in the world and the author can take legitimate credit for his vision.

'Postscript' is couched in highly philosophical tones. Even though Tan Sri Kamil claims that he would try to avoid forcing Malaysia's foreign policy into any theoretical mould, be it described as 'predictive, scientific or deductive', he is not unmindful of the challenges coming from global governance, trans-nationalism, power politics versus issue politics. He unhesitatingly states that it would not be in Malaysia's national interest to 'compartmentalise our practice of diplomacy, into being Islamic and non-Islamic' as Malaysia's existence 'is founded on cultural pluralism and social justice, built upon communal tolerance and individual dignity'. Prima facie, it has to be 'based on the need 'to protect, defend and promote its national interests' while ensuring that 'communitarian and normative values form part of that world'.

The book is a mine of knowledge on Malaysia's foreign policy over a period of four decades, told in a candid and transparent manner. Through the book, Tan Sri Kamil conveys a personal message of satisfaction, as in his diplomatic career he was able 'to combine my moral quest' with the 'practice of my profession'. He could thus fulfil his urge for 'moral values', while pursuing the 'national interests' of Malaysia. It is a blend of the heart and the head, a solid work written in a dispassionate manner, but with passion from a committed and successful diplomat. I would rate it as a must read book for any diplomat or student of foreign policy on Malaysia.

**Paramjit S Sahai**
*High Commissioner of India to Malaysia 1996–2000*
*Honorary Principal Advisor, Centre for Research in Rural and Industrial Development (CRRID), India*

CHAPTER 1

# Childhood

It was during the Japanese Occupation[1], at the age of three or four, that I started being aware of things around me. I particularly remember the blaring of the siren mounted on the roof of the Survey Department not far from where we lived. It would go off to warn people of approaching Japanese aircraft. My father, with the help of my eldest sister and brother, would gather us younger ones and make a dash for a clump of rubber trees lining the front of the government quarters, called *the barracks*, where we lived. Government employees living in the vicinity, shopkeepers, moneylenders, and others would also seek refuge there. The scare happened often, but for me it was great fun, like a game of hide-and-seek.

The year was 1941, the date 8 December. The Pacific War had arrived in Malaya. News soon reached our town that Penang Island and Butterworth[2] had been bombed. Japanese forces had already landed and occupied Kota Bharu on the east coast, and were moving south through Kuantan heading for Johor. On the west coast the Japanese were advancing south from the Thai border along the main trunk road through Alor Star, Penang and Ipoh. They were to join the forces advancing from the east coast heading towards *impregnable* Singapore to complete their victory over the British, and to take control of British Malaya, and thereafter the other—French, Dutch and American—colonial possessions in Southeast Asia. This became the Greater East Asia Co-Prosperity Scheme. What it meant was control of all the natural resources of the region to feed Japan's war effort.

The two or three aircraft flying over our town were looking for military targets in and around Kulim. Luckily there were no such things there. The Civil Defence Force, in which my father and many others in the town were volunteers, had already been disbanded. The British colonial authorities had concluded that it would be of no help in the war effort. Kulim was thus spared, at least from the air. But a detachment of Japanese forces, on foot and on bicycles and motorised vehicles, took control of Kulim and established it as the administrative centre of southern Kedah.

It was at this point that my father made the decision to move his family out of Kulim. Years later my elder brother Mohamad Khir told me that my father had been vocal in his dislike of the Japanese. He had had no qualms about telling the Japanese barber in town what he thought of his countrymen. As soon as the Japanese arrived in Kulim the barber was revealed to be a member of the Japanese military intelligence, the *kempeitai*. My father considered it prudent to leave Kulim.

We went to Kampung Pasir, the home village of my maternal grandfather. Kampung Pasir is situated in the district (*mukim*) of Merbok. My grandfather was a person of some means, having acquired tracts of rubber land in the '30s when he had helped with survey work for the land office in Sungai Petani, the centrally located second largest town in Kedah. He had also large parcels of prime land in Kampung Pasir and plots of paddy fields. He agreed to host my parents and make sure that his grandchildren were out of harm's way.

For the journey to Kampung Pasir we were packed into two bullock carts and then transferred into two small river boats (*perahu*). But I also remember that it was during this journey that my mother gave birth to my brother Abbas in the house of an Indian family known to my father. My father, with the help of the friend's wife, acted as midwife, and when, after some days, it was decided that mother and child were strong enough to continue the journey we pushed on towards our final destination.

Kampung Pasir was the ideal place for a young child to grow up. I still remember how impressed I was when tens of able men from the kampong used their shoulders and sheer physical strength to lift the house that would be ours for the next three and a half years and put it down not far from my grandfather's. It was also here that I learned to ride a buffalo. After many trials I became quite good at it. I also remember life in this kampong, roaming freely with some friends but also helping my mother pound padi into rice and my father make rope from coconut husk. Although rope-making was not big business it helped us get by. But the thing I enjoyed most was going to the paddy field to catch fish. I would put my hands into the water and feel for the fish until I could catch their wriggling bodies in my hands. It was a thrilling sport for me and it also allowed me to bring home some much needed food for dinner. My grandfather had given my father a small plot of land to grow rice. So throughout those years of the Japanese occupation we were never short of rice or chicken, or vegetables that my parents planted close to the paddy fields.

It was also here that I started school. The schoolhouse was located in Merbok, about four miles of good walking from Kampung Pasir. What we were taught or what I learned during those years completely escapes my mind today. However, the one thing I cannot forget was the compulsory ritual at every morning assembly—we had to sing the Japanese anthem, the *Kimigayo*, and we had to bow to the over-sized Japanese flag, the *Hinomaro*, as it was hoisted up the flagpole.

In the final year of my university life many years later, I revisited this region. One of my subjects was archaeology and, accompanied by Professor Alistair Lamb[3] and a handful of my course mates, we went to Merbok and Bukit Batu Pahat to see the ruins of ancient Hindu temples, or *chandi*, and also to Kedah Peak or Gunung Jerai, where an ancient *chandi* sits atop the hill. The *chandi* served as a beacon for incoming ships. Merbok lies in the Bujang Valley and is one of the earliest places where the Hindus, arriving from India, set up settlements and to where they transplanted their culture and religion.

The Bujang Valley is rich in historical sites. It is an area of about 400 square kilometres in the Merbok basin bounded by Gunung Jerai and Muda Valley. Historical evidence of about 50 excavated Hindu temples points to the existence of the Bujang Kingdom that, according to historical sources, preceded the Sri Vijaya Empire. Little did I realise back then, as my family hid out from the Japanese occupation in Kampung Pasir, that I was living in the cradle of a great Hindu civilisation.[4]

In August 1945 the Pacific War ended.[5] No one was happier and more excited than my father at the news of the Japanese surrender. Some days later he took me to Sungai Petani to watch Japanese POWs being marched through town to the internment camp. I remember the townspeople throwing verbal abuses at them. It was a good time to vent their anger. This was as close as I got to the Japanese soldiers. Later that day my father took me to the cinema in town to watch documentaries on Allied victories in Europe and in the Pacific.

Soon after the Japanese surrender I became aware of the MPAJA, the Malayan People's Anti-Japanese Army, when they established their base in Merbok filling the void left by the departure of the Japanese and the late return of the British Military Administration.[6] The MPAJA came out of the jungle and took over the police stations and administrative offices of most of the small towns in the peninsular. Merbok was one of them. This was the first time I came face to face with the MPAJA. But I can only relate my own experience in Merbok and in Kampung Pasir. It was a time to exact revenge on those the MPAJA saw as Japanese collaborators. In Merbok and in adjacent towns and villages people talked about cases of collaborators being hunted down and dealt with in the harshest of brutality resulting in death. I heard of a case where one person, who today might be referred to as a Pakistani, was beaten to death by the MPAJA. I rushed to the scene but I was too late. The body had already been removed but I could see traces of blood on the ground. The townspeople and the villagers referred to the MPAJA as 'Bintang Tiga', meaning three stars, because of their flag, which had three yellow stars on a red background. Some members wore the stars on their arm bands and caps. The fact that in Merbok they were all Chinese and the collaborators mainly Malays did not help the situation and racial tension started to simmer. By then my father had moved us all back to Kulim.

My father was fortunate enough to be able to go back to his former job at the Survey Department in Kulim. After waiting a few months, living temporarily in Pondok Labu, a village which was actually my place of birth back in 1937, we were allowed to return to the government barracks in Kulim where we had lived before the war. Thanks to my grandfather, and the resourcefulness of my father and mother, our family survived the war years relatively unscathed. It was after the war that the real struggle started for my parents.

While in Kampung Pasir two more children were born—my sisters Mahani and Hamisah. Providing for this large family was already a challenge. But after the war, my parents' main concern was schooling. Before the war my elder siblings, sisters Arbaaton (the eldest in the family), Maimunah (the third child), Khiwalah (the fifth child, raised by an aunt on my mother's side) and brothers Mohamad Khir (eldest boy) and Omar (the fourth child, raised by another aunt) had been sent to religious schools, according to tradition and the wishes of my maternal grandparents. And my father had complied with this.

However, I believe the war years and the turbulent situation in Malaya after the war made him realise that a different kind of education would be needed for his younger children to compete in the changing world. I think that his own background also played a role in his determination and change of attitude.

My father originated from Deli in Sumatra where he had been brought up, not by his own parents, but by relatives who were connected to some obscure royal house in that part of Sumatra. When he was still a young teenager, he left Deli and came to Malaya to the care of his uncle, a cousin of his mother. This uncle Haji Mohamad, better known as Che Mat Deli, like my father, came from Deli. He was already well established and well connected in Sungai Petani, Kedah. Among his several passions was horse racing and on race days he would slip to Penang to satisfy his passion and all that came with it. More remarkable though is the fact that without knowing a word of English he would finally become the District Officer of Sungai Petani, a post which in the State of Kedah was usually reserved for the royal family or those connected to the royal house. But in those days English was not a requirement to join the Kedah Civil Service.

He took my father under his wing. He put him to work in the Survey Department as a *peon*.[7] He also arranged his marriage to my mother, the daughter of Haji Abaid bin Haji Abbas in whose kampong we took refuge during the Japanese occupation. My father, though not schooled in English, picked up on his own a smattering of the language during his years at the Survey Department. Even in Sumatra he had tried to learn it as he prepared himself to seek a new life in Kedah.

In his own life my father had escaped a stagnant backwater in Sumatra and the uncertainty of his own future and sought an opportunity in Malaya. After the upheaval of the war years and with the British back in Malaya there were new ideas and conflicts in the air and nothing would ever be the same. It must have seemed to him that fundamental changes were coming and he had to prepare his children to meet them.

Education for his children now meant an English education. Starting with me. It meant defying my maternal grandparents' religious and Malay conservatism and arguing against their suspicion and criticism of English schools. He got me admitted to a school in Bukit Mertajam about six miles west of Kulim. Although Kulim was a major town in the south of Kedah it did not have a reputable school. Since there was no English school at all for girls in Kulim he sent all my younger sisters to St. Margaret's Convent in Bukit Mertajam, in the British-administered colony of Penang.

Kulim itself was an important urban township in southern Kedah, with plantation and mining industries. For me, coming back to Kulim as a boy of nine, it was my first experience of life in a town. Kulim was founded by Malays in the middle of the 18th century and about 100 years later it experienced a boom when iron and tin ore were discovered in the area. This in turn brought many Chinese settlers there. When we returned the lucrative mining activities in and around Kulim had all but stopped and had been taken over by the production of rubber, a business which was dominated by large British and other foreign-owned plantation companies, with smaller Chinese-owned estates on the periphery.

We were lucky to be allotted the same government barracks where we had lived before. It was a semi-detached house raised about three feet above ground. There was a cluster of about five similar barracks in our little corner of Kulim, all identical. Each had a living room, two bedrooms, a kitchen, a bath and a separate toilet, and a fenced-in void where laundry could be hung out to dry and where odds and ends could be stacked against the wall.

How was it furnished? Well, my family had to start with the bare minimum. In the living room we had a dining table with six chairs, items my father considered useful when we did our homework under his supervision. There was a sideboard where some odd books were kept. Not many. Later, when he could afford it, he bought a radio, a British-made Bush. He was really proud of this acquisition. Like all of us in the family my parents slept on the floor, and some years later when he could afford it my father bought a simple metal bed for him and my mother. My two brothers and I slept on the floor in the same bedroom as my parents. In the other bedroom, also on the floor, the eight sisters slept. My eldest brother Mohamad Khir slept by himself in the living room. I am afraid I did not pay much attention to how the kitchen was equipped. It was probably equally basic but adequate enough to allow my mother, who was a very good cook, to prepare excellent meals on the rare occasions the budget ran to it.

Those first few years, after the war and after our return to Kulim, were the most difficult period for my parents. Three more children, my sisters Nazirah and Sakinah and brother Zubir were born. By now our family had probably the largest number of children among all the families in the barracks around us. My father's meagre salary was certainly not enough to feed and clothe so many of us. Even when combined with the small income my mother derived from the lease of the rubber land that she inherited money was often not enough for our most urgent needs.

I recall that my father lost his bicycle as a result of repossession by the *chettiar*, the Indian money lender, who had set up shop on the main road in front of our house. And on several occasions my mother had to visit the only pawn shop in town. Breakfast for us before going to school would be a slice of bread with condensed milk, and sometimes dinner would consist of one or two sweet potatoes. But it was not all gloom. There were occasions when we were thrilled to see our father come home with a trishaw full of durians or something else in season that he could afford. And before the Hari Raya celebration he would return from Penang with bales of cloth for the girls' dresses, the balance of which was turned into window curtains, and also cloth to make Malay *baju*[8] for the boys. All the cutting and sewing was done by my mother. She was also good at this, almost professional, I would say. Years later when my father could afford it he bought her a hand-operated sewing machine.

Despite the fact that my belly was sometimes empty my days were full and I was happy. There were many children in the homes around us and I had no shortage of friends. But I have to confess that sometimes with my friends I would steal a neighbour's rambutans, and on one occasion I stole a chicken to sell to get money for cinema tickets. It was here that I befriended, among others, Chandran Jeshurun. Chandran became a professor of history and distinguished himself as a scholar in regional history and international relations. It was also in Kulim that I started my love affair with badminton and football. There was a football field, the only one in town, just a short walk across the street from the house and it became a favourite hangout of mine. My eldest brother Mohamad Khir was a good football player and he started coaching me in the game. It was also he who, when I had expressed an interest in badminton, prepared a rustic badminton court just outside our house so that we could play together.

This came about after our national team, with great players like Ooi Teck Hock and Wong Peng Soon, returned home with the Thomas Cup. Malaya became the first nation to win the cup in 1948. The euphoria of winning reverberated throughout the country, and I was caught up in all of it. Despite our very tight situation, and without it ever being expressed in words, I know that my father supported all these activities and not only for his sons. Two of my sisters also became successful in sports. Maybe he understood the importance of a well-rounded education, a concept rarely discussed in Malay society in those days.

On hindsight I now realise that—while I was passionately involved in games—the nation was going through a time of political turbulence. Malay fears of British post-war intentions were exacerbated when the incoming British administration in 1946 unveiled the plan for Malayan Union, which would give equal citizenship rights to all races and remove the special position of the Malays. With unseemly haste and secrecy, the British bullied each of the Sultans into signing a document removing their sovereignty over their states and their Malay subjects. The assumption of power by the MPAJA after the Japanese surrender and their brutality galvanised a fierce Malay response that led to the resistance to the Malayan Union scheme. Malay communities organised themselves against the Malayan Union proposal and developed unprecedented links across states that led to the formation of UMNO[9] under the leadership of Dato' Onn Jaafar in May 1946. Even I, whose main passion was tearing around a football field in Kulim, was swept up in this excitement.

My brother Mohamad Khir was a staunch supporter of independence from British rule, and I still recall that he brought me along to attend an anti-Malayan Union rally. I vaguely registered that the air felt stiff with emotion and the people jostled about in united agitation. On another occasion he took me all the way to the Merdeka Bridge, which straddles the states of Kedah and Penang, to listen to Dato' Onn Jaafar, the founder of UMNO. It took the British less than a year to abandon the Malayan Union proposal in the face of this unprecedented resistance from Malays all over the country. After a series of secret talks with the Sultans and with UMNO, a committee was formed to redraft a constitution which would 'be acceptable to Malay opinion' and would lead gradually to independence.

The cooperation between the British and the Communist leaders to defeat the Japanese did not long outlast the victory parade in London. The core group within the MPAJA was the Malayan Communist Party (MCP) led by Chin Peng, and by 1948 the MCP had been directed to abandon united front tactics and launch a violent struggle for independence. The British administration declared a state of Emergency against this communist insurgency. Many of the former MPAJA guerillas dug up their guns and went back into the jungle. For people in the 'black areas'[10], where the MPAJA were strong, the early years of the Emergency were a time of turbulence and fear.

The state of Kedah, where I lived, was not declared a black area. Still, in and around Kulim, we were often reminded of the communist threat. On two occasions the police station in Kulim was under siege by the communist terrorists (CTs). Both times the British military detachment stationed in Kulim came to its rescue, and, in an effort to win the confidence of the people and to demonstrate that the government was on top of the situation, dead CTs were displayed in full view of the public. On such occasions I would make a dash for the police station. But not only CTs lost their lives. Once I rushed to the hospital to watch the unloading of bodies of the members of the Special Constabulary, created to assist police work particularly in the rubber estates that ring Kulim District. Ambushes were frequent and anyone could be a target.

Despite the declared emergency and the communist threat life in Kulim seemed to continue with a semblance of normality. The estate managers could be seen in their armour-plated vehicles heading to Kulim for a break. They usually ended up at the Kulim Club, which was open only to white members and out of bounds to locals. For the locals there were two other clubs for the Public Works Department staff and the Survey Department staff. Kulim also boasted a nine-hole golf course which was only opened to locals when the whites were not using it. It was not well maintained but still attracted players from as far as Bukit Mertajam, six miles away. And it attracted me since it gave me a chance to be a bag boy for a few cents, and ten cents[11] was big money for me in those days.

Life in Kulim ended when my father retired in 1956 from the service. He decided, for financial reasons, to move the whole family to Bukit Mertajam. Most of his children were still in primary school and the schools were in Bukit Mertajam. No more bus fares. But I was moving further away. I was 19 years old and would continue my schooling at the Malay College in Kuala Kangsar, the royal town of Perak.

### Endnotes

1    December 1941 to August 1945.

2    The town on the mainland opposite Georgetown about ten miles west of Kulim.

3    The Professor of Archaeology at the History Department, University of Malaya, then.

4    Wikipedia: The Bujang Valley or Lembah Bujang is a sprawling historical complex and has an area of approximately 224 square miles. Situated near Merbok, Kedah, between Gunung Jerai in the north and Muda River in the south, it is the richest archaeological area in Malaysia, and it existed long before neighbouring empires such as Majapahit (1200 AD) and Sri Vijaya (700 AD).

5    Japan's Emperor Hirohito announced its surrender on 15 August, 1945, ending the Pacific War. The Allied Forces took occupation of Japan on 28 August. The formal and official surrender of Japan took place on 2 September, 1945.

6   The first detachment of Allied forces landed in Penang on 3 September, 1945 and the official surrender of Japan took place on 12 September, 1945 in Singapore when Lord Louis Mountbatten, the Allied Supreme Commander, accepted the instrument of surrender.

7   An office boy or general purpose helper.

8   Outfit.

9   United Malays National Organization.

10   Black Areas were areas deemed by the security agencies to be infested with insurgents and a threat to security.

11   That was the caddy fee!

# CHAPTER 2

# School Years

*In the cold and frosty North*
*There are ancient schools we hear,*
*Famous sons have sailed forth*
*Borne their honour far and near.*
*Some have fought and conquered "dragons",*
*Others nature's secrets won.*
*Here within our sun-kissed province*
*Deeds are waiting to be done.*

One of the deeds waiting for Mr. Edgar de la Mothe Stowell, who wrote this song, was the founding of High School Bukit Mertajam, the first government school in Province Wellesley.[12] He was the first Headmaster when the school opened in 1927, and the lyrics are part of the school song. It was closed during the Japanese occupation, from 1941 to 1945, and thus in early 1946, at the age of nine, it was possible for me to start my schooling there in Primary One. I got no credit for the few years I had spent in the Malay school in Kampung Pasir and as a result was among one of the older boys in the class. I was two years older than most of my peers whose schooling had not been disrupted by the

Japanese occupation and I had to start afresh from Primary One. The same fate applied to quite a few of my classmates but this bore no stigma at all. As Mr. Swan, the Headmaster, put it, "All the boys who were keen to pick up the broken threads of their education again were enrolled, irrespective of their age. The High School spirit had revived and the school flourished again…"[13]

The major difference from the kampong school was that English was the medium used in all subjects and in all extra-curricular activities—until my last two years when a few hours a week of Malay language were included in the syllabus. I spoke no English at all at that point. I still remember the drills we had to go through, moving all muscles in our faces so that we could pronounce the new sounds. But at that age we learned quickly, and guided by very dedicated and stimulating teachers a new exciting world opened up to us.

This was the school my father had chosen for me. Both my parents had agreed that in the realities of the country at that time all their children of school-going age should go to English-medium schools. My eldest brother Mohamad Khir had gone to an Arabic school in Penang after which he had to start working as my father lacked the means to send him to the Muslim College in Kuala Kangsar. My two elder sisters Arbaaton and Maimunah went to a Malay-medium school in Kulim. My brother managed to teach himself English but the two elder sisters have always regretted not having the chance to learn the language.

However, my parents had to face the opposition of my maternal grandmother, a very religious lady, and try to assuage her fears that her grandchildren would not become proper Muslims if they were exposed to foreign schooling. High School Bukit Mertajam was sensitive to such feelings and decided not to include (Christian) religious classes in the syllabus. However, all my six younger sisters, who were sent to

St. Margaret's Convent, had to participate for a while in catechism. My sisters, like all the other girls, had no choice but to attend these classes, until it was decided that Muslim girls need not attend. My father involved himself very actively in our schooling especially that of the girls. He even got himself appointed to the School Board of Directors and often found himself at loggerheads with the nuns, who were teachers in the Convent, particularly over the need for Muslim girls to be subjected to catechism classes.

High School Bukit Mertajam, or HSBM for short, was the first government school in Province Wellesley. Its founder and first Headmaster Mr. Edgar de la Mothe Stowell sought to create a replica of the famous Sedbergh Public School in Cumbria, England, which he himself attended, a school known for its stringent discipline. I am sure that fact appealed to my father, who also was quite the disciplinarian and tougher than any of our teachers! I can remember many days at home spent at the table, not enjoying a good meal but struggling to commit multiplication tables to memory, with my father standing over us. We would have preferred any one of our teachers.

The purpose of the English-medium schools established in Malaya by the British was to educate a corps of civil servants who could be employed to serve and support the British administration and the British commercial houses. The British system, which included the fostering of ethical values, was something that found acceptance among the Malays, who also valued discipline and a respect for traditional values. For me this turned out to be an environment where I thrived along with my schoolmates.

The school itself sits on a hilltop close to the railway station. Bukit Mertajam is in fact a railway town, being the junction of the major railway lines to the north and south. The town was populated by Chinese,

Indians and Ceylonese (Sri Lankans), who were mainly engaged in running the Malayan Railway, while Malays were more numerous in the surrounding rice-growing areas. Our rivals in other Penang schools used to call HSBM students 'Hill-Side Black Monkeys'. While the nickname stuck, we were no hillbillies when it came to sports and games—we *monkeys* certainly knew how to go after the trophies!

A school day for me, as for many other kids from Kulim, began very early in order to catch the bus to Bukit Mertajam. It was too far to walk. Upon returning by bus from primary school, there would be time only for a quick lunch before I had to take off again, this time for religious instruction. These classes took place in Kulim, but I was already tired from schoolwork and travelling and did not much like them. We were taught recitation of the Qur'an and other religious fundamentals and as far as I can remember it was mainly rote learning. I had to attend these classes almost throughout my primary school years. In secondary school, school work and extra-curricular activities became too demanding for me to continue my religious classes.

As far as my school results were concerned I managed to be placed in the top ten of all my classes throughout most of my 11 years in the school. But towards the end of the Fourth and Fifth Forms the competition from other students became stiffer and I got more and more distracted by sports.

The school system required that each student participate in at least one extra-curricular activity. I first chose gardening from the many choices and later also joined the Red Cross Society. At the same time I was intensely involved in football and rugby and furthermore managed to join the school Cadet Corps, despite my father's disapproval—anything that smacked of military training would make his hackles rise.

It was one of my teachers who introduced me to what the Red Cross

Society stood for. I was immediately attracted by the possibility of being able to help and to render first aid to those who needed it, and it also made me proud to be part of the larger British Red Cross community. It is still a mystery to me why this same teacher selected me to go to Penang for an interview, the purpose of which was to select two local representatives to a gathering of the Australian Red Cross Societies in Melbourne.

No interview since has ever felt more important to me than that one. One of the questions I was asked was what hobbies I had and could I tell a bit about them. 'Hobbies' was a pretty arcane idea to a boy from Kulim—we did not have the time or the money. "Aero-modelling," was my smart reply and I proceeded to tell them all about it. Of course, this was stolen goods. One of my teachers sometimes invited me and a friend of mine to help with *his* hobby, which was aero-modelling, gluing and pasting the tiny parts. Nobody called my bluff, and, together with another boy from Kuala Lumpur,[14] I was chosen to represent Malaya at the Australian gathering. About a week later my teacher, responsible for the school Red Cross activities, came all the way to my house to tell my father that I had been selected and, with his permission, would travel to Australia. It was an immensely proud moment for us all.

My 'career' in the Cadet Corps was not as illustrious. After about a year I managed to have two stripes stitched onto my sleeves which meant that I had become a corporal. As such I was entrusted one day to take charge of the drill. Of course, here, too, I had a role model. It was the police officer who had been training us, and whose colourful language fascinated me. "Stand straight! Even my grandmother can stand straighter than you fellows!" I barked at the top of my voice at the platoon, using the same words which had so often been thrown at us. Of course, I knew, as well as my fellow cadets, where they came from and first I, and then all of us, cracked up laughing. Little did I know that the cadet teacher was standing nearby. I do not think that I managed to explain to my poor dear mother why she had to unstitch one of the stripes which, not long ago, she had taken such trouble to stitch on!

My first encounter with the game of football was a day in my ninth grade, Form Three, when I was asked to stand in as a goalkeeper for my house team, the Cheeseman House. I was just idling along the side of the football pitch when the teacher noticed me and pulled me over to keep goal. I complied. On that occasion I let in four goals. The games teacher was hopping mad at my performance. He vowed I would never play in that game, or any game, again. "You have no sporting talent at all," he told me. This was a serious and brutal blow to my ego.

I decided to prove a point. I would not be a defeatist. I told my father what had happened and how much I really wanted to give it a try. He must have sensed my determination for, at the end of that month when he had received his salary, he took me to Penang to have a pair of football boots made for me. In those days you could not buy them off the shelf. There were none. I also got help and encouragement from my eldest brother Mohamad Khir, who was already playing for the state. Football and soon after rugby became my favourite sports.

I ended up being appointed the school football captain and, with another friend M. Kupan, who later played for the national team, was selected to play for the Penang combined school team. My greatest ambition was to play for the state. And I had that career all mapped out. I had gained admission to Penang Free School, one of the earliest and best regarded schools in Malaya, and hoped to continue playing for Penang and eventually get into the state team.

However, fate and politics thwarted my plans. On 1 January, 1957 Georgetown, Penang was conferred city status. There was no euphoria. Many Penangites did not want to be part of the Federation of Malaya.

There was even some talk of seceding and creating an independent island state. I, together with some friends, happened to be in Georgetown on that New Year's Day when some took their unhappiness to the streets. We could actually feel the tension between the Malays and the Chinese to the point that we quickly decided to return to the mainland. The disturbances did not develop into riots; still, to be on the safe side, the Penang Free School closed for about a month. A couple of weeks after our outing to Georgetown I received a letter from the Penang Education Department informing me that I had been redirected to the Malay College in Kuala Kangsar, Perak, where I would spend two years to complete my A-levels education.

I must have been the unhappiest new boy heading to this elite school as my father and I travelled by train from Bukit Mertajam to Kuala Kangsar and then walked the short distance from the railway station. He produced me to the Headmaster J.D.R. Howell. But as we walked through this beautiful school, built in pseudo Greco-Roman style, I started to feel proud of it. The main school house, the Big School, was flanked by two recently added wings which were the dormitories for the boys. In front of the Big School was, and is until today, a magnificent rugby field. Next to it was the football field, flanked by the hockey pitch. That immediately made things right for me. And casting its benevolent long shadow across the rugby green was the loveliest rain tree I had ever set eyes on, with its large branches stretched out magnificently over the fields. It stood, and will hopefully still stand for a long time to come, outside the East Wing of the College.

It was easy for me to adjust to my new school and the new environment, even though it was my first experience at being a boarder. But then it was not just any boarding school, having been built in the early 20th century and meant exclusively for royals and elite Malays.

Some even referred to it as the Eton of the East.[15]

It was also the first time I was in an environment where all pupils were of one race and one religion. The school admitted as boarders Malay boys as young as 12 years old and gave them an English Public School education. The medium of instruction was English and the major subjects were from the regular English curriculum, except in the lower grades leading up to O-levels. There the mandatory *foreign* language was Malay and there was a test in Koranic studies. But I, like many other pupils, had arrived here from other schools to finish our A-levels and the curriculum for us was entirely British. It was easy to make friends and I bonded in a special way with Razali Ismail and Sallehuddin Alang, who arrived a couple of weeks after me, and also with Dalil Awin and Khalil Yaacob who both were already long-term pupils at the school. The five of us became a close-knit *gang* and remain until today in touch and very dear friends. Razali joined the Foreign Service at the same time as me and rose to be Malaysia's Permanent Representative to the United Nations. He was elected President of the UN General Assembly in 1996. Sallehuddin had a most adventurous and colourful life. Having failed to complete his studies in Ireland he joined the French intelligence service and was seconded to the French Foreign Legion serving in North Africa. He died of a massive stroke after his return to Malaysia. Dalil did not complete his studies at the University of Malaya in Singapore but ended up as a senior executive of Motorola in Kuala Lumpur. He died in 2011. Khalil gave up his diplomatic career midway and went into politics. He held several ministerial posts and is presently the Governor of Melaka.

Dalil and Khalil were appointed prefects because by then they were seniors and were good students and natural leaders. Razali, Sallehuddin and I were made prefects after about three months into the semester, perhaps because we had been prefects at our old schools. As prefects we were put in charge of the dormitory where we took turns to be on duty. Every Friday afternoon it became our duty to accompany the boys to the mosque located next door to the school. Once that duty was done, we could, as it was also our day off, slip out for a quick treat in town.

Sunday was our day out, and the gang would troop to town for lunch and also to watch movies at one of the two cinemas in Kuala Kangsar. One of our duties was to collect laundry money from the boys in our dormitory at the beginning of each month. But before we handed the collection to Ah Cheng, who ran the laundry service, we would use part of it for a boyish fling in Ipoh. In a rented car we would drive down to Ipoh. Razali was the only one among us with a driving licence. The balance would be handed over to Ah Cheng with a promise that we would make good the shortfall when we received our allowance.

When on duty we would have dinner with the duty master of the day at the high table which served food of more variety and taste than the tables on the floor. Dinner was followed by prep, which meant going back to classes until 9.30 p.m., giving us just enough time to get ourselves ready before lights-out. There were occasions when the pangs of hunger would take us downstairs to forage for any kind of snack or to ransack the kitchen store. And sometimes we would sneak out after lights-out and enjoy fried *mee* (yellow wheat noodles) or *char kway teow* (fried flat rice noodles) or the famous Kuala Kangsar *pao* (dumpling with a stuffing of meat or mashed beans) at the nearby stalls.

Anthony Burgess was one of the teachers at MCKK from 1956 to 1957. He was known to us as Mr. Jack Wilson and was a most colourful personality. His tempestuous relationship with his wife was widely known to the staff and the senior boys of the school. He was not a teacher of any of my subjects but since he lived on the school grounds we were all very aware of his eccentricities.[16]

On 31 August, 1957 Malaya became an independent state. One might have expected that this would be regarded as a particularly important day for us at the College. But it passed by like most others. We were informed about the important event. There was a ceremony to raise the new flag of the Federation of Malaya and we sang the newly introduced national anthem at the school assembly. This was not difficult as the melody was close to the Perak State anthem. But there were no congratulatory and certainly no political speeches; maybe understandably so as the College was essentially a British institution with scores of British and Anglophile teachers in charge of an equally Anglophile curriculum.

Most of Malaya's post-independence leaders received their education at this College and in this environment. Nobody ever doubted their nationalism and national pride, but it must have flowered after they left the College. The British educators certainly deserve our admiration and respect for moulding these leaders.

Life at MCKK left me with many fond memories. It was a very happy period of my life despite the fact that my visions of glory as goalie for Penang State were dashed. I was hoping to continue to keep goal for the first team at MCKK. This was not to be since the school head boy was both the captain of the team and its goalkeeper. This was Malik Salleh who played for the north Perak combined school team when I was playing for the Penang combined school team. I first met Malik Salleh while still at HSBM when we met on a football pitch playing against each other.

Having been relegated to the second team at MCKK I put my whole effort into rugby, winning the school rugby colours at the end of my stay there. At that time rugby had just been reintroduced to MCKK by our history teacher N.J. Ryan, who became headmaster of the school from 1959 to 1965. He literally put MCKK on the rugby map of the country.

The two years at MCKK passed by very quickly and it was time for me to think seriously about my life as a grown-up. I had high hopes of getting a scholarship to go to England—with all that British-style education in my pocket, England was to me the ultimate in education— but the scholarship I was granted was to the University of Malaya, so that was where I went.

I went to the University of Malaya (UM) with much youthful enthusiasm and great expectations. UM had its genesis way back in 1905 from the establishment of the King Edward VII College of Medicine[17] and Raffles College[18] in Singapore in 1928. These two tertiary institutions were merged to form the University of Malaya (in Singapore) in 1949.[19] Two years after independence, in 1959, the university was divided into two campuses, one to remain in Singapore, the other one to be established in Kuala Lumpur.

It was to this brand new and not quite completed Kuala Lumpur campus that I, together with Razali, Dalil and Khalil, arrived to begin our tertiary education. Like MCKK the setting for the campus was impressive. It was a huge area of pristine rolling hills. Down in a small valley was a lake into which a river flowed. Surrounding the lake were the buildings for the Engineering Faculty, the Arts Faculty, the Science Faculty and the Agricultural Faculty as well as the Library. There were only about 200 of us in this very first batch of students. We were housed in the only residential college, called the First Residential College, which was a mixed college with girls occupying one wing and boys the other two wings. There were so few of us that we quickly got to know each other by first names. We were also a happy group free from religious or ethnic prejudices and divisions.

The gang spent the first week settling down and choosing the subjects that we wanted to study. Having done English Literature, History and Geography at principal level, and Malay Studies at subsidiary level in my matriculation examination in MCKK, I wanted to continue studying the same subjects—except for Malay Studies. I was accepted to all three departments, but when I saw the reading list for English Literature I quickly opted out and took Islamic Studies instead. I had no idea what the course was all about or how it would develop.

The first year was a serious year for all of us. The results would determine whether we would be placed in the honours stream or in the general stream, which in turn would have an important influence on our professional and financial futures. Even I worked hard. It paid off and I could then choose to do either honours in History or in Islamic Studies. I chose History, a subject close to my heart and one I was comfortable with.

However, being serious about my studies during the first year did not prevent me from also spending time on the fields playing football and rugby. Here at UM I was once again keeping goal and for three consecutive years I was elected captain of the university football team. My greatest thrill came at the 7th Inter-Varsity Biennial Games of 1960 when I was elected to represent the combined team made up of players from the three universities of Malaya, Singapore and Hong Kong. That was a very proud moment for me.

The non-sporting activities in which I found myself involved in would sometimes be the kind that would get me into trouble—like the 'panty-raid' on the ladies wing of the First College. Of course I was quickly identified, betrayed by my outstanding height! There was talk of expulsion, but the masters of the residential college were an understanding and broad-minded lot. We were forgiven but not until we agreed to make a humbling public apology to the girls.

There were also times after a night out at Poon's Bar, in the adjoining old town of Petaling Jaya, when we would struggle to return to campus and just about manage, with the help of those more sober, to reach our beds. On such occasions Errol Foenander would be the most boisterous and noisy. I had met Errol at one of the social evenings organised by the Students' Union. He was properly drunk on that evening and got himself into a fight with the band boys. We in the gang struggled to separate the fighting young men and were helped by another student, Michael Matupang.

That evening was our first proper introduction to Errol and Michael. Errol Foenander was from Pahang and of mixed parentage, according to him a mix of English, Dutch and Burmese. Michael Matupang was from Kelantan, a Batak whose parents had moved there from Sumatra. The Gang of Five had become the Gang of Four when Sallehuddin left for Ireland to continue his studies there. And now with Michael and Errol it became the Gang of Six.

Having been slotted into the honours stream for the second and third year, with exams only at the end of the course, I found that I had a lot of time on my hands. I was not about to use it in the Library. I went full throttle into my sporting activities; I even got myself elected General Secretary of the University Athletic Union. This was a very pleasant period of my student life; time went by very fast and suddenly my final and thus most crucial year had arrived. I realised too late that I had spent more time playing than studying for the final exams.

I went through a miserable period after the exams, fearing I must have done badly. Finally, I screwed up my courage and asked to see Anthony Short, my European history lecturer, before the results were announced. Anthony Short had, at my invitation, been the coach of the university rugby team, and I had on several occasions invited him to be part of the team. Rugby was his passion and he was pleased to be included. I hoped he would be kind to me.

I entered his office. To this day I can hear his words. "You have flunked your exams!" Then he looked up at me and continued, "Since you have been active on the sports field I have recommended to Professor John Bastin[20] that you be given a third class honours. Now go out and get yourself a job!"

Over the years I have never forgotten his benevolence. We became good friends and when he came to Bangkok to do some research work at the Chulalongkorn University during my time in Thailand he stayed with me for a good two weeks.

*Aut Coepisse Noli Aut Confice.*[21] Accomplish Or Do Not Begin. I had begun and I had accomplished… but only by the skin of my teeth!

It was the early 1960s… and I was thrust into the world of working adults.

## Endnotes

12  The narrow stretch of rectangular territory across the Island of Penang that is now known as Seberang Perai. Its original name Province Wellesley was named after Richard Wellesley, then Governor of Madras and Governor-General of Bengal (1797–1805). Penang was part of the British East India Company territory under British Bengal then. This territory was originally part of the State of Kedah but ceded in perpetuity to the British East India Company in 1798 for an annual sum of 10,000 Straits Dollars which the State of Penang still pays to Kedah (now Ringgit Malaysia 10,000).

13  En.wikipedia.org/wiki/Bukit Mertajam High School.

14  Ang Seng Kiat.

15  After Eton College, the renowned British public school founded in 1440.

16  John Burgess Wilson (25 February, 1917–22 November, 1993)—who published under the pen name Anthony Burgess—was an English author, poet, playwright, composer, linguist, translator and critic.

17  Notes from National Library of Singapore: The King Edward VII College of Medicine was established in 1905 as the Straits and Federated Malay States Government Medical School. It was renamed the King Edward VII Medical School in 1913, and then the King Edward VII College of Medicine in 1921.

18  Notes from National Library of Singapore: Raffles College was set up at 469 Bukit Timah Road in 1928 as a college for higher education in the arts and sciences. The establishment of Raffles College was the result of a scheme to commemorate the centenary of the founding of Singapore by Sir Stamford Raffles.

19  Notes from National Library of Singapore: In 1949, King Edward VII College of Medicine and Raffles College merged to become the University of Malaya, and the medical school became the Faculty of Medicine. The university split in 1959 to form the University of Malaya in Kuala Lumpur, and its counterpart, the University of Malaya in Singapore.

20  Professor John Bastin was the Head of the Department of History.

21  Motto of High School Bukit Mertajam.

# CHAPTER 3

# Baptism of Fire

*We offer our youth, To the world we build,*
*With courage and truth, And love fulfilled,*
*Proudly we'll serve, And with faith we'll strain,*
*Muscle and nerve, And heart and brain,*
*Till wisdom descends, Like a silver dove,*
*Till evil ends, And the law is love.*

*Anthony Burgess'* Ode to the Malay College

The 1960s was a convulsive period for the country. It was just at the dawn of Independence and the new country was grappling with external threats as well as the continuing communist insurgency. Britain's decision to withdraw from East of Suez and the escalation of the war in Vietnam shook the region. Konfrontasi by Indonesia was a direct threat to the country.

Malaya was thrown into the deep sea of international politics by these regional developments. The price of independence was having to guard its national security and hold the country together through its own efforts and with its own resources. The juggling of relations with super powers and neighbours was of utmost importance and necessitated great skill.

The nation's very survival was at stake following the historic formation of Malaysia in 1963. This was something that was violently opposed by Indonesia, which was demonstrated by their launching armed incursions into Sarawak and Sabah. Konfrontasi by Indonesia tested the country's resilience to its core. There was also the deep political schism that hightened racial tension between the political leadership of Malaysia and Singapore and culminated in the separation of Singapore from the newly enlarged federation on 9 August, 1965. Konfrontasi also ended shortly thereafter. The peace treaty between Malaysia and Indonesia ending Konfrontasi was signed on 11 August, 1966.

Then in the wake of Britain's announcement in 1967 of its intention to withdraw East of Suez, the Five Power Defence Arrangements[22] were set up as a framework to safeguard the security and national integrity of Malaysia (and Singapore). The Vietnam War also finally ended in April 1975. Malaysia emerged from these external threats and turmoils more self-assured and confident of its ability to meet external challenges.

Meanwhile within the country the communists shifted tactics to fomenting urban unrest which sharpened political and racial divisions. The decade ended with the 13 May, 1969 race riots that brought the country to its lowest point yet, and shattered much of its efforts at nation building. Answers had to be found to save the country from chaos. But the problems were not totally solved, and the underlying discontent continued to have a divisive impact on the country.

It was against this tumultuous background that a young man, who was always more interested in football and rugby than politics, found a career in the Foreign Service. I got there in a roundabout fashion. I had first applied to join the Police Force. My motive was not borne of any altruistic desire to fight the communist menace, or to combat evil and bust lawbreakers. I just wanted to continue playing sports.

I was called for the interview, I was accepted, and was then told that I would have to serve a probationary period of three years during which time recruits would not be allowed to get married. That forced me to step back. While at university I had already made plans to get married to Zil, who became the mother of my two children Anis and Tariq. I quickly abandoned my plans to join the Police Force. Nobody was more relieved than my father and I, myself, have never regretted that decision.

Soon after the final results came out I had also applied to join the Malaysian Civil Service, the MCS.[23] My application to this highly regarded service was successful and I was posted to the Ministry of Agriculture and Cooperatives. I soon found my day-to-day tasks tedious, having to deal for the most part with answering letters from farmers and deciphering their handwritten Jawi script.

One of my gang Razali Ismail, who was already working in the Ministry of External Affairs,[24] talked me into applying to join that service. And so I did, and was delighted when I was offered a position.

The Ministry of External Affairs, as it was known then, was a wholly different service from the Malaysian Civil Service. It was a fledgling service and we were all new recruits with only the vaguest notion of what we might have to do—except that we hoped to be sent abroad.

The Ministry of External Affairs was then housed in the Sultan Abdul Samad Building, commonly referred to as the Selangor State Secretariat Building. It occupied two floors in one corner of this huge building and consisted of an open office and a *restricted*[25] office in which all the confidential work was done. The Prime Minister, Tunku Abdul Rahman Putra, was then also concurrently the Foreign Minister. Professionally the Ministry was headed by the the Permanent Secretary, the redoubtable Tan Sri Ghazali Shafie,[26] affectionately referred to as King Ghaz, with Tengku Ngah Mohammed[27] as his deputy. This meant that foreign policy formulation and execution was largely the product of the interaction between the Tunku and King Ghaz, the two working closely together to direct the foreign policy of the nation.[28]

Compared to the Ministry of Agriculture, the Ministry of External Affairs was a small world with not more than a dozen diplomatic officers attached to a few divisions—political and information, consular and immigration, administration and financial, and protocol.

I liked the work and quickly set about familiarising myself with the work culture and practices. It is generally recognised that the early batches of the Malaysian Foreign Service were the product of Tan Sri Ghazali Shafie's moulding. His aggressive and inquisitive style, coupled with his quick temper, put a fear in our young hearts. Those who survived the full blast of his temper when things went wrong were later transformed into a dedicated and professional core of officers that would serve the country well right into the 21st century. Tan Sri Ghazali Shafie made great demands on us all and once you learned to face the challenge you began to appreciate and value his style of on-the-spot training, even when it felt like a whipping. Yes, he whipped us into shape. Those who could not take it left.

But one never learns quickly enough. One fine morning I was summoned to his office. Presenting myself like a schoolboy waiting to be disciplined, I was instructed to draft a 'minute' to the Prime Minister regarding an overflight by a Russian military aircraft. The Ministry had received a request from the Soviet Union and I was to draft a recommendation to allow for the overflight. I had been in the Ministry for only a month or so and it was the first time I had heard of a 'minute'. After being told by a senior colleague what a 'minute' was, I drafted the recommendation as instructed. On my own I added that the Soviet aircraft should be tracked and its flight monitored by our air force. I was quite pleased with myself. I brought the file containing the draft 'minute' to Tan Sri Ghazali Shafie and the next instant the file came flying back at me. "What air force?" he shouted. I quickly realised that we had plenty of airspace but no air force.[29]

I had some other minor brushes with him, but the one that caught me shivering in my pants was when I returned one day to the Ministry after a lunch of rice on banana leaf at the Ceylon Restaurant at Jalan Melayu. The door to my room was locked and the guard who was posted along the corridor outside pointed upwards towards Tan Sri Ghazali Shafie's room when I asked him for the key. I meekly went up to retrieve my key.

Of course, the key came flying back at me. More shouting, only this time it was about security of the room and the confidential matters lying on my desk. I still remember that I was writing a cabinet information paper on the Kurdish uprising in Iraq. The next morning at the 'morning prayers'[30] I was banished to the police training depot at Jalan Gurney to be trained in security. I was there for close to ten days. Upon my return I had to account in detail what I had learned.

That is how I began my diplomatic education. But it was the incident at the Blue Boy Mansion that decided how soon I was to leave on my first foreign posting. It happened very suddenly—and it was not a reward.

It was the evening of Chap Goh Mei, the 15th day of the first month (full moon) of the Chinese New Year. There were four of us, Dalil, Errol, Razali and I, trying to finish off what the little fridge in the flat could offer us to drink, which was not much. The flat was rented by Razali and me and two others who were not with us that night. It was on the sixth floor of an apartment complex called, strangely, the

Blue Boy Mansion. In 1962, it was an upmarket apartment complex located in an almost totally Chinese area. Situated at the junction of Jalan Pudu and Jalan Bukit Bintang, our 'mansion' was flanked on the northwest by Tung Shin Hospital and the Chinese Maternity Hospital, and on the other side by the Pavillion Cinema, which screened only Chinese movies. Further up on Jalan Bukit Bintang was the Federal Hotel, built purposely for the dignitaries, so we were told, who came to attend the celebrations of Malaya's independence in 1957. Adjacent to the hotel was the Bukit Bintang Amusement Park, commonly known as BB Park. It belonged to the same owner as the Federal Hotel. Not far, but further up on Jalan Pudu, stood a row of Chinese shop houses, emblazoned with the bold words Rumah Tumpangan—guesthouses for the flesh trade.

The crackling of firecrackers broke the silence of the night, sending a cacophony of intense and unbridled noise into the air as if there was a competition between the shops. Having nothing more to drink at home the four of us filed out of the flat heading straight for BB Park. We might as well join the fun and be part of the Chap Goh Mei celebrations. It was well past midnight when we struggled home, exhausted after a night of merriment. Each one of us had a packet of fried *mee* or *char kway teow* clutched in our hands looking forward to enjoying a late supper. Now that the celebrations were over everything was peaceful again. Or so it seemed.

Closer to home we suddenly noticed that, instead of firecrackers, mechanical lights were flashing from several fire engines in the grounds of our Blue Boy Mansion. There were firefighters ready to deal with some fire somewhere nearby, we thought. We had no idea where it was and in our state of near exhaustion and dizziness we could not have cared less.

We took the lift[31] up to our sixth floor and, opening the door of our flat, got the shock of our lives. The fire was in our flat! Wide awake now, we threw some of the burning furniture out from the balcony and pulled the rest into the only bathroom in the flat and got the shower running full blast. Feeling pretty pleased with the way we had dealt with the problem we settled down to tackle our still warmish food packages. Then came a loud knock on the door. I got up to open it and there, glaring menacingly at me, was the Fire Chief backed by several of his firefighters. "Where is your warrant?" I demanded. "You can't come in here without a warrant."

The next morning we were told to report to the Campbell Road (now Dang Wangi) Police Station. We were told to write a full report of the incident. Only Razali and I were involved—Dalil and Errol were not required to since they had been our guests and both of them quickly made a dash back to Singapore where they were studying.[32]

This was my first serious brush with the law. I had obstructed a fire officer in his duties, which was a criminal offence. Our status as officers in the Foreign Service saved the day. The Deputy Public Prosecutor (DPP) from the Attorney General's Chambers reported us to Tan Sri Ghazali Shafie. The DPP recommended that to save our skins both of us be immediately posted out of the country. The DPP was Harun Hashim[33] who became a distinguished judge later in his career.

Razali was posted to India and I to Thailand.

**Endnotes**

22   Wikipedia: The Five Power Defence Arrangements (FPDA) are a series of defence relationships established through bilateral agreements between the United Kingdom, Australia, New Zealand, Malaysia and Singapore signed in 1971, whereby the five states will consult each other in the event of external aggression or threat of attack against Peninsular Malaysia (East Malaysia is not included under the FPDA) or Singapore.

23   The Malaysian Civil Service was later renamed Perkhidmatan Tadbir dan Diplomatik (PTD) in Bahasa Malaysia (the literal translation is Administrative and Diplomatic Service).

24  As the Foreign Ministry was initially called.

25  Access to this area was only for officers who had received security clearance from the Central Security Agency.

26  After his retirement, he was conferred the title Tun.

27  A senior career diplomat who served until his retirement in the late 1980s.

28  Chandran Jeshurun, *Malaysia: Fifty Years of Diplomacy 1957–2007*, Petaling Jaya, The Other Press, 2007, p. 4.

29  Or rather we did have an air force, but the only planes were *burung pipits*—one- and two-seater trainer planes!

30  Daily morning house-keeping meeting of senior officers.

31  Yes, lift despite the fire hazard!

32  They were not allowed to continue at the University in Kuala Lumpur because of poor results in their First Year examination. They were admitted to the Law Faculty in the University in Singapore.

33  He was later conferred the title Tan Sri. He retired as a Judge of the Supreme Court.

# CHAPTER 4

# Early Postings

## Bangkok, City of Angels

I was sent on my first posting in 1962, landing in Bangkok on 5 August to serve abroad for the first time. I had asked to be sent there because my marriage plans were imminent and I preferred to be close to home. My request was granted. Without much briefing, I was instructed to read whatever I could find to inform myself about Thailand, and off I went. I was told that the Ambassador would brief me further. There was no briefing by the Ambassador. As was the case in those days, young officers just went along with whatever was decided without further ado.

In those days in the '60s Bangkok was far smarter and more developed than Kuala Lumpur. Having flown out from Kuala Lumpur Airport in Sungai Besi I could not but be impressed by the sheer size of Don Muang International Airport and how busy it was. My attention was further drawn to the almost unbroken *klongs*[34] hugging the highway on both sides. These *klongs* formed a network crisscrossing this huge metropolis. It was this system of *klongs* that made the Thais proudly call Bangkok 'the Venice of the East'. In the early days they were the main means of transportation and were joined to the bustling Chao Phraya River. Later, when I was able to tour the city during weekends and public holidays I was even more struck by the sheer size of this capital, as well as by the Grand Palace, the Temple of the Emerald Buddha, and many other monuments of national pride. I was like a kampong boy who had wandered into a land full of excitement and bewildering wonders. This was the city of angels, the regal Krung Thep Maha Nakhon,[35] a name that King Rama III had granted his new capital.

The general culture and embracing friendliness of the Thais filled me with admiration for the people. When my son was born in Bangkok I was pleased when his Thai godfather gave him a Thai name, a name which in later years was dropped, much to my son's great relief.

Although I was representing a newly-independent country in a neighbouring state with whom we had historically enjoyed special[36] relations, at the time I did not have any convictions about what I was representing to the world nor how I wanted the world to see me. None of us did. My work was straightforward—I did information and media work, like showing movies on Malaya to the Thais. It was a step-by-step learning process on how to represent and promote my country, and there was nothing elaborate or remarkable about it.

Thus my first posting to Thailand slowly opened my eyes to what diplomacy really means. Being a diplomat, I learned, was first of all to be observed as a representative of one's country and only in second place as an individual. As a representative of my country I was to be aware of the politics of the host country as well as the general situation in the region and how they related to my own country.

At that time things were happening in the region, which were quite disturbing. The Philippines began the year 1963 by calling for the 'restoration' of Sabah, then known as British North Borneo, citing historical links to the Sultanate of Sulu. Meanwhile, by July of 1963 President Sukarno was screaming from his pulpit, with his Foreign

Minister Subandrio in full support, that the soon-to-be formed Malaysia was a British neo-imperialist plot and should be "chewed up and spat out" (*ganyang* Malaysia).

The formation of Malaysia, comprising Singapore, Sabah and Sarawak, directly clashed with Sukarno's ambition for a greater Indonesia, Indonesia Raya, comprising all the Malay lands. It was easy to see why Tun Dr. Ismail Abdul Rahman referred to Sukarno as the *Führer* of Jakarta.[37] While the Philippines' claim hounded us for many years, it was Konfrontasi, an undeclared war by Indonesia, that posed the greatest security threat to our young nation.

At a meeting in Tokyo, on 30 May, 1963 between Indonesia, Malaysia and the Philippines, including a bilateral meeting between Sukarno and Tunku Abdul Rahman, it was announced that Sukarno was ready to reconsider his opposition if Malaya agreed to a UN assessment of public support for the enlarged Federation. In order to move the process forward, Malaya did so. Following its assessment of support on the ground by the people of Borneo, the Security Council endorsed the formation of Malaysia.[38]

But inexplicably, at the last minute, we pre-empted the disclosure of the UN findings by announcing on 29 August that Malaysia would be formed on 16 September. The UN findings were due on 14 September.[39] Although the findings corroborated our stand that Malaysia's formation was fair and was agreed upon by a consensus of the majority of its people, it still intrigues me to this day as to why we did this—and gave cause to Indonesia and the Philippines to withhold recognition of Malaysia, and, in the case of Indonesia, to aggressively oppose it.

I was in Bangkok when the seriousness of this development struck the country. We were now in a war situation, in Konfrontasi with our much bigger neighbour. Throughout my time in Bangkok I was only too aware of the threat posed by Indonesia. My life as a diplomat somehow became enmeshed with the life of our young nation as it tried to figure out an articulate language to handle all these developments.

Our nation's foreign policy was just beginning to mature. I, too, was just starting my own journey of discovery of what being a diplomat was all about. Indonesia's Konfrontasi and the Philippines' claim to Sabah together marked the sharpest challenges to our country since gaining independence. It pulled into focus the need to *rethink* our foreign policy directions and options.

In the first years following independence, our foreign policy may be described as ad hoc responses, and, for various reasons, most of them were just echoes of British and Commonwealth stances. We had inherited an insurgency movement aimed at overthrowing the government by force. We had to respond. Our 12-year struggle to defeat the communist insurgency and to rid the country of communist influence had pushed us into strongly anti-communist and pro-western standpoints.

We inhabited a different world compared to Indonesia, which had fought and won a war against the Dutch colonialists and whose communist party was part of the government. Indonesia was a natural leader in the Third World and in the non-aligned movement, and its anti-Malaysia propoganda was initially effective in isolating Malaysia in the Third World caucus.[40]

Malaysia's first reaction to Konfrontasi, and the parallel threat from the Philippines, was to fall back on the Defence Agreement with Britain. But we soon realised that it was imperative for us to find new friends and create more natural allies to safeguard and promote our national interests. We began to seek allies in Asia and Africa, open many more embassies in the developing countries and become more active in international forums.

Thus from a knee-jerk pro-western position we began to explore options for a non-aligned and pro-development policy. As a fresh practitioner of diplomacy, posted in the region but not at home, I was able to look at things with some measure of detachment. When Singapore left Malaysia in 1965 to become an independent republic, I could work out that it was perhaps forcibly removed. As Tunku himself said, "It was a gangrenous toe severed from the body for the sake of its overall health."

In all this unfolding drama Thailand offered its good offices to mediate and to help bring Konfrontasi to an end. Thanat Khoman, the Thai Foreign Minister, was fully engaged in negotiations between Malaysia led by Tun Abdul Razak, the Deputy Prime Minister, and Indonesia led by Adam Malik, their new Foreign Minister.

By the time the peace treaty was signed in August 1966 in Bangkok, President Suharto was fully in control. An abortive coup by the powerful Partai Komunis Indonesia (PKI) on 30 September, 1965 gave the army the opening to sideline and then depose Sukarno and launch a brutal campaign to eliminate the PKI and its supporters.[41]

I was actually there to witness the signing of the peace agreement with Indonesia on 11 August, 1966. Considering the drama that preceded it, the actual signing was almost banal. We were all crammed into a small room, made even smaller and hotter by lots of pressmen and members of the media. The document was signed, appropriate but brief statements were made, photographs were taken, and that was it. It is difficult to imagine that this undramatic moment in a crowded Bangkok room signified the end of a huge conflict. Thailand's mediatory role was helpful and valued by us and reflected the good neighbourly relations we had worked hard to achieve.

Malaysia nevertheless emerged from the events during this period with a more matured approach to diplomacy which was reflected by the peaceful separation of Singapore from the Federation on 9 August, 1965 and the end of Konfrontasi a year later. We bacame more aware of our national interests and concerns in the conduct of our international relations and diplomacy.

Thailand is a neighbouring country with whom we have had traditionally strong and *sensitive* ties. The four northern Malaysian states of Perlis, Kedah, Kelantan and Terengganu had, at one time, been under Thai suzerainty. These four states were given back to Thai control during the Japanese occupation as a reward to the Thais for allowing Japanese forces to transit their country to invade British Malaya. They were returned to Malaya after the Japanese surrender. The Japanese period served a fear that Thailand still had its eye on the four northern Malaysian states. On the other hand, the Thais were suspicious of Malaysia's intentions towards the largely Malay and Muslim population of Thailand's southern provinces of Narathiwat, Yala, Pattani and Satun.

Thailand has a proud history of never having been colonised. This was so because the two competing colonial powers, France and Britain, had agreed between themselves that they needed Thailand to be a buffer state. However, it has never forgotten the Anglo-Siamese Treaty of 1909, imposed by the British and French, which resulted in the loss of the four northern Malaysian states. And as it faced problems with its own Muslim minority in the south, it casted shifty glances over the border to Malaysia. Despite mutual suspicion Malaysia and Thailand were able to cultivate good neighbourly relations which remain until today.

From the time of our independence the Thai government and its leaders were more than helpful and supportive of whatever assistance we requested and always underlined the *special* ties between us. Maybe it helped that Malaya's first Prime Minister Tunku Abdul Rahman had a Thai mother and had, for a brief period, gone to school in Bangkok as a child. There was indeed a feeling of closeness at all levels among the political leaders of the two countries. The Malayan Embassy at that time before Malaysia was established was referred to as *Setantut Melayu*, Malay Embassy, an expression of a historical closeness between us.

The leaders of the countries, especially Tunku Abdul Rahman and Tun Abdul Razak, maintained a close and abiding friendship with Thai Prime Ministers Sarit Dhanarata and his successor Thanom Kittikachorn as well as with others like Air Chief Marshal Dawee Chulasapa, and Thanat Khoman, the Foreign Minister, who in his youth had studied in Penang. To further underline this closeness, Tunku's brother-in-law Syed Sheikh Shahabuddin was appointed Malaya's first Ambassador to Thailand.

The situation in the region at the time gave Bangkok a new feature with the presence, in large numbers, of US soldiers on R&R from the Vietnam War front and from the American bases in Thailand. The Americans were receiving all the attention of the locals in the service industries. Taxis and shops clambered to the Americans over other foreigners. The reality on the ground spoke volumes about how deeply the Thais had compromised their sovereignty with the American presence and their membership of the American-engineered Southeast Asia Treaty Organization (SEATO). Knowing how geographically close they were to the Vietnam War and the uncertainty about how that war would turn out, the Thai position seemed understandable.

To cater to the needs of the foreign troops the Patpong district, close to the famous Lumpini Park, as well as the area beyond the British Embassy on Sukhumvit Road and the extension of Petchburi Road, were developed into the red entertainment districts in Bangkok. Bars, nightclubs and massage parlours sprouted all around this area. Thai entreprenuers were minting money catering to the needs of the foreign soldiers and other *farang*.[42]

The lure of Patpong did not escape the attention of our own Malaysians, VIPs included, who would come to Bangkok to seek a taste of this excitement. I remember a senior Cabinet Minister who arrived in Bangkok unannounced. When the Embassy learned about his presence, I was instructed to go and meet him at his hotel. Despite his visit being unannounced he was displeased, in fact angry, that he was not met at the airport. I told him that we did not have any information about his arrival but that his wife had called the Embassy twice to find out if he was in Bangkok. He suddenly became friendly. It turned out that he had told his wife that he would be in Alor Star, the capital of the northern Malaysian state of Kedah, checking on the progress of some projects.

A few months after my arrival the chancery[43] of our Embassy moved from a rented bungalow to a brand new building, the first built by our government overseas and built on our own property. Our new chancery had its own shallow moat which surrounded it entirely. This made it quite beautiful, especially at night, when the lights would dance off the water, illuminating the building and its curved Minangkabau roof. However, as always, beauty comes with a price, and ours was that our fancy roof did not have a ceiling underneath it. As for the walls, these were unwisely made almost entirely of glass. The combination of the roof and the glass walls meant that the heat of the hot summer months was conserved so efficiently that no amount of air-conditioning could cool the interior down. As for our moat, its beauty rapidly faded when the rains came, and we were regularly flooded.

Bangkok was a veritable crash course for me in diplomacy. Malaysian foreign policy was maturing and so was I. During my three years in Thailand, Malaysian diplomacy had moved from an anti-communist, pro-Western stance to one that was more neutral. We were establishing diplomatic contacts with countries throughout the world, regardless of their ideology. Now my next stint, in Germany, was going to show me the Cold War from the other perspective.

## Bonn: A World Polarised

I was posted to Bonn, Federal Republic of Germany, in August 1967. Germany was not an immediate neighbour nor was it a political global power that could have any security impact on Malaysia, at least not at that time. The Marshall Plan had helped rebuild its battered economy after World War II and it was on its way to becoming an economic powerhouse of the future. Our relations with Germany, therefore, were premised on obtaining technical assistance and at the same time attracting German investment and economic cooperation.

So I started to learn about strings. The '60s were a time when Germany was actively using its new-found economic leverage to pursue its political goals. It was still a politically divided country: the German Democratic Republic (GDR) which was communist-ruled and within the Soviet sphere of influence, and the Federal Republic of Germany (FRG) which maintained western-style democracy. The rivalry and antagonism between these two parts of the divided country were intense, a product of the Cold War.

I arrived in the Federal Republic of Germany just as the Malaysian Government was moving towards recognition of the other half of Germany, the GDR. This was part of the trend noted earlier, where Malaysia saw itself as part of the Third World, and not an appendage of either power bloc, and was building relationships pragmatically according to its national interest. In 1967 we established diplomatic ties with the Soviet Union and undertook several trade initiatives with countries in

Eastern Europe. From the mid-60s to the end of that decade we had a newfound interest in establishing links with non-aligned countries and the hitherto closed communist world. This interest had not gone unnoticed, certainly not by the United States, whose intelligence in 1965 reported that both Malaysia and Singapore 'were headed in the same direction with regard to their foreign policies: toward closer relations with non-aligned and communist countries'.[44]

When we announced recognition of the GDR in early 1968, we fell foul of the Hallstein Doctrine, a key doctrine put in place by West Germany (FRG) to discourage countries from establishing relations with the GDR.[45] At the time Malaysia was negotiating a financial and technical assistance package to set up the University of Malaya Teaching Hospital. We were also looking towards Germany for assistance in other future projects. The German side suddenly started asking hostile questions. Why did such a small country as Malaysia require an up-to-date and expensive hospital? Tun Abdul Razak, on an official visit to Germany, enquired about the response to our requests for assistance. I told him that we were running into some difficulties as a result of our recognition of East Germany.

The recognition came as a rude blow to me personally. I was called to the German Foreign Ministry on the morning of our announcement of ties with GDR. The Ambassador, on grounds of illness, had directed me to stand in for him, knowing that it was to be a session for receiving the wrath of the Germans. He had chickened out. The Germans registered a strong diplomatic protest and made known their displeasure. They told me Malaysia may forfeit any future assistance and threatened to invoke the Hallstein Doctrine, in other words revoke diplomatic relations. However, that did not happen, nor did the German Government cut economic assistance to Malaysia. The Hallstein Doctrine was never fully applied and by the time of Willy Brandt (1969) it had become obsolete.

The meeting at the German Foreign Ministry was very tense and I had walked into it blind. I felt bitterly let down at that time for not being told beforehand of our decision to recognise the GDR. It may have been an omission by the Ministry back home in its contacts with the Embassy, or that the Ambassador was informed but failed to grasp the implications. The Ambassador then was Haji Khalid Awang Osman, a politician and ex-deputy minister who had no flair nor understanding of the intricacies of diplomacy. For a number of reasons I found it hard to do an honest job, much less get along with him in terms of managing the Embassy. Within less than two years, at my persistent request, I was posted out of Germany, this time heading closer to home.

## Singapore: Pains of Separation

I left Bonn for Singapore at the end of 1968, at a particularly sensitive time in Malaysia-Singapore relations. Singapore had been forced out of Malaysia three years before. In Malaysia an election was approaching, where the DAP (Democratic Action Party), heirs to the Singapore ruling party the PAP (People's Action Party), would fight on a platform of 'Malaysian Malaysia', claiming equal rights for all and challenging the 'special privileges' of the indigenous Malays. The outcome of that election in May 1969 was the worst ethnic rioting that the country had seen since the end of the Japanese Occupation.

Relations with Singapore were 'laced with the antipathies of history and ethnicity', to quote Saravanamuttu's phrase.[46] There was an excess of emotion emanating from both sides; we viewed each other with suspicion and hostility. Sometimes the hostility was warranted. For example, the Singapore newspaper *The Straits Times* insisted on publishing weekly articles criticising Malaysia. This, obviously, was not helpful in dispelling suspicion and establishing closer relations with us. These emotive as opposed to rational elements in our relations remain to this day.

It is no surprise then that our relations with Singapore were often simmering although the objective of both sides was that peace be maintained. The most important outcome of these strained relations was the severing of Singapore from Malaysia in August 1965. In 1968 the strain was again critical. It was critical not just because the very goal of maintaining peace was threatened but because whatever action we took would be observed and judged by others in the international community.

Relations were often made worse by Prime Minister Lee Kuan Yew's tactless remarks about Malaysian leaders, and his government's habit of dealing directly with our respective ministries without first clearing with our Foreign Ministry. It took time for both sides to be fully conscious that the two countries were now separate national entities. At that time it was common for ministries of both countries to communicate directly with one another without the involvement and often without the knowledge of the foreign ministry of either country.

At the functional level we still tended to regard one another as colleagues, but in times of stress this led to many a diplomatic *faux pas,* often having nothing to do with foreign policy or strategy. For example, one incident took place in 1970, when I had already been posted out of Singapore. At the Malaysia-Singapore causeway check-point Singapore authorities detained three Malaysians and gave them each a haircut. They were enforcing a Singapore law forbidding long hair for young men.[47] Malaysia was incensed by this, but instead of proffering some conciliatory offering, Lee Kuan Yew postponed his visit, further stirring up ill-will between our two countries.

In spite of all the challenges facing our two countries, I enjoyed my Singapore posting, brief though it was. I liked being there. It was close to home and it was like home. And in spite of the numerous and seemingly insurmountable problems our respective countries were having with one another, our mission enjoyed the best of relations with the foreign and other ministries. Our Head of Mission was on extremely good terms with the Singapore Cabinet ministers and I was also on close terms with senior members of the Singapore Foreign Office.

Coincidentally, my time spent in the Ministry of Agriculture back then being busy with farmers' letters was fortuitous because Rahim Ishak, the brother of the Minister of Agriculture Aziz Ishak, was Singapore's Minister of State for Foreign Affairs while I was posted to Singapore. Rahim and I were on excellent terms. And another Ishak brother Yusof Ishak became President of Singapore, making it all the more ironic that here we were, getting along famously, in the midst of these most trying of times between our two countries.

Neither this problem nor my meagre overseas allowance of RM50 prevented me from occasionally sharing a good lunch with Mr. S.R. Nathan, the Deputy Permanent Secretary who later became the Singapore High Commissioner to Malaysia and eventually President of Singapore. Whenever he came to Kuala Lumpur, even as President, he would not fail to get in touch with me. Our friendship has remained firm throughout these many years.

On 13 May, 1969 racial riots broke out in Kuala Lumpur. I had again encountered difficulties with my High Commissioner, and had requested a transfer back to KL. Of course, my own human relations problems paled in comparison to those of my home country with Singapore. So although I was more or less on my way out of Singapore when the riots erupted, I remained there a while longer.

The origins of the riots are well known and much has already been written about them. For me personally, experiencing the drama close at hand from the 'enemy camp', as it were, there was nothing much that was particularly new. Racial riots had broken out in Singapore before; in July 1964 riots there had left several dead and hundreds wounded. But on that occasion the situation in KL had remained calm and peaceful. What was new in 1969 was the shocking and completely unexpected way in which unrest exploded in Kuala Lumpur on 13 May.

During weeks of election campaigning sensitive communal issues had stirred up tensions in the capital enough to explode in shocking acts of violence of a kind never experienced before. None of us was prepared for it and the significance of how it might affect our relations with Singapore was not lost on any of us. But what we focused on was not so much on the actual factors behind the initial outbreak of racial unrest as on those elements that would serve to prolong such violence if they were allowed to continue. One of these elements was the importunate refusal of the Singapore leadership to recognise the relevance of racial politics in Malaya/Malaysia which involved the question of Malay special rights and language privileges.

In regional development our testy relationship with Singapore had also been evident back in 1966 when Indonesia announced in April of that year that it would recognise Singapore as an independent state, while it was still refusing to recognise Malaysia. Tunku was greatly offended. Fortunately Tan Sri Ghazali Shafie managed to persuade Adam Malik[48] to withhold Indonesia's recognition of Singapore until it had settled its confrontation problems with us.

Our Singapore mission was preoccupied with reassuring Malaysians in Singapore that their security was our priority. This came about because the riots had spilled over into Singapore, with Singaporean Malays being attacked by the Chinese there in retaliation for what was happening to the Chinese Malaysians in Kuala Lumpur.

Coincidentally at this time our Naval Chief was in Singapore visiting the Malaysian Naval base in Woodlands, at that time its operational Headquarters. Although still a young practitioner of diplomacy, I was alert to the implications and the possible repercussions. I quickly called our Ministry and spoke to Zain Azraai, then the Special Political Officer at the Ministry to inform him that the Naval Chief's presence, viewed against sensitivities at this time of crisis, might be misread by the Singapore Government. My concerns must have found resonance because the Navy Chief was instructed to return home.

By the time I was back home in Kuala Lumpur in the latter part of that year, busy helping the Foreign Ministry to restructure itself, the happy corridors and grounds of my alma mater in Pantai Valley were filling up with mobs of angry student demonstrators. They were angry at numerous things but it came out as anger toward Tunku Abdul Rahman. It became clear that his leadership had lost much of its authority among the Malays. He was not included in the National Operations Council (NOC), hastily formed when Parliament was suspended in the immediate aftermath of the riots. Tun Abdul Razak and his right-hand man Tun Dr. Ismail took over the running of the country. When Parliament finally reconvened in early 1971, Tunku had already retired as Prime Minister on 22 September, 1970.

With Tun Razak in office the cautious moves in foreign policy towards non-alignment became much more confident. Gone was Tunku's cautiousness. It was Tun Dr. Ismail, as a backbencher, who had earlier articulated this new approach: "The time is ripe for the countries in the region to declare collectively the neutralisation of Southeast Asia. It is time that the countries in Southeast Asia sign non-aggression treaties

[and] declare a policy of co-existence in the sense that [they] should not interfere in the internal affairs of each other and accept whatever form of government a country chooses."[49] The alternative, he told Parliament, was becoming pawns of the big powers, a regional arms race and increased tension and subversion in the region.

And so, together with neighbours in our region, we began more and more to talk about neutrality, which was easier for us than for those with planes taking off regularly from American military bases in their countries.[50] Since we had no such bases non-alignment rang true. It was therefore easier for us to subtly embellish our non-alignment policy.

In actual practice, there was, of course, already high tension in the region with the war in Vietnam, which gave impetus to our search for peaceful co-existence and the strengthening of regional ties. In the next few years, while I was based back home in Kuala Lumpur, Malaysia would be accepted as a member of the non-aligned movement, we would support the seating of China in the United Nations and ASEAN would adopt neutralism as its basic policy. The culmination of these developments was the recognition of the People's Republic of China and Tun Abdul Razak's historic visit there in 1974. I was lucky enough to be involved in all these events.

## Endnotes

34 Canals.

35 Thai for City of Angels.

36 *Special* in diplomatic parlance infer to relations bearing special attention, either because of the exceptional nature of the diplomatic ties or the sensitivity of the relations.

37 See Ooi Kee Beng, *The Reluctant Politician: Tun Ismail and His Time,* Singapore, Institute of Southeast Asian Studies, 2006.

38 See Johan Savaranamuttu's Timeline in App.4.1, in his book *Malaysia's Foreign Policy The First Fifty Years: Alignment, Neutralism, Islamism,* Singapore, ISEAS Publishing, 2010, pp. 107–112.

39 United Nations Malaysia Mission Report to the Secretary-General—Final conclusion of the Secretary-General. General Assembly 18th Session.

40 In 1964, Malaysia was denied a seat at the Non-Aligned Conference in Cairo, largely because of Indonesian influence. See Johan Saravanamuttu, *op. cit.,* p. 89.

41    This event was code named Gerakan September Tiga Puluh, acronym GESTAPU 30. It was brutally put down by the Army and President Sukarno himself was accused of complicity.

42    Foreigners.

43    The administrative section of an Embassy.

44    Chandran Jeshurun, *op. cit.* p. 87.

45    Wikipedia: The Hallstein Doctrine, named after Walter Hallstein.

46    Johan Saravanamuttu, *op. cit.*, p. 18.

47    Ibid., p. 99.

48    Foreign Minister of Indonesia then.

49    Quoted in Johan Saravanamuttu, *op. cit.* p. 90–91. This speech was made in 1966. Although this foreign policy stance did not have the full backing of Tunku at the time, it became the policy of the new leaders in UMNO after 1970.

50    Thailand and Philippines.

# CHAPTER 5

# Years of Policy Involvement

The days of diplomatic apprenticeship and back rooming soon gave way to a more direct involvement in policy implementation. Having gone through the mill for five years, in three politically and geographically distinct postings, I was now thrust into assignments calling for profundity of judgement and insight. Gone were the days of British slanted policy that we had inherited just after independence. The new Prime Minister Tun Abdul Razak was moving towards non-alignment and neutrality, an evolution towards clearer national objectives.

My first assignment was to assist in the formation of the Organization of the Islamic Conference, a name that was later changed to the Organization of Islamic Cooperation (OIC). In the wake of a decision made in Rabat on 22 September, 1969 at a summit of Muslim Heads of State and Heads of Government there was a decision to form the first official grouping of Muslim countries that would meet every three years. The proposal arose from the unhappiness among leaders of Muslim nations over their status especially in the wake of the 1967 Arab-Israeli War. They had had several meetings earlier but these had no proper form, with no secretariat nor secretary-general.

The decision of the Rabat Summit would provide a structure that would give them a permanent voice in the international arena. The Summit decided that a First Islamic Conference of Foreign Ministers meet in Jeddah in March 1970. Subsequently at the Jeddah Conference the decision was made to appoint a Secretary-General to head the Islamic Secretariat. Even more momentous was the decision that this new Secretariat would be headed by a Malaysian.[51] The Conference further decided that the Second Islamic Conference of Foreign Ministers be held in Pakistan at a date to be arranged that same year which was later set for December 1970.

In this, as in many matters requiring action in our early days of diplomacy, we had no precedent to fall back on. We were a small Muslim country, newly independent, and far from the axis of Islamic civilisation, but we were about to spearhead the creation of an Islamic body. It was in preparation for the Karachi Conference that Dato' Ali Abdullah[52] and I were hastily despatched to London in October 1969 to begin preparations.

Why London? The Tunku had a particularly high regard for the organisation and structure of the Commonwealth Secretariat and instructed us to study its set-up. We would adopt something along the line of this Secretariat but *with Muslim emphasis.* Ali and I spent almost two months in London doing this. We were pleased and relieved when both Tunku and Tan Sri Ghazali Shafie, the Permanent Secretary of the Foreign Ministry, accepted our draft for the structure of the secretariat and the draft declaration for the forthcoming conference.

Back in KL from London I was instructed, within only a few days, to proceed to Islamabad and attach myself to the Pakistani Ministry of Foreign Affairs to work out details for the impending OIC Foreign Ministers Meeting. Working closely with my Pakistani officials we were to draw up the *modus operandi* for the Tunku to be elected as Secretary-General of the OIC. In September 1970 Tunku Abdul Rahman was about to step down formally as Prime Minister and he had set his sights on becoming the first Secretary-General of the Islamic Secretariat. Following our footwork and hard lobbying the Islamic Foreign Ministers Meeting held in Karachi elected Tunku Abdul Rahman Putra as its first Secretary-General. The Tunku said, *"Now begins his service to his faith, having served his people and his country all his political life."*

Following the conclusion of the Conference in Karachi, the Tunku and the pro-tem secretariat officials, which included Dato' Ali Abdullah and me, left for Jeddah to look at sites to house the Secretariat as had been promised by the Saudi King. The first site offered was palatial, in fact a mini palace, more suited to a king. The Tunku commented that the secretariat could not work in a palace and subsequently a more functional building was offered and accepted. Jeddah was not the best of places for me. It was both climatically and in other ways *dry*. I had to find a way to ease myself out of further involvement with the OIC. Pleading that my father was old, I managed to get permission to return to KL.

Back in Kuala Lumpur in early 1971 I was appointed Director-General of ASEAN. Our task was to build a community among the five ASEAN members, which at that time were Indonesia, Malaysia, the Philippines, Singapore and Thailand. In those early years the five nations were still setting up their respective national secretariats and finding a basis for functional cooperation. The emphasis was on economic rather than political cooperation. It would turn out to be quite an effort to lay down the groundwork for this new entity considering the diverse perception of what the member countries expected from ASEAN.

There was also the Vietnam War hanging like a dark cloud over all of us. There was serious concern of what could happen if North Vietnam won the war. We were talking about the domino theory[53] and the regional impact of a victorious North Vietnam. Most of the five ASEAN members were antagonistic to the government in Hanoi, and none had helped it through the decades of war against the crusading and overpowering Western powers. Some had even sided with the Americans by providing bases for their use.

The ASEAN fear of a belligerent Vietnam was real and the impetus for ASEAN was to find some common ground to forge a common strategy for the region. After emerging from Konfrontasi and with the relations with Manila still strained by its territorial claim, our priority at first was building confidence within ASEAN and learning to work together.

For me personally, the assignment was both enjoyable and challenging. There were regular meetings rotating between the respective capitals to discuss and explore commonalities. It started modestly and simply by trying to identify projects that would benefit two neighbouring countries, like creating a bridge over a common river. At the foreign ministers' meetings there was a series of speeches by the ministers, all in the same vein, expressing expectations of common benefits from ASEAN. But the goals were as vague as the speeches and many meetings took place without clear direction.

Then the spark was lit. Tun Abdul Razak, the Prime Minister, returned from the Non-Aligned meeting in Dar-es-Salam, Tanzania in September 1970 with a proposal calling for Southeast Asia to be declared a zone of peace, freedom and neutrality. This idea gave the impetus for ASEAN to move forward. I was tasked with preparing the draft paper setting out the parameters and framework of the concept. I started discussions in Bangkok with my good friend Bhira.[54]

Bringing the idea to fruition was not without difficulties. Not least among these was how to get around the fact that some member states had military pacts with the US. The biggest obstacle was the Manila Treaty, binding Thailand and the Philippines to the Southeast Asia Treaty Organization (SEATO). This Treaty was foisted on Thailand and the Philippines by the US as part of its Cold War strategy. Under this treaty the two countries were obliged to support the American war in Vietnam, and later in Laos and Cambodia.

But despite strong and differing perceptions of how ASEAN should shape itself, the subsequent meeting in KL, chaired by Tun Abdul Razak, agreed to adopt a final document on the establishment of ZOPFAN (Zone of Peace, Freedom and Neutrality). This document was short and brief, and it contained serious weaknesses that in later years made it less easy for ZOPFAN to move forward.

In order to pursue the ZOPFAN initiative further, I was instructed to attend the Non-Aligned Bureau meeting in KL as an observer. Malaysia was part of this Bureau, and among issues to be considered was the impending foreign ministers meeting in Georgetown, Guyana. It was for this reason that Shridath Ramphal, the Guyanese Foreign Minister, attended the meeting, although it was at the level of senior officials, usually permanent representatives based at the United Nations in New York. This was my first contact with the Non-Aligned Movement in which I would be greatly involved when I took up my posting in New York a couple of months later.

The Non-Aligned Bureau, based in New York, is a standing committee in between ministerial and summit meetings. Because our permanent representative to the UN at the time was concurrently accredited to Canada, and almost always in residence in Ottawa, I represented Malaysia at most of the Bureau meetings. Among the burning issues of the time was the admission of the People's Republic of China (PRC) to the United Nations. Malaysia voted in favour of the Albanian Resolution to admit China, and it passed the General Assembly on 25 October, 1971 by a vote of 76 to 65. The PRC became a member of the United Nations on that day. This happened before I arrived in New York.

The positions taken by the Non-Aligned Movement (NAM) on many issues at the UN were close to the positions of the Soviet Union and China, and coupled with the membership in NAM of countries like Cuba, gave rise to the jibe by the United States of the 'alignment of the non-aligned'. On the other hand NAM was accusing the United States of interfering in the internal affairs of a number of their member countries. The muscular diplomacy of the US, backed by military might, was only too obvious in Asia, as they strong-armed countries into backing their war in Vietnam.

In March 1970, the US engineered the removal of Prince Sihanouk and the installation of Lon Nol as head of state in Cambodia. To most of the members of NAM, this made Cambodia a puppet state of the United States. This had serious repercussions at the NAM Foreign Ministers Meeting at Georgetown, Guyana in 1972.

The majority of the Ministers wanted to expel Cambodia from NAM. Tan Sri Ghazali Shafie argued that the movement should leave the decision to the regional member countries in Southeast Asia. When he did not get his way, Tan Sri Ghazali Shafie and the Malaysian delegation walked out of the meeting. So did the delegations of Laos and Burma. Tan Sri Ghazali Shafie and others of the Malaysian delegation flew out of Georgetown the same day leaving Tan Sri Zakaria Ali[55] and me to monitor the meeting from the corridors. Both Tan Sri Zakaria and I viewed the walk-out as a hasty and negative action which made Malaysia even more suspect of playing footsie with the Americans.

The meeting in Guyana was followed by a Bureau Meeting in Kabul in 1973 to make the final preparations for the Summit in Algiers, Algeria. Already at that time there was a strong and widespread rumour of an impending coup in Afghanistan. Barely a week after the meeting, when all delegations had left for home, the King[56] was deposed and went into exile. In place of the monarchy a government backed by the Soviet Union was installed.

The Malaysian delegation to the Non-Aligned Summit in Algiers from 5 to 9 September, 1973 was led by Tun Abdul Razak, the Prime Minister. There are always two levels of meeting at Summits. The meetings of Heads of Delegation, the Plenary, were held as scheduled. The meetings at official level, however, were usually late, and in Algiers, started after 10.00 p.m. and went on until morning. The reason for this was that time was needed to put the documents into four different languages as well as to accommodate bilateral or group discussions over differing points of view.

On one of these stretched-until-morning sessions Anthony Yeo[57] and I trudged half asleep to Tun Razak's residence to brief him before he left for home. He was surprised to see us so early in the morning until we told him that our meeting had just ended. I briefed him on the problem we faced insofar as ZOPFAN was concerned. I explained to him that the meeting had failed to endorse the ZOPFAN declaration. He sounded disappointed, of course, for the very concept of peace, freedom and neutrality came out of the Non-Aligned Ministerial Preparatory Meeting in Dar-es-Salam, Tanzania in 1972.

I informed him that it was not Malaysia they were questioning, although to some degree we were already suspect. It was the fact that ZOPFAN included Thailand and the Philippines who were members of SEATO. After all, American military aircraft and navy were using bases in these countries to fight the Vietnam War. But lines were being drawn within NAM eroding its position as a third force. The assassination of the popularly elected President Salvador Allende of Chile, in a 11 September, 1973 coup inspired by the CIA, further raised tensions within the movement.

When Tun Abdul Razak left Algiers after our briefing, Anthony Yeo and I were left again to monitor the remaining part of the Summit. It was not without compensation. As the most senior national representatives of the country we got to sit among the Heads of State and Government for the rest of the Summit. Thus we found ourselves among the likes of President Gaddafi of Libya, and Idi Amin of Uganda. Following the conclusion of the Summit I returned to New York via London where I briefed Tun Razak on the final outcome of the meeting.

Notwithstanding some lapses in judgement and occasional internal bungling our country did exert an independent pro-active policy at the international level. Our non-alignment and subtle neutrality showed that the direction we had chosen for our foreign policy was to emphasise, in both regional and global contexts, our philosophy of peaceful co-existence with all countries. We had initiated networks of cooperation in Southeast Asia, and among Muslim countries and countries of the Third World. We had tried, not without difficulty, to adhere to our policy of equidistance through all the mine fields of the Cold War.

## Endnotes

51   See the OIC, 'Final Declaration of the First Islamic Conference of Foreign Ministers', Jeddah, Moharram 1390 H., March 1970.

52   A senior colleague in the Foreign Ministry.

53   Wikipedia: Imagine that if one state in a region fell to communism, then the surrounding countries would follow in a domino effect, thus the domino theory. This argument was used by successive United States administrations during the Cold War to justify American military intervention in Southeast Asia. President Eisenhower was the first to refer to countries in danger of Communist takeover as dominoes, in a 7 April, 1954 news conference. Eisenhower's domino theory of 1954 was a specific description of the situation and conditions within Southeast Asia at the time, and he did not suggest a generalised domino theory as others did afterward.

54   M L Bhirabongse Kasemsri, then special assistant to Thanat Khoman. M L—Mom Luang—is a Thai royal title.

55   Then Permanent Representative to the United Nations in New York.

56   Mohammed Zahir Shah (15 October, 1914–23 July, 2007) was the last King of Afghanistan, reigning from 1933 until he was ousted by a coup in 1973. Following his return from exile he was given the title 'Father of the nation' in 2002 which he held until his death.

57   A Senior Foreign Service Officer who later rose to become Secretary-General of the Ministry of Labour.

# CHAPTER 6

# The Region Riven by Conflict

On 27 January, 1973 the United States, the Democratic Republic of Vietnam (North Vietnam), the Republic of Vietnam (South Vietnam), and the Provisional Revolutionary Government of the Republic of South Vietnam (PRG) signed the Paris Peace Accords,[58] which ended direct US military involvement and became the prelude to the establishment of peace in Vietnam.

A little more than two years later, Saigon fell to the combined troops of North Vietnam and the PRG. This was a humiliating defeat for American military power. It signalled the collapse of their wider strategy of containment of communism, at least in Asia. For Southeast Asia it fundamentally reshaped the political landscape in ways our foreign policy had to come to terms with.

In Vietnam, Cambodia and Laos, communist governments took power. Vietnam was reunified as the Socialist Republic of Vietnam, with a large and battle-tested military force. It was a victory for the steely resolve of the Vietnamese people fighting for their freedom and dignity. But what would they do next?

It was inevitable that the war in Vietnam would expand into Laos and Cambodia. The Ho Chi Minh trail[59] ran through these two countries. The Ho Chi Minh trail was a logistical system that ran from north to south Vietnam that provided support to the National Front for the Liberation of South Vietnam (Vietcong) and the North Vietnamese Army. North Vietnamese forces and the South Vietnamese Liberation Forces had set up bases along their borders straddling Laos and Cambodia. In Cambodia, Prince Sihanouk had been deposed in an American-inspired coup in March 1970 that brought in Lon Nol as the head of a new regime.

With the objective of buying time for South Vietnam the US launched a massive bombing campaign on Cambodia hitting at the bases of the North Vietnamese and of the South Vietnamese Liberation Forces along the Cambodian-Vietnamese border. US forces also carried out massive bombings of Laos, in particular targeting North Vietnamese and Pathet Lao bases. On the ground in Laos the CIA was given the order to recruit a force of thousands of Hmongs[60] to be trained by the US and assisted by the Thai military. It was commanded by General Vang Pao to stem the tide of communist expansion. By the end of the war Laos was the most heavily bombed country ever in the world.

On 17 April, 1975 Phnom Penh fell to the Khmer Rouge. Soon after on 30 April Saigon fell to the North Vietnamese forces and the National Liberation Forces of South Vietnam. The events in these two countries brought about political pressure on the coalition government in Laos. It provided the Pathet Lao the opportunity to consolidate its power and take full control of the country. After the collapse of the coalition government and the establishment of the Lao People's Democratic Republic, Kaysone Phomvihane became Prime Minister and Souphanouvong, the Red Prince, became its President.

Laos, as far as Malaysia was concerned, did not pose any threat, and the change of government there did not cause the same panic as did

Vietnam and Cambodia—Vietnam, because it had the largest battle-hardened army in Southeast Asia, and Cambodia, because of the butchery of the Khmer Rouge regime that sent thousands of their people to their deaths. Both these countries became the source of fleeing refugees, by boat and by land, in the thousands. To Thailand, in particular, the threat from these two neighbouring communist countries was immediate.

In the mid-1970s Thailand was going through a period of soul searching in both its domestic politics and in its foreign policy. The past decades of military dictatorship and pro-US policy needed urgent adjustment in view of what was happening in Indochina. During the Vietnam War Thailand had staunchly allied itself with the US and other western countries. It was a member of SEATO. US military aircraft were taking off from their bases in Thailand to bomb Vietnam, Cambodia and Laos. Now they were face to face with their victorious neighbours and had to make adjustments to their policy with the three governments

Well before the fall of Saigon public unhappiness with the military dictatorship had forced them from power. M R Kukrit Pramoj, a multitalented politician of Royal descent (he is a direct descendant of King Rama II), and leader of the Social Action Party, was elected Prime Minister in 1975. He took over from his brother M R Seni Pramoj from the Democrat Party, whose premiership had lasted not quite one month. Kukrit was the author of the 1974 Constitution which formed the basis of representative government following the student revolt that overthrew the military dictatorship in 1973. He was also a literary figure who wrote novels and, through his newspaper, published his critique of social and political conditions. He once also acted in a movie, *The Ugly American*, portraying the prime minister of a country that kicked out the Americans. And when, in real life, he became Prime Minister of Thailand, he did the same thing. He kicked the Americans out of Thailand. Irony or dream realised?

One of Kukrit's first promises to the electorate was to rid Thailand of all foreign troops. As Prime Minister he issued a statement of national policy to this effect on 19 March, 1975, giving one year for compliance. The United States, which at the height of the Vietnam War had about 50,000 troops in Thailand, was the target of his policy. But it hit other targets as well.

The Malaysian Police Field Force Unit was stationed in southern Thailand as part of our bilateral border cooperation agreement to monitor the activities of the Malayan Communist Party (MCP). The MCP used bases in southern Thailand to enter the jungles of Malaysia to lay their anti-personnel mines and at times engage the Police Field Force in hit-and-run skirmishes. We were, of course, both concerned and angry to be told to remove the Police Unit. Our understanding was that we were fighting a common enemy together with Thai forces. We were thus outraged to be equated with the American forces. This prompted Tan Sri Ghazali Shafie, then Minister of Home Affairs, to declare that Malaysia reserved the right to attack MCP bases in southern Thailand if Malaysia deemed it necessary. It was an outburst of anger and frustration.

I recall clearly, in the wake of this, the Ambassador Tan Sri Abdul Rahman Jalal was summoned to the Thai Foreign Ministry by the Permanent Secretary Anand Panyarachun. I accompanied him. I was then on my second posting to Bangkok from March 1975 to August 1976. I knew Anand from when we were both stationed in New York. Anand, a distinguished and brilliant Thai diplomat, later became the Prime Minister of Thailand. He told us that public opinion demanded that all foreign forces be removed from Thailand and the government could no longer ignore the pressure from the people and the media.

While the Ambassador maintained a cultured politeness, I took on the role of devil's advocate, taking advantage of our friendship established in New York, and bluntly retorted that the demand for us to withdraw would be a setback in our relations and that Malaysia naturally would view this as a step backwards that was opposite to the understanding between the two countries presently in force.[61]

The Thai euphoria at getting rid of the military government manifested itself in a more critical view of Malaysia, especially in the media. Articles harshly and unjustifiably criticising us began to appear in both the English language and Thai vernacular papers. I remember one journalist who went out of his way to criticise Prime Minister Tun Abdul Razak for cancelling his visit to Thailand, which was scheduled to take place in January 1976. At the end of 1975 Tun Abdul Razak had travelled to London and was still there. We informed the Thai Government that his visit might not take place as planned. In his article this journalist lambasted Tun Abdul Razak, accusing him of prolonging his stay in London to enjoy life there. Then the news came that Tun Abdul Razak had passed away in London.[62] When I met the journalist soon after he apologised to me, admitting that he had misread the whole situation. The knowledge that Tun Abdul Razak suffered from leukaemia had been kept secret from the public.

The military coup of October 1976 ended the period of democratic government under M R Kukrit Pramoj. General Kriengsak Chomanand became Prime Minister and brought back military government to Thailand. Although, during my second stay in Thailand, the governments swung from military to democratic and back again to military, our relations continued on an even keel and the underlying strength of our bilateral ties stood the test. We also realised that while the role of the military in politics was deeply entrenched, there was now a need for us to seek out and establish relations with other interest groups in the country.

But Bangkok gave me other stranger duties. It was during my short stay in Bangkok that Tunku Abdul Rahman, our first Prime Minister, came to Thailand to seek permission to exhume the remains of his brother Tunku Yusoff. His brother had served in the Thai police and had died many years earlier from malaria. He was buried in the Muslim cemetery. It was the first time I heard the Tunku speak Thai—although this should not have come as a surprise. His Thai mother had seen to it that he was schooled in Bangkok for at least a brief period during his childhood.

The Tunku wanted to take his brother's remains home and have him reburied in the Royal Mausoleum in Alor Star, Kedah. The person in charge of the mosque informed me that the Thai Muslim community was not pleased with the idea. Perhaps that explained why no one was there to assist us with the exhumation. So it was left to me and the embassy staff. On that particular evening the weather was treacherous with a hurricane-force thunderstorm, howling wind, and deafening thunder and lightning. This was a horror movie re-enacted in real life. We at first had difficulties locating the grave but were helped by the person in charge of the mosque. By midnight, after some hours of exhausting digging, we broke the top of the tomb which over the years had sunk into the soft ground. The next morning when Tunku was at the graveyard with the Ambassador we finished the job. The bones were collected and washed, followed by prayers before being prepared for the flight to Kedah. I never for one moment imagined that my job would include grave-digging.

During this time the unfolding events in Cambodia were seriously disturbing to many of us in the region. Lon Nol, the military dictator and

US stooge, fled to Hawaii from Phnom Penh shortly before Cambodia's fall to the Khmer Rouge on 17 April, 1975. He was accompanied by his family and immediate associates, including Long Boret, the Prime Minister of his regime. I had met Long Boret in Georgetown, Guyana, during the Non-Alligned Foreign Ministers Meeting. We met again in New York when as Prime Minister as well as Foreign Minister he attended the debate on the Non-Aligned Resolution on Cambodia at the General Assembly. I met him again in Bangkok on his way from Hawaii returning to Phnom Penh. At a dinner in Bangkok we discussed the situation in Cambodia. I asked him why he wanted to return to his country, since he was fully aware that his name was at the top of the Khmer Rouge execution list. He told me that he had no choice but to return home because his family was still there in ·Phnom Penh. In any case, he believed he 'could negotiate with the Khmer Rouge on the transfer of power'. He truly believed he could work things out with the enemy. Much later I was informed that when he was about to leave with his family his helicopter was shot down by his own soldiers who felt betrayed at being left to face their terrifying fate at the hands of the Khmer Rouge.

Anticipating the imminent fall of Phnom Penh we had to quickly evacuate our embassy staff back to Kuala Lumpur. However, Ismail Ambia, the Chargé d'Affaires, was directed to position himself at the Embassy in Bangkok to monitor the developments from a closer but safer distance. Early one morning he received a message from the Thai authorities saying that a few hundred Malaysians had gathered at the Thai-Cambodian border seeking permission to cross into Thailand. Ismail hurriedly drove to the border and found a group of Muslim Chams desperate to escape the savagery that was already taking place in their country.

. According to records the Cham empire once stretched from Hué in central Vietnam to the Mekong delta.[63] There are remnants of the Cham community in south Cambodia, and in Kelantan and Terengganu in Malaysia. But this group was not Malaysians. What Ismail did without a moment's hesitation—and without any clearance from home—was to accept them as Malaysians. Luckily for them Ismail did not follow his head but instead followed his conscience and his heart. They were placed in transit camps in Thailand before finally being sent to Malaysia. We continued to receive more Chams after this incident and continued to integrate them into our society. What Ismail did was laudable.

This was not the easiest of periods to be handling affairs of the region. The immediate effects of the post-Vietnam War were just beginning to sink in. Southeast Asia now was divided into communist and non-communist countries. There was a conscious effort on our part to work out how to deal with this new situation. Uppermost in our minds was how to rebuild confidence between us and the three victorious, but utterly devastated, countries of Indochina.

For nearly three decades Malaysia, and all of the ASEAN member countries except Indonesia, had sided with the pro-American regimes in these countries that had just been defeated by the victorious parties now in power. True, they were presented to us as democratic regimes and therefore tilted towards the US and western powers in our perception of the geopolitics of the region. We were also influenced by our own struggle against the communist insurgents. In his book *My Side of the Story* Chin Peng[64] related that the Vietnamese and the Laotian communist parties facilitated his communications and movements between Malaysia and China. So the suspicion and enmity generated by this history was mutual and would take some time to neutralise.

Nonetheless, facing reality, we took steps to extend our hand in friendship to the new regimes. We initiated diplomatic overtures first in Hanoi by early 1973,[65] soon after the signing of the Paris Peace Accords in January of the same year, and with Phnom Penh soon after when we established representation in Beijing. We had always had an embassy in Vientiane, Laos. After the liberation of South Vietnam in 1975 Malaysia was among the first[66] members of ASEAN to recognise the Provisional Revolutionary Government of South Vietnam on 29 July, 1975. In 1976, after the formal reunification of Vietnam, Malaysia and the Socialist Republic of Vietnam opened Embassies in each other's capitals. Our diplomatic assessment of Hanoi's attitude towards Malaysia during this initial period was one of cold formality. But we hoped over time that Vietnam would see and appreciate the sincerity of our actions.

Towards this end the Foreign Minister Tengku Ahmad Rithauddeen made official visits first to Hanoi and Vientiane, and later after a short break, to Phnom Penh. I accompanied him as Under Secretary for Political Affairs, a position I had just occupied upon my reassignment from Bangkok. The short break between our visit to Hanoi and Vientiane and Phnom Penh was necessary taking into account the animosity between Vietnam and Laos on the one hand and Cambodia on the other. The visits were to inform the three governments of our intention to invite Prime Minister Fukuda of Japan to the ASEAN Summit in Kuala Lumpur in 1977 and to explain to them that in doing so we had no hidden agenda and that ASEAN was not ganging up against them.

The only way to fly directly to Hanoi was by our own military aircraft. In Hanoi the devastation caused by three decades of war against first French and then American imperialism was striking. It struck us just how much the Vietnamese had sacrificed to gain their freedom. We were well received and met with the Prime Minister Pham Van Dong and his Foreign Minister. In our discussions, apart from telling them of the upcoming visit of Mr. Fukuda, we expressed our readiness to be of some assistance in the rehabilitation of their battered economy.

Our second visit was to Vientiane where we met with the new leaders including the President Prince Souphanavong. Vientiane was a small town in those days. It looked more like a village than a capital city. The people were extremely poor and appeared undernourished and some even stunted. Within their limited means the reception was cordial and friendly and we were happy with their acceptance of the case we were making.

A couple of weeks later we flew to Phnom Penh also in our own military aircraft. We did not, however, get to meet Pol Pot, but we met Khieu Samphan, the Head of State, and Ieng Sary, the Deputy Prime Minister. I had earlier met Ieng Sary when he visited Kuala Lumpur and we had talked about relations between our two countries. Here in Phnom Penh he was as chummy and friendly as he was in Kuala Lumpur, but beneath that façade was a brutality we could hardly have imagined. Khieu Samphan on the other hand appeared stern and unsmiling with a penetrating gaze.

Phnom Penh was as scary as a ghost town and eerily deserted. At the guest house where we stayed were four very young boys, hardly in their teens, armed with AK47 assault rifles, responsible for our security. The accommodation was as basic as the meals were. In the evening we were entertained to a stage performance by young girls and boys. The next day we flew to Siem Reap in their aircraft to visit Angkor Wat. During the war Angkor Wat was used by the Khmer Rouge forces as their western headquarters. We were taken on a brief tour of Angkor Wat and treated—to our immense surprise—to a champagne lunch in the open at the main entrance of the Wat.[67] And again, in Phnom Penh, we had the same discussions here as we had had in Vietnam and Laos.

We could not be sure what the Vietnamese, the Laotians and the Cambodians really thought about the ASEAN Summit and Fukuda's presence at it. But by going out of our way to pay them a visit and to brief them and give them assurances of our genuine desire for good relations we felt we had done our part in nurturing trust and friendship.

In the case of Vietnam there was a feeling that we had made some headway. Our offer to train some 30 or so of their cadres at our Rubber Research Institute in Kuala Lumpur was readily accepted. In addition we also provided them with new clones of rubber seedlings and coconut plants to help rehabilitate rubber and coconut plantations in the south. These were delivered to them in December 1978 by our naval ship *RMN Hang Jebat*. The ship went directly to Haiphong in a symbolic recognition of Hanoi as the capital of the Socialist Republic of Vietnam (SRV). The crew was given a tour of Hanoi before going south to Ho Chi Minh City to deliver the cargo. Tan Koon San, the Counsellor at the Embassy, accompanied them to Ho Chi Minh City.

Then in early 1978, a few months after our return from Indochina, the Foreign Minister Tengku Ahmad Rithauddeen told me I was to be posted out. He gave me the choice of Jeddah, Tripoli or Hanoi. It was not a difficult choice to make. Our relations with Vietnam were among our top priorities, and I knew I would have meaningful work to do. Going to Vietnam was to be a natural extension of my work as Under Secretary for Southeast Asia and Oceania at the Ministry. I would also have to handle the challenging problem of the boat people,[68] an influx of refugees by sea from Vietnam, which had become a huge problem for the ASEAN countries.

During my tour in Hanoi from August 1978 to July 1980 I saw some of that stiff formality collapse. Vietnamese leaders had thawed a bit and become friendlier. One gesture was to allow me in 1979, as Ambassador of Malaysia, to drive to Hué to visit the old imperial capital. Similar requests by the Thai and Philippine ambassadors had been turned down by the Vietnamese Foreign Ministry. I was also lucky that the personal chemistry worked well between me and some of the senior Vietnamese leaders. I had long and rewarding discussions with Deputy Foreign Minister Nguyen Co Thach[69] and Vice Minister Phan Hien on bilateral as well as regional issues. At times these discussions were combative but they were full of give and take and constructive. I got the impression that we all enjoyed these exchanges and that we were successfully building a basis of trust.

Six months into my sojourn in Hanoi the Sino-Vietnamese conflict boiled over on a series of issues including demarcation of their common border. On 17 February, 1979 China began its invasion to 'teach Vietnam a lesson'. This was China's response to the 1978 Vietnamese invasion and occupation of Cambodia. Following initial gains by the Chinese the invasion stalled and the Vietnamese claimed that they had contained the Chinese advance. Our own thinking at the time was that China had no intention of scaling a slap into a war, although the government in Hanoi was prepared to fight on. The conflict ended with each teaching the other a lesson.

On 6 March, 1979 the Chinese unilaterally withdrew.[70] I was one of the ambassadors invited to the border area to be briefed on the Vietnamese success in the war. The trenches dug out along kilometres of the border were reminiscent of the Vietnamese tactics against the French in Dien Bien Phu in 1954. The Vietnamese steely resolve to uphold its national integrity had not changed in three decades. But the people of Vietnam paid a heavy price.

Hanoi, and much of the country, reflected this. There were hardly any cars in the city—but thousands of bicycles. Those cars on the roads were government or military vehicles or cars belonging to the diplomatic corps. The most trustworthy means of transportation were the trams brought there by the French and still rattling, windowless, through the city, endlessly ringing their bells warning pedestrians and cyclists to get out of their way. Most of the buildings were in disrepair and there was an acute shortage of accommodation. All of the French mansions that had survived the war now housed multiple families. The roads were littered at regular intervals with open manholes that had served as bomb shelters.

The US had used the Gulf of Tonkin incident[71] to trigger massive aerial bombing of Hanoi. Using the alleged attack, President Lyndon Johnson conned the American people into supporting the war and the world into justifying the bombing of the North. The famous bridge that crosses the Red River, built by Eiffel Gustave of Eiffel Tower fame, was badly damaged. But despite the damage, Hanoi held, and still holds, a special charm, exuding a timeless grace. The people were poor but they bore a stubborn pride in having won their freedom against immeasurable odds.

We were all too aware of the difficult times the country was going through. Our Embassy was housed at the very rundown Thong Nhat (Reunification) Hotel, formerly Hotel Metropole.[72] Communications between Wisma Putra[73] and the Embassy, as well as with the outside world, were a serious problem. Most infrastructure had been totally destroyed and telecommunications were primitive. I was to suffer from this. It took the Ministry three days to reach me with the news that my father had passed away. Today it would have taken me only a few hours to reach home. In those days I had to board an Air Vietnam flight to Nanning in Southern China, then a CAAC[74] flight to Guangzhou where I had to stay overnight. Early the following morning, I took the Chinese train to the Hong Kong border and walked across the border to catch the Hong Kong train for Kowloon until, at last, I got a flight home. So near and yet so far and so long to travel!

In the second half of 1978, there was a flurry of diplomatic initiatives from Vietnam to ASEAN. Vietnam's Deputy Foreign Minister Phan Hien visited Kuala Lumpur early in July 1978 and met with Tun Hussein Onn, the Prime Minister, to discuss the zone of peace, freedom and neutrality. Phan Hien assured him of Vietnam's sincere desire to establish friendly relations. Then a few months later the Vietnamese Foreign Minister Nguyen Duy Trinh visited Malaysia and three other ASEAN countries, to reiterate their friendly intentions. Shortly after, while I was in Hanoi as Ambassador, I was informed of the intention of Prime Minister Pham Van Dong to visit the ASEAN countries later in the year.

Before returning home for his visit[75] I called on him. At that meeting he raised questions about ASEAN that gave me the impression that he felt the regional organisation was still tainted by western bias. I tried to disabuse him of this notion and mentioned that visits undertaken by his foreign and deputy foreign ministers to ASEAN countries earlier showed a positive perception of the organisation. I stressed the point that ASEAN was not a military organisation and that ASEAN's zone of peace, freedom and neutrality gave the space needed for the interests of all countries involved to be protected.

I asked him, outright, now that Vietnam was reunified and had the largest standing army in the region, what would be Vietnam's intentions? He told me to inform Prime Minister Tun Hussein Onn that the priority for Vietnam was to rebuild the country. "Our soldiers will not cross our borders," he assured me. They would be tasked with the rebuilding.

Soon after his visit to ASEAN, he made a visit to the Soviet Union where, on 30 November, 1978, a Treaty of Friendship and Cooperation was signed between Vietnam and the Soviet Union.[76] Under this treaty Vietnam was guaranteed of Soviet military assistance should China intervene in the conflict between Vietnam and Cambodia. Soon after his return from Moscow, at the end of 1978, Vietnam launched a full-scale invasion of Cambodia.

His visit to the ASEAN countries seemed to me, in hindsight, as an exercise to soften whatever negative reaction ASEAN countries would have over the invasion of Cambodia. His soldiers had crossed the borders. He had lied comfortably.

The Vietnamese invasion of Cambodia became a conflict of conscience for us. On the one hand we were silently pleased about the removal of the Khmer Rouge regime. On the other hand the Vietnamese invasion was a serious violation of the UN Charter pertaining to the sanctity of sovereignty and integrity of a state. And it changed the balance in the region to the detriment of the ASEAN states. After ousting the Khmer Rouge regime Vietnam installed the People's Republic of Kampuchea, which was pro-Vietnam with Heng Samrin as its Head. In response to the invasion the Coalition Government of Democratic Kampuchea (CGDK) was established in exile. It comprised the three Cambodian factions of Prince Sihanouk's FUNCIPEK Party, the Khmer Rouge, and Son Sann's National Liberation Front Party. The CGDK was established in June 1982 in Kuala Lumpur.

The invasion of Cambodia certainly revived our mistrust of Vietnam's military intentions and the region continued to be riven by conflict. However, considerable effort was made to reconcile the different groups and move forward the Cambodian peace process. We had hoped that the willingness of the parties to reach a settlement would lead to peace. But it was not until the signing of the Comprehensive Political Settlement nearly a decade later that these hopes were realised.

The human aftermath of the Vietnam War was embodied in its boat people. This would be a saga stretching across my career... and beyond.

## Endnotes

58   The negotiations that led to the accord began in 1968 after various lengthy delays. The main negotiators of the agreement were United States National Security Advisor Dr. Henry Kissinger and Vietnamese Politbureau member Le Duc Tho. The two men were awarded the 1973 Nobel Peace Prize for their efforts, although Le Duc Tho refused to accept it.

59   Wikipedia: According to the United States National Security Agency's official history of the war, the Trail system was 'one of the great achievements of military engineering of the 20th century'.

60   The Hmong are an ethnic group from the mountainous regions of China, Vietnam, Laos and Thailand. The Hmongs in Laos were known to be fierce jungle fighters. After Saigon fell, America abandoned this secret army, and it was not until 1997 that Washington officially acknowledged the valor of the Hmong soldiers.

61   In diplomatic parlance this is deemed a very strong statement.

62   On 14 January, 1976.

63   Wikipedia: The Cham people are concentrated between the Kampong Cham Province in Cambodia and central Vietnam. Cham form the core of the Muslim communities in both Cambodia and Vietnam. The Chams are remnants of the Kingdom of Champa (seventh to 18th centuries). At its height in the ninth century, the kingdom controlled the lands between what is now modern Huê, to the northern reaches of the Mekong Delta in Southern Vietnam. The Vietnamese expansion in 1720 resulted in the total annexation of the Champa kingdom. The last king, Pô Chien, gathered his people in the hinterland and fled south to Cambodia, while those along the coast migrated to Terengganu (Malaysia). A small group fled northward to the Chinese island of Hainan where they are known today as the Utsuls. Their refuge in Cambodia where the king and his people settled still bears the name of Kampung Cham.

64   Chin Peng, *My Side of the Story*, Singapore, Media Masters, 2003.

65   Vietnamese Embassy website June 2012: Vietnam and Malaysia officially established diplomatic relations on 30 March, 1973.

66   Together with Indonesia.

67   The Temple.

68   See Chapter 7.

69   Nguyen Co Thach had a solid revolutionary background. He joined the Viet Minh and rose to the rank of Colonel in the army before turning to diplomacy in 1954. He played a leading role in the 1973 Paris Peace Accords which led to the US military withdrawal from Vietnam preceding Hanoi's final victory on 30 April, 1975. He became Foreign Minister in 1980 and an alternate member of the Politburo in 1982 and a full member in 1986. In 1987 he became Deputy Prime Minister. He fell from favour in 1989 but retained the respect and admiration of many of those who had dealt with him as an intellectual among the leadership and though a tough ideologue and nationalist he had a pragmatic approach to problems. Many were drawn to his personal charm and linguistic ability.

70   The practice of unilateral withdrawal after a brief penetration was not new for the Chinese.

71   Wikipedia: The Tonkin Gulf incident was concocted by the US National Security Agency. It was said to have occurred on 4 August, 1964. Congress passed the Gulf of Tonkin Resolution, which granted President Lyndon Johnson the authority to assist any Southeast Asian country whose government was considered to be jeopardised by 'communist aggression'. The resolution served as Johnson's legal justification for deploying US conventional forces and the commencement of open warfare against North Vietnam. In 2005, an internal National Security Agency historical study was declassified; it concluded that the *Maddox* had engaged the North Vietnamese Navy on 2 August, but that there were no North Vietnamese Naval vessels present on 4 August. The report stated regarding 4 August: ... it is that no attack happened that night. In truth, Hanoi's navy was engaged in nothing that night but the salvage of two of the boats damaged on 2 August.

72   Today it has been restored to its colonial glory.

73   Wisma Putra is commonly used to refer to the Malaysian Foreign Ministry. It is actually the name of the building that housed the Ministry.

74   Civil Aviation Authorities of China.

75   It is common practice for an accredited Ambassador to accompany the visiting Head of State/Head of Government on official visit to their home country.

76   The treaty could have been aimed at neutralising Chinese threats as the Sino-Soviet Treaty of Friendship of 1950 (which actually expired in 1979) prohibited either party from attacking an ally of the other. At the same time it provided a protective umbrella against Chinese attacks by the provision of mutual defence assistance. By the Treaty the Soviet Union was granted access to the facilities at Da Nang and Cam Ranh Bay naval port. The use of the bases represented substantial strategic gain for the Soviet Union whose naval bases in the Pacific had until then been limited to the Soviet Far East. It was certainly strategically disturbing to the regional countries and ASEAN as the Soviet presence could trigger potential super power military rivalry in the region.

CHAPTER 7

# The Challenge of the Boat People

The first encounter I had with the refugee problem was when Ismail Ambia, our Chargé d'Affaires to Cambodia residing in Bangkok,[77] rescued hundreds of Chams at the Thai-Cambodian border by accepting them as Malaysians. A few days later, I travelled with Ismail to the border area and visited the camp. It was a makeshift camp crammed with Cham refugees in the hundreds. They were in a wretched state of health made worse by the primitive conditions of the camp. By this time news of the boat people from Vietnam arriving on Malaysian shores and also the shores of other ASEAN countries was making headline news in Bangkok.

On my return to Kuala Lumpur, I assumed my duties as Under Secretary for Southeast Asia and Oceania and was now facing the enormity of the problem of the Vietnamese boat people.

According to the UNHCR archives the first 47 refugees from Vietnam arrived in Malaysia in May 1975. The last remaining Vietnamese refugee left Malaysia more than 30 years later on 28 August, 2005. The trickle had turned into a flood and in the end a quarter of a million refugees had landed in Malaysia. The lives of these people impacted three decades of Malaysian history, touching many lives in the process, including mine.

This human tragedy was a direct result of the fall of Saigon, Phnom Penh and Vientiane in 1975. Following the fall of Saigon, retribution began against those who had worked or fought for the defeated government of South Vietnam or those who had in any way been involved in supporting the American forces. Many were sent to prisons or re-education camps and had their properties confiscated. Businesses and livelihoods collapsed across the south. Thousands took to rickety wooden boats to flee this persecution and hence came to be known as 'Boat People'.[78] They risked their lives and many lost them. Taking to the open sea they further exposed themselves to harassment and untold misery. As documented by the UNHCR, a sizeable number became victims of Thai fishermen masquerading as pirates, seeking booty, who mercilessly attacked the boats, killing the men and taking the young women and girls to use and sell. Malaysia and other ASEAN countries were pushing them out from their shores, in some cases repairing their boats so they could continue their endless journey.

The first response of ASEAN to this crisis was a fumble. At a meeting of officials just before the Kuala Lumpur ASEAN Summit 1977, before my posting to Hanoi, we discussed a common ASEAN position. But no agreement was reached. There was no common position. The default position was to let each country respond individually and independently of the others. And so, in the end, the only response we had, which was common to all ASEAN countries, was pushing the boat people back to the open sea.

In early January 1979 the ASEAN Foreign Ministers at their meeting expressed 'grave concern' about the rising flow of boat people. They threatened the peace and stability in the region and were causing 'serious economic dislocation' for ASEAN countries. In May that year Vietnam and the UNHCR signed a Memorandum of Understanding on the Orderly Departure Programme (ODP). Under the ODP, about half a million people left the country legally for resettlement, mainly in Western countries. But even that did not stem the 'disorderly' flow of refugees to Malaysia and Thailand.

The international community had to do more. In July of the same year, the Secretary-General of the United Nations Kurt Waldheim called for a Geneva Conference on Indochinese Refugees. By that time I was in Hanoi as Ambassador. At a meeting organised by the Vietnamese Foreign Ministry and the UNHCR Representative, attended by most of the ASEAN ambassadors and Australia, I argued strongly that Vietnam, as the source of the refugees, could not but attend the meeting in Geneva. I was backed by the UNHCR representative in Hanoi, Sergio de Mello[79] who had asked for the meeting. Vice Foreign Minister Phan Hien started by saying that Vietnam would not attend the Geneva conference and was not obliged to do so. A few days later I called on him at the Foreign Ministry to try again to persuade him. One week later he telephoned me at the Embassy to inform me that Vietnam would attend the conference.

The Geneva Conference of 1979 was the starting point in the search for a comprehensive and final solution to the problem. The Conference laid down a framework. Initially, there was a drop in the number of arrivals. But the early euphoria was short-lived and the numbers began to peak again in an alarming way. Malaysia and other ASEAN countries expressed concern at what seemed to be an unstoppable flow.

Malaysia—and also Thailand—came under a lot of criticism for their 'cruelty' towards the boat people. Of course, pushing desperate people back to sea in leaking boats was morally reprehensible. I felt that acutely at the time. But Malaysia's argument was that we did not create this problem; we were the victims of it. It was the military intervention of the US and its western allies in Indochina which was the root cause. Then retribution in Vietnam against those who had supported the Americans generated this flood of human misery that was hitting our beaches. We felt that it was totally the responsibility of the US and its allies to resettle all of these refugees and to work through international agencies to stop the flood of refugees at source.

The Geneva conference set up a framework for this to be achieved. But countries receiving the boat people for final settlement were suffering from 'compassion fatigue'.[80] For some time the resettlement rate was slower than the number of new arrivals. Western agencies picked out the refugees they wanted, those who were educated and healthy—and left the rest in our camps.

At the height of this massive flow, the domestic political situation in Malaysia was very tense, our people not taking kindly to these arrivals and the economic burden they imposed. Those that arrived on our shores were mainly Vietnamese of Chinese origin, running away from possible harassment and likely retribution. They could not be settled in Malaysia without upsetting the racial balance. There was strong pressure on the government not to allow any settlement. We continued to maintain our position that they were illegal immigrants and not refugees, and therefore could not qualify to be accepted as such. Malaysia had not signed the 1951 United Nations Convention Relating to the Status of Refugees nor the 1967 Protocol. Legally, we had no obligation.

While the pressure at home continued to mount we were also at the receiving end of international pressure. We could not ignore this pressure. We could argue that we were free from any obligation to the UN-endorsed 1948 Universal Declaration of Human Rights, and its principal of *non-refoulement*,[81] but that would make us look callous in the eyes of the world. We had to tread nimbly between domestic and international pressure and this set up tension between Wisma Putra and politicians addressing their domestic supporters. At one point Dr. Mahathir Mohamad, at that time the Deputy Prime Minister, was quoted as saying, "We will *shoot* whoever lands on our shores illegally". This remark immediately created a furore in the international community. Quickly Tan Sri Ghazali Shafie, as Minister of Home Affairs, issued a clarification that Dr. Mahathir had been misquoted and had actually said that he "would *shoo* whoever…". This episode served one positive purpose for us, in that the issue grabbed international attention and put our plight in focus.

At the time, there was an internal debate between the hard-line position strongly espoused by Tan Sri Ghazali Shafie, Minister of Home Affairs, on the one hand, and Wisma Putra on the other. There were occasions when he and I locked horns on this issue. I could understand that he was working with his domestic constituency in mind, while we at Wisma Putra were trying to maximise the advantages of working closely with the UNHCR. We knew that in the final analysis the United Nations was the only organisation with the capacity to resolve this human tragedy. In the end we were vindicated by the successful resettlement of the boat people from our shores through working closely with the UNHCR and the UN.

To get control of the numbers and quarantine the refugees away from the local population the government gazetted Pulau Bidong, an island off the Terengganu coast, as a refugee camp and it became off limits to the public. The Malaysian Red Crescent was put in charge of feeding, housing and schooling refugee families and organising access to interviews for resettlement. I visited Pulau Bidong in its early days and I could see that it was the beginning of a consolidated effort by the government to treat people humanely until they could be sent to final destinations. At its height Pulau Bidong hosted 40,000 refugees at any given time. In June 1982 the Sungai Besi camp in the outskirts of Kuala Lumpur was likewise gazetted and it held in total about 60,000 people.

The boat people was a central issue in my diplomatic career and I was involved in it at many points for more than two decades. From my first visit to the Cham refugee camp in Thailand to my defence of our position as Secretary-General, my involvement had stretched over 27 years. I was deeply involved as Ambassador to Vietnam and equally embroiled as Political Under Secretary in Kuala Lumpur. When I returned from my posting in Tokyo in 1989 to head the Ministry of Foreign Affairs as Secretary-General, 14 years after the fall of Saigon, the problem was still with us. Lakshamana Chetty poignantly described the era as 'The Age of the Uprooted' and 'The Century of the Homeless Man'.[82] The boat people presented a situation which wrung the heart; but my job was to use my head to protect the interests of my country.

Now back in Kuala Lumpur and heading Wisma Putra, I could feel the restlessness of the ASEAN countries and understood that they had reached the limit of their patience. Within their own countries they felt the enormous weight of the refugees, eating at their resources and applying pressure on their political and social fabric. Refugees were still arriving in boats, but now they looked less like people running away from persecution and more like people running towards a better life.

So in June 1989 the UN Secretary-General Javier Perez de Cuellar, responding to the ASEAN call, convened the second Geneva Conference. I attended that meeting with Dato' Abu Hassan, the Foreign Minister. Malaysia was elected to chair the conference, and I remember clearly that the US Deputy Secretary of State Lawrence Eagleburger met with Dato' Abu Hassan at a meeting where I was present. We showed him the draft of the chairman's final statement which we had carefully crafted to take into account the views of all the countries attending. He was happy with the statement. The French had initially disagreed with parts of the draft. After being told that the US delegation had already accepted it, the French finally accepted the draft statement without any reservations. We had a smooth passage at the meeting.

The results of the conference were a success in terms of Malaysian interests. The conference adopted the Comprehensive Plan of Action (CPA), which called for effective steps by Vietnam to deter 'organised, clandestine departures', to expand and to speed up the Orderly Departure Programme (ODP), to establish temporary refuge for all asylum seekers, and to repatriate those regarded as non-refugees. It also provided for the creation of regional holding centres. As a result of this conference the resettlement countries agreed to double their intake.

However, it was another seven years, and after my retirement, that the final chapter of the boat people was written. By then more than 250,000 refugees had landed on our shores. In 1991 Pulau Bidong was closed, and the Sungai Besi transit camp in 1996. This brought to a close this human saga, and when the very last refugee left in 2005 Malaysia heaved a huge sigh of relief.

### Endnotes

77    See preceding Chapter.

78    A. Lakshmana Chetty, 1991, 'Resolution of the Problem of Boat People: The Case for a Global Initiative', *ISIL Year Book of International Humanitarian and Refugee Law*. Professor A. Lakshmana Chetty is Director of Centre for Studies on Indochina & South Pacific, Sri Venkateswara University, Tirupati.

79    De Mello was killed by a terrorist bomb which blew up the UN headquarters in Baghdad on 19 August, 2003.

80    A. Lakshmana Chetty, *op. cit.*, p. 4, quoting Stephen Chee, "Southeast Asia in 1988: Portents for the future," *South-east Asian Affairs 1989*, Singapore, Institute of Southeast Asian Studies, 1989, p. 24.

81    Wikipedia: *Non-refoulement* is a principle of the international law, which forbids the returning of a victim of persecution to their country/government. *Non-refoulement* is a key facet of refugee law that protects refugees from being returned to places where their lives or freedoms could be threatened. Unlike political asylum, which applies to those who can prove a well-grounded fear of persecution based on membership in a social group or class of persons, *non-refoulement* refers to the generic repatriation of people, generally refugees back into war zones and other disaster areas.

82    A. Lakshmana Chetty, *op. cit.*

# CHAPTER 8

# China: A Transformational Journey

After having been in Switzerland for almost three years, following my tour in Hanoi, I received word that I might soon be posted out, but the source of this information did not reveal where my next posting would be. I was interested in getting back to Bangkok and I tried to pass word back home to that effect, hoping it would reach the ears of the Foreign Minister Tan Sri Ghazali Shafie. Bangkok was my first posting and I went back there again in 1975. The friendships that I had earlier established there would serve me well, I thought, as some of my Thai friends were now sitting in senior positions at the foreign ministry. However, the decision had already been made. I was to proceed to Beijing and concurrently accredited to North Korea.

I was not in the least unhappy. I was one of the members on the negotiating team for the establishment of diplomatic relations with China in 1974, a team that was ably led by Tan Sri Zakaria Ali,[83] then Permanent Representative to the UN. China was still an enigma, mysterious and out of reach for Malaysians. Tours to China were still in the future; only a few Malaysians went there for medical treatment. We were all curious about it. Adding to my excitement, this was a time of geostrategic change taking place in the global community. Not only was China a great country with an old civilisation, it was emerging as a strong player in the global world.

A major and distinct shift in Malaysian foreign policy had begun when Tun Abdul Razak took the reins of government from the early 1970s. Malaysia had opted for a policy of equidistance among the major powers and a newly open and inclusive foreign policy. Malaysia dismantled its pro-west stance and discarded its anti-communist phobias. The country rapidly expanded its diplomatic relations with several other countries including those in the eastern bloc.

It was within this foreign policy shift that Tun Abdul Razak saw the inevitability of relations with the People's Republic of China. In the spring of 1974 Tun Abdul Razak and Chinese Premier Zhou Enlai signed the Joint Communique that established diplomatic relations between the two countries, the first country in ASEAN to do so. This was a historic landmark in Malaysia's foreign policy. China, by the time I arrived, in the late 1970s and through the 1980s was well on the road towards modernisation, fully committed to its policy of economic transformation. The state launched an aggressive campaign of reforms aimed at attracting foreign investment and providing business opportunities.

Trade between our two countries had existed for centuries and was fairly well-established. After diplomatic relations were established and up to 1983, the year I landed in Beijing, there was a steady growth in bilateral trade. The two countries complemented each other. China wanted Malaysian natural resources, petroleum, rubber, wood and palm oil, all critical to their drive towards modernisation. Malaysia was happy to import manufactured and semi-finished products from China. But there was still a huge, unrealised potential for increased trade and investment. I therefore set my mind to explore this potential.

However, standing in the way of improved relations was the

Chinese policy of state-to-state relations on the one hand and party-to-party on the other. Even during the negotiations for the establishment of diplomatic relations the question of CCP and CPM[84] relations became a sticking point. It continued to bedevil our bilateral relations. This matter was raised by Tan Sri Ghazali Shafie during his visit to China following Dr. Mahathir's visit in 1985.[85] During this visit, after dinner at my residence, Tan Sri Ghazali Shafie and the Chinese Foreign Minister Wu Xuqian got into a heated debate. Tan Sri Ghazali Shafie accused the Chinese of 'shaking our hands and kicking our backsides at the same time'.[86] The Revolutionary Voice of Malaya (Suara Revolusi Malaya) was still operating their shortwave broadcast as late as 1983, supporting the activities of the CPM, which had by this time moved their centre of operations to Betong in southern Thailand. Members of the CPM who had taken refuge in China were well provided for by the CCP.[87] It was against this backdrop that I had to operate.

After a brief break at home I left for Beijing, transiting Hong Kong and taking a CAAC flight. On the flight we were served with an excuse for soup, a concoction slightly better than hot water with a pinch of salt and pepper. Suddenly the folding tray of this aging aircraft of Soviet vintage gave way and the entire contents of the bowl poured straight onto my crotch. This was my Chinese baptism!

I was received at the airport by the Chief of Protocol, as was the normal diplomatic practice, as well as some senior staff from the Embassy. From the airport we drove on what seemed to me like a country road into the city of Beijing. As we drove through the city I was overwhelmed by the waves of humanity on bicycles.

I soon arrived at the Embassy located at Sanlitun. The street was lined on one side by embassy buildings with sizable compounds built by the Chinese government on long lease to the diplomatic missions. We were hemmed in by the Australian Embassy on the right and the Spanish Embassy on the left. Two blocks away was the Cambodian Embassy (CGDK)[88] whose Ambassador was a Khmer Rouge with whom I had many dealings throughout my stay in Beijing. Standing guard at the gate was a PLA (People's Liberation Army) soldier, not so much to secure the Embassy as to prevent Chinese citizens from entering it.

Having settled in as quickly as I could, I began to plan my work, particularly visits to several provincial capitals to explore economic opportunities. China's early modernisation was focused on the eastern seaboard cities of Shenzhen, the newly established industrial city Zhuhai which adjoined Macau, Shantou in the Guangdong province, and Xiamen in the Fujian province. These cities were to spearhead the opening up of China to foreign investment. Other cities, like Shanghai and Tianjin, along the northern seaboard had already been targeted to play a major role in attracting the global market. Steering this national effort, known as *socialism with Chinese characteristics* was Deng Xiaoping, strongly backed by Premier Zhao Ziyang, and General-Secretary of the Party Hu Yaobang.

Many other countries were sniffing out opportunities in China, so I quickly got to work. I travelled to several major cities to meet and discuss with the governors, mayors and bureaucrats charged with economic management at provincial level. I was well received and these officials were equally eager to establish economic links with Malaysia. The discussions also provided me with a clear economic picture on the ground. I could see a rich range of opportunities. But I also learned that there were hardly any uniform rules or regulations governing business partnerships between Chinese and foreign corporations. For a long while this was to be the bugbear of doing business in China.

Travelling in China in those days was a hassle, not only from the point of view of getting from one place to another, but also of confirming hotels. Air travel in China was monopolised by the CAAC and confirmed tickets were only issued from point A to point B. A new ticket from point B to point C would have to be purchased *at* point B, and so on. I could not rely on such an arrangement as you could be stranded for days at any of the points along the route. It was only through the intervention of the Service Bureau[89] that I managed to string together an itinerary with secured bookings on the CAAC flights. I made my journey to Chongqing, Xian, Xiamen, Guangzhou, Shanghai and back to Beijing. I visited Shenzhen at a later stage taking advantage of my trip to Hong Kong for the bag-run.[90] Later I drove to Tianjin, the port city that serves Beijing. On my return, I submitted my report and recommendations to Wisma Putra. I recommended that the political problem of party-to-party be put aside for the time being. I knew there were voices who could not understand why Malaysia should have much to do with communist China at all. But as many other countries were already knocking on Chinese doors and eyeing the rich opportunities there Malaysia could not be left behind. I strongly recommended that the Prime Minister visit China and that he bring with him entrepreneurs and businessmen to begin our entry into this new market.

Soon after, Dr. Mahathir arrived in the autumn of 1985 at the head of a more than 200-strong delegation including cabinet ministers, government officials, and private sector businessmen and entrepreneurs. His official visit took him from Beijing to Shanghai, Suzhou, Xian, and finally Guangzhou.

The official meeting, which took place the following day, was held at the Great Hall of the People at Tiananmen Square next to the Forbidden City. This impressive building constructed in 1959 in less than a year was a monument to the indomitable spirit of the Chinese. It consists of several magnificent halls, among them the Congress Hall where the Chinese People's Political Consultative Conference (CPPCC)[91] and the National People's Congress (NPC)[92] meet. The meeting between the two leaders was as frank as it was polite. The charm and easy manner of Zhao Ziyang was beguiling and certainly put Dr. Mahathir at ease and set the tone for an agreeable and pleasant discussion. The one looming political problem, the relationship between the CCP and CPM, was not mentioned at the meeting. Dr. Mahathir decided not to raise it. He explained later to the business leaders who accompanied him that it was pointless to include it as "we are fully aware of each other's position". I was happy with the position he took, the one I had earlier recommended to the Government.

A number of agreements were reached including the need to establish direct trade relations and issues of economic expansion. The Agreement on the Avoidance of Double Taxation was signed during the visit. These broad agreements worked out during the meeting were to pave the way in later years for the signing of a Trade Agreement, Agreement on Investment Protection, and Shipping and Air Transport Agreements which laid the foundation for robust economic and trade relations.

As was normal practice Zhao Ziyang threw a lavish banquet at the Great Hall of the People for his guests. Dr. Mahathir reciprocated the gesture by having a dinner in honour of Zhao Ziyang at the Great Wall Hotel, one of the newest western-style hotels at the time. While we were seated to be served I was summoned to the main table and once there Dr. Mahathir whispered into my ear, asking what he should do as Premier Zhao Ziyang and other Chinese guests on the main table had requested beer, and I suspected that *maotai* was also included in the request. I whispered back to him that as host it would be embarrassing for him to say no, and that I would sort things out once everything was over. And so, the host was at ease and guests were happy, and the dinner went well.

The next day Dr. Mahathir called on Deng Xiaoping at Zhongnanhai,[93] (literally meaning central and southern sea) a complex of beautiful old buildings adjacent to the Forbidden City where the leadership had their residences and offices. The lakes are artificial, the first of which (the northern lake) was constructed during the Jin Dynasty (1115–1234), a northern dynasty formed by the Tangut Jurchen tribe from Manchuria coexisting with the Song Dynasty (960–1279), for the leisurely pleasure of the emperors. Subsequently the succeeding Yuan (1279–1368) and Ming (1368–1644) dynasties added other lakes. Around the lakes pavilions, shrines, temples and a number of palaces were built in the most exquisite Chinese architectural style.

Since the early days of the People's Republic of China Zhongnanhai has served as the nerve centre of the government. More structures have been added to house, among others, the Central Committee of the CCP, as well as the State Council. The complex provides maximum security and privacy and to this day is shrouded in mystery as it is closed to the general public.[94]

The meeting with Deng Xiaoping was held in an amicable atmosphere with friendly exchanges on ways to enhance bilateral relations. He seemed knowledgeable on Malaysia expressing confidence that relations between the two countries would flourish. On this subject he was most effusive giving the impression that already relations between the two countries were on the right track. Deng Xiaoping was a chain smoker and kept a spittoon at his side, and used it frequently, which was his normal practice during his official meetings with foreign dignitaries. On the way back in the car with Dr. Mahathir, I jokingly observed that our relations could not be bad as Deng Xiaoping had only spat three times during the whole meeting. Dr. Mahathir looked at me and smiled.

Dr. Mahathir also met President Li Xiannian and General-Secretary of the Party Hu Yaobang. The discussion with these leaders touched on bilateral relations and also regional and international issues. It was indeed a rare honour for a visiting Prime Minister to be given the opportunity to meet the top four personalities in the Chinese hierarchy. I felt that the long and hard discussions I had had with the Chinese Foreign Ministry had paid off. I was pleased.

Interspersed with the official functions the private sector had its own set of meetings with counterparts and business corporations, exploring avenues and opportunities for the expansion of economic and trade relations and providing them with the window to do business in later years. These private sector meetings were repeated in Shanghai and Guangzhou with regional and city authorities. Visits to the Great Wall, the Ming Tombs, and a tour of the Forbidden City were arranged for Dr. Mahathir and his wife.

In Shanghai, apart from the official meeting with city officials and provincial authorities, the Chinese had organised a tour of the old section of the city that reflects, through their different and distinct architectural characteristics, the presence of foreign powers in the second half of the 19th and first half of the 20th century. The old section was carved up during the period of European and Japanese intrusion, referred to in history as the 'cutting of the Chinese melon'. These were the concessions made by the Chinese as a result of the unequal treaties imposed upon them by the Western powers then.

Dr. Mahathir and his wife were also invited to witness a major abdominal surgery carried out using acupuncture to anaesthetise the patient. Throughout the surgery the patient was conscious and indeed was carrying on a conversation with the nurse seated at the head of the operating table. Only a small screen placed on the upper part of the patient's chest prevented him from seeing how badly he was being cut up. It was my first, and thankfully, only such experience.

After Shanghai the delegation left for Suzhou for a short break in the official visit, where Dr. Mahathir and his wife were the guests of Robert Kuok[95] at his newly-opened Shangri-la Hotel. From there the journey took them to Xian to visit the famous Terracotta Army of Shi Huangti, the Qin Dynasty Emperor (221 BC–210 BC). Dr. Mahathir and wife also visited the magnificent old mosque in Xian, which at a first glance would be mistaken for a Chinese temple instead of a mosque. It is beautifully crafted in the Chinese architectural style. Finally the last leg of the official visit took Dr. Mahathir to Guangzhou where, after two days of official meetings with city authorities and private sector meetings, the delegation left for Kuala Lumpur.

A Malaysian car company hoping to showcase Malaysia's breakthrough in heavy industry, no doubt to please Dr. Mahathir and hopefully to impress the Chinese, brought in two units of Proton Saga to be exhibited in Beijing. The Chinese were not impressed. They were already producing their own cars, the Hongqi, the Red Flag, a gas-guzzling mammoth of a car, used by the top leaders for official functions. The local Chinese were simply not interested in cars. Private ownership of cars and motor vehicles was not yet heard of. Their blunder arose from lack of consultation with the Embassy and very poor market research.

The visit of Dr. Mahathir was the turning point in our bilateral relations with China. It set the stage for more visits, both official and private, seeking business opportunities. As relations multiplied, along with mutual trust and confidence, more private visits took place, visits which were no longer controlled and monitored by Malaysia's Special Branch.[96] There was by now a relaxation on travel to China. Dr. Mahathir's visit marked the beginning of a more constructive and robust engagement that saw Malaysia and China enter a new stage of bilateral economic and trade relations.

Following Dr. Mahathir's visit, Tan Sri Ghazali Shafie,[97] then Foreign Minister, led a delegation smaller in size but still with the same purpose. This was later followed by a delegation of key businessmen led by Tun Ismail Ali, the chairman of PNB.[98]

Wherever our delegations went the Chinese were unabashedly happy to receive us. I am sure they were equally happy to receive delegations from other countries. After the official discussions, a good meal followed with beer and *maotai*, all at the expense of the state. I, too, enjoyed the meals.

Living in China in those days was altogether an exciting time for me. Life was not uncomfortable. There were a few outlets where foreigners could shop; the main one was the Friendship Store where purchases were settled by foreign exchange certificates issued by the Bank of China. There was, however, not much to be had, so, from time to time, we had to fall back on our regular bag-runs to Hong Kong to bring in foodstuff and other items needed for diplomatic functions. The few open markets that were allowed by the authorities catered more to the needs of the locals.

But still Beijing offered some excellent local cuisine. Worth mentioning are the three duck restaurants, which were frequently patronised by foreigners and diplomats. One was the 'Big Duck' simply because it was the biggest of the three, one the 'Small Duck' for obvious reasons, and the third the 'Sick Duck' because it was located close to a hospital. There were also a few Muslim restaurants ran by Han Chinese Muslims while others were run by Muslims from Central Asia, mainly the Uighurs. The newly-opened western-style hotels, The Jianguo Hotel, the Great Wall Hotel, and the Holiday Inn became favourite spots for diplomats and foreign visitors. The Grand Old Lady of Beijing, the Beijing Hotel, continued to serve a wide variety of excellent food most of the time.

An old mosque serving the local community was also a meeting point for Muslims, diplomats and others. I had, by this time, befriended the *imam* of the mosque and at times sat down with him to exchange views on current affairs, particularly those touching on the Muslim community in China.

Islam has a rich heritage in China with a Muslim population today of 140 million. Its history goes right back to the seventh century during the Tang Dynasty when an embassy arrived there, supposedly sent by the third Caliph only 20 years after the death of the Prophet. The *imam* took great pains to relate to me how, during the Cultural Revolution, mosques were defaced and destroyed and the Quran burnt, all in the hope that their faith would be destroyed. He went on to say that under threat of death he and his followers were forced to eat pork. He, however, survived this tumultuous period because his faith, he said, was unshakeable.

In between taking care of the increasing flow of visitors from Malaysia and the frequent diplomatic dinners and functions, with the occasional game of *sepak takraw*[99] and badminton, sometimes with Prince Sihanouk[100] at his palace in Beijing, there was not much to do. There was hardly any social interaction with the foreign ministry officials or officials of other ministries.

Finding myself with ample free time I tried my hand at learning Chinese. The only Chinese I knew till then were some unprintable words in Hokkien[101] that I learned from mixing with my *no-good* schoolmates in Bukit Mertajam. However, I found the language puzzling and I failed completely. As if trying to learn Chinese was not ambitious enough I started taking lessons in Chinese brush painting. Soon these lessons were also left by the wayside. I became bored with painting the lotus and its leaves, or rocks, for days, weeks and months on end. The final straw was when I was told by my art teacher that calligraphy on a Chinese painting is as important as the painting itself. Both these adventures put an end to some of my self-delusions.

China was going through some interesting changes. Although the investment zones on the coastline had little visible impact on people in Beijing or the hinterland, there was a perceptible easing of restrictions, both from the point of view of private business as well as movement of people from one region to another. Migration from the interior to the economic centres, particularly the eastern seaboard, was taking place in double-quick time. While the CAAC was painfully slow in upgrading its services and its aging fleet of Soviet aircraft, the railway continued to provide the best mode of transport and the best service, always comfortable and always on schedule.

I was able to travel about quite extensively on my own. The greatness and vastness of China, both ancient and modern, is something to behold. I observed that most of its people had adequate housing and did not seem to go hungry as I had seen in other countries. Despite past disasters, both natural and man-made, the country that Chairman Mao bequeathed to his people was a nation that had gone through a series of political, social and cultural convulsions, and had finally decided to move forward. Of course, directing and managing every step was the Chinese Communist Party.

As I look back today I am gratified at how our relationship developed to the extent that both countries could take pride in it. Twenty-six years later China's highest officials still remembered it.

In April 2011, the Chinese Premier Wen Jiabao in an interview with Malaysian and Indonesian journalists, said, "I cannot help but recall two major historical events in the history of exchanges between China and Malaysia. The first is that when China was in its most difficult moments, Malaysia was the first ASEAN member to establish diplomatic relations with China. The second event is that Malaysia proposed to ASEAN 20 years ago to begin a dialogue with China. As an ancient Chinese proverb goes, 'do not forget what favours others have done for you' and we have never forgotten these."[102] Tun Abdul Razak laid the basis for recognition of China by moving Malaysia towards a more independent and proactive foreign policy. Then in the '80s, China opened up its seaboard provinces to foreign capital and Malaysia moved decisively to seize these opportunities. Dr. Mahathir embraced the idea of doing business with China—and put the politics of China's support for the MCP on the backburner. This not only brought immense economic benefits to Malaysia, but in the end helped solve the political problem as well. In December 1989, three years after I had left Beijing, a peace accord was signed between the Malaysian Government and the CPM. The last impediment to our bilateral relations was removed.

In December 1989, barely two months after CHOGM, I travelled to Haadyai, South Thailand to witness the signing of the peace accord between the Malaysian Government and the CPM. The accord came about as a result of efforts by General Chavalit Yongchaiyudh who was Deputy Prime Minister and Defence Minister of Thailand at that time and Dr. Mahathir. It marked the end of the communist insurgency carried out by the CPM, first against the British Colonial power and later against the Malaysian Government. With the stroke of a pen Chin Peng's dream of establishing a People's Democratic Republic of Malaya was forever buried.

For me it held a special significance. Finally, the Emergency was put behind us after decades of destruction and discord. I remember the dead bodies at the Kulim Police Station of both communist terrorists and ordinary policemen. I remember buses ambushed and burnt, estate managers roaring into the Kulim Club in their specially armoured vehicles. Then later, young Malaysians in the urban areas losing their liberty and even their lives as they joined the CPM to fight the government. And throughout these years, Special Forces were dying from anti-personnel mines and booby traps laid along the Malaysian border with Thailand. Now this hopeless struggle was over. Social and political conflict had moved into legal structures and peaceful channels. And the impediments and irritants in our bilateral relations with China were removed.

## North Korea

Within the general policy of equidistance and balanced relations with all countries whether east or west, I was also concurrently appointed ambassador to the Democratic People's Republic of Korea (North Korea). I requested for a date to present my credentials to the Great Leader Kim Il Sung. It was quite a wait but finally we were told that a window of about a week was available and possible for the presentation of credentials.

On this first visit I was put up in a hotel that was supposed to be the top hotel in Pyongyang. There were four other ambassadors from African countries who were to present their credentials at the same time. The five of us were the only guests. Meals were served in a massive dining hall made more massive by the absence of other diners. I asked at one point if we could move to another table which was more pleasingly located. The answer was a definite no. It took me some time to figure out that perhaps our table was bugged and at the other end of the listening device were English or Malay speakers.

We waited for three days without a word about the presentation. I made it known to the protocol that, whatever happened, I and my staff would return to Beijing as planned. Finally, late on the fourth day we were told to be ready to fly out of Pyongyang to an unknown destination for the presentation of credentials. I learned later that the Great Leader was at Samjiyon, a village in the northeast of the country with a beautiful huge lake surrounded by the Baekdu mountains. It was situated close to the Chinese border.

We flew in an aircraft big enough to take about 12 people. The other ambassadors were there accompanied by their wives. We were already on the tarmac when the door of the aircraft was opened for us to board. The others scrambled on board leaving me and my accompanying staff and the Foreign Minister on the tarmac. I gestured to the Foreign Minister that he should board the plane before me. He turned to me and remarked that there certainly was a great cultural difference between the Asians and the Africans. I smiled.

The next day was the big moment. In the presentation ceremony I was given precedence over the other ambassadors, even though they were more senior to me by virtue of the fact that they had been in Beijing long before I arrived. I would never know if the incident at the airport had anything to do with this out-of-order presentation. In the brief meeting after the presentation the Great Leader was charming enough and pleasantly smiled as he asked about Malaysia. I could easily have been taken in by his friendly demeanour. But this was a man with absolute power over his people.

We were taken on a little tour of this beautiful mountain village and ended up at one farm where I commented on the farm machine they were using. The farmer, who was probably head of the commune, immediately shot back saying that they considered themselves fortunate because these machines "were given to them by the Dear Leader". Not wanting to antagonise him or the official guide I nodded as if in recognition of this great contribution by the Dear Leader.[103]

We returned to Pyongyang the next morning and onwards to Beijing the next day. During the days of hanging about waiting for the meeting, I managed to sight-see a bit of Pyongyang, including the fabulous underground railway station that looked more like a palace in a lost city than a train station. We were, of course, guided throughout the tour.

I also had the opportunity to call on the Indonesian Ambassador who was the only resident ASEAN Ambassador in North Korea. He was kind enough to invite us to lunch at his residence. He told me how frustrating life was for a diplomat in Pyongyang from a professional point of view. There was very little contact with the Foreign Ministry and hardly any contact with the people.

I made two more visits to Pyongyang, the second time to get myself acquainted with some senior officials in the Foreign Ministry as well as with other ministries dealing with economic and trade matters. There was nothing to talk about in terms of trade or economic relations. I was just going through the motions, giving the impression that Malaysia was interested in expanding our bilateral relations.

During this visit I was taken to Panmunjom.[104] It was an unforgettable experience. The border guards from both North and South Korea were facing each other just a few feet apart staring at each other in the face and looking menacingly stern and serious. The whole area was enveloped in eerie silence. I was taken into the meeting room, demarcated with a white line painted across it and across the table to show the division between the two countries. It was the strangest thing I had ever seen.

After a brief tour I was taken back to the Peace Museum and was asked to write something in the book meant, I suppose, for foreign visitors. I desperately cracked my mind to come up with some neutral statement which I would dare to leave behind in written form. The best I could do was to pen, "It is the supreme duty of everyone to defend the sovereignty and integrity of one's nation".

During this second visit, as it was during my third and final visit, I was invited by Prince Sihanouk to stay at the annex to the palace given by the North Korean Government for his use.[105] I could only speculate why North Korea had made such a gesture to the Prince. My final visit was to say goodbye as part of normal diplomatic practice. I was, however, not given an opportunity to take leave of the Great Leader or of the Dear Leader. However, a farewell dinner was hosted by the Director of the Asian Department in my honour.

My memories of Pyongyang are vague since I never did much more than formalities there. What stuck in my mind were statues, always images of the Great Leader and concrete billboards, huge pieces of socialist artwork, exhorting the people to reunite the country and become patriots of the Korean Workers Party.[106] Others depicted the Korean people's victory over Japanese imperialism. Standing tall in a prominent part of the city was an obelisk-like tower soaring into the sky with a concrete *juche*[107] torch at the top, with the flame painted in bright red, symbolising the national ideology. Also in the main square was a massive portrait of the Great Leader hanging under a giant DPRK flag. Everyone had, without fail, a pin on his or her chest bearing the image of the Great Leader. Unlike the moving mass of Chinese on bicycles in Beijing, here in Pyongyang was a moving mass of Koreans endlessly walking.

It left me with a lasting imprint of a self-described 'socialist paradise on earth' that was so secretive and isolated that it was truly a hermit country. The people were subject to paralysing doses of delusionary propaganda about the virtuous benevolence of the regime and how it was bravely resisting the evil threat from the imperialist world. There was no access whatever to alternative sources of information. So whatever was gurgled out by the regime's propaganda bureau had to be swallowed in toto. It would be treason to do otherwise.

## Endnotes

83   See Chapter 5.

84   CCP: Chinese Communist Party; and CPM: Communist Party of Malaya.

85   See below.

86   Quoting Tan Sri Ghazali Shafie at the after-dinner discussion.

87   Chin Peng, *op. cit.*

88   Coalition Government of Democratic Kampuchea.

89   The Department at the Foreign Ministry in charge of all the needs of foreign missions.

90   This refers to the weekly routine when Home-based staff of the Embassy take turns to deliver our diplomatic bag, containing all our confidential official correspondence to the home ministries and agencies by secured means to our Consulate in Hong Kong for onward transmission to Kuala Lumpur.

91   The Chinese People's Political Consultative Conference (CPPCC), also known as the PCC, is a political advisory body in the People's Republic of China. The organisation consists of delegates from a range of political parties and organisations, as well as independent members. The proportion of representation of the various parties is determined by established convention, negotiated between the parties. The Conference is, to a large degree, controlled by the Communist Party but it is intended to appear to be more representative and be composed of a broader range of interests than is typical of a government office in the People's Republic of China. It typically holds a yearly meeting.

92   The National People's Congress is the highest state body and the unicameral legislative house in the People's Republic of China. The National People's Congress is held in the Great Hall of the People, Beijing, capital of the People's Republic of China; with 2,987 members, it is the largest parliament in the world. The NPC gathers each year along with the People's Political consultative Conference (CPPCC) whose members represent various defined groups of society. NPC and CPPCC together are often called the Lianhui (Two Meetings), making important national level political decisions.

93   Zhongnanhai is an area in central Beijing, China adjacent to the Forbidden City which serves as the central headquarters for the Communist Party of China and the State Council (Central Government) of the People's Republic of China. The term *Zhongnanhai* is closely linked with the central government and senior Communist Party officials. It is often used as a metonym for the Chinese leadership at large (in the same sense that the term White House frequently refers to the President of the United States and his associates).

94   Source: Wikipedia.

95   Malaysia's richest man and an entrepreneur with global business interests.

96   The intelligence arm of the Royal Malaysian Police.

97   See reference at beginning of Chapter.

98   Permodalan Nasional Berhad (PNB) is Malaysia's biggest fund management company.

99   Wikipedia: Sepak takraw is a popular game in Southeast Asia where players use only their head, chest, knee and feet to touch a rattan ball.

100    Following the coup of 1970 when he was deposed by Lon Nol, Prince Sihanouk spent most of his time leisurely in Beijing and Pyongyang, where both the governments of China and North Korea provided him with lavish accommodation and hospitality, with occasional breaks in Paris.

101    A Chinese dialect of Fujian Province that is also commonly spoken in Bukit Mertajam and the northern states of Peninsular Malaysia.

102    *The Star*, 27 April, 2011. I was a member of the negotiating team for both events.

103    Dear Leader referred to the son and heir apparent to the Great Leader, Kim Jong Ill.

104    Panmunjom is located in an abandoned village on the *de facto* border between North and South Korea, where the 1953 Korean Armistice Agreement that halted the Korean War was signed. The building where the armistice was signed still stands though it is north of the Military Demarcation Line, which runs through the middle of the Demilitarised Zone. Its name is often used as a metonym for the nearby Joint Security Area (JSA), where discussions between North and South still take place in blue buildings that straddle the Military Demarcation Line. As such, it is considered one of the last vestiges of the Cold War.

105    But I did not, viewing it as improper to visit a host country and stay in a third party premise.

106    The official name for the Communist Party.

107    *Juche*, loosely translated means self-reliance.

# CHAPTER 9

# Japan: Ethics and Esthetics

Thus far, I had not been to Japan. So while still in China I asked for and obtained permission to take a few days of leave to travel to Japan as a tourist. Tokyo was, after all, just a short hop from Beijing and there were daily flights available.

I arrived there in the later part of February 1986 quite unprepared. After all I was on holiday and there was not much tourist information about Japan in Beijing. My plane landed at Narita airport and it did not take me long to realise I was among a people who lived by a code of conduct and shared values to a degree I had never experienced in any other country. From the very first I was struck by a consummate sense of orderliness, cleanliness and politeness in the Japanese.

We were ushered through immigration and customs by airport attendants in white gloves, bowing deeply, who showed us what to do. It all conveyed to me a feeling of ease and safety, which remained with me throughout my stay. I was overwhelmed by the politeness and helpfulness shown by people I met in the streets and in the restaurants. They spontaneously came up to me and offered to help with instructions, street maps and menus, all written in Japanese. Although there was time to spend only a few days in Tokyo I was filled with admiration for the country and its people and I left wishing that on some future day I would be able to return for a longer visit.

So it is easy to imagine my delight and pleasure, and perhaps also surprise, when soon after my return to Beijing I received the news that my posting after China would be to Japan.

I began my assignment in Tokyo in April 1986 looking forward with great anticipation to knowing Japan in more depth. I knew something about its eventful history from the period of the shogunate to the Meiji restoration in the mid-1800s, the rise of the military and the subsequent challenge to the West, and finally its rise from the devastation and destruction of the Second World War, to become incontrovertibly, a world economic power, second only to the US. And I was intrigued at how the country deliberately opened itself to outside influences and thereby became economically prosperous and technologically advanced.

But culturally, the Japanese themselves remained strongly anchored to their proud cultural heritage. Despite the upheaval of the war, for the Japanese the present is irrefutably bonded to the past. I learned this had to do with its homogenous population who shared common values and felt a collective responsibility for the well-being of their country. The Samurai warrior code of courage and pride and the practice of the Bushido code of honour, was guided by Shintoism, the creative or formative principle of life.[108] This seemed to instil in the Japanese tenacity, fortitude and discipline, and all these collectively contributed to their indomitable spirit and passionate drive to advance their national goals and to carry the country forward. These attributes greatly captured my admiration. I undertook my accreditation to Japan energised by this attraction and determined to advance the already strong bilateral ties.

Malaysia's diplomatic relations with Japan date back to 1958, one year after Malaya gained independence. The newly-independent

Malaya then looked to Japan for much needed financial assistance in order to implement the country's development plan. Even though Japan then, in the late 1950s, was just on the way to recovery itself, over the next two decades it did provide valuable developmental assistance and cooperation.

Attitudes towards Japan in Malaya were coloured by wartime experiences. The Chinese community, at least for a couple of decades after the war, felt a legitimate bitterness over the atrocities committed by the Japanese Occupation forces. But the other communities did not harbour any deep-seated resentment against the Japanese. On the contrary. For most countries in Southeast Asia, except perhaps for Singapore, it was the victory of Japanese forces that destroyed forever the myth of colonial invincibility. It stirred their minds and made the rise of nationalism and finally independence possible. Thus, sentiment and pragmatism moved Malaya to establish diplomatic relations with Japan. Bilateral relations have since flourished and, indeed, the two countries continue to be on the best of terms, diplomatically, economically and culturally, to the present day.

When I arrived there in 1986 strong political bonds already existed. This allowed me to narrow my focus to strengthening economic and trade relations. For several decades both countries had enjoyed robust economic growth. Japan was, and remains, one of Malaysia's major trading partners. Exports to Japan include LNG (liquid natural gas), timber and, later, manufactured electronic products produced by Japanese companies operating in Malaysia. The list of import items to Malaysia is long and includes heavy equipment and machinery, automobiles, electronics of all sorts as well as manufactured goods. Malaysian farmers were calling their tractors *kubota* and their water pumps *suzuki*, demonstrating how ubiquitous and useful Japanese products had become.

In turn, Japan has found conditions in Malaysia attractive for investment, and a number of well-known Japanese companies have set up operations in Malaysia, particularly in the states of Selangor and Penang. These companies then re-export their products to Japan and to other countries. FDI (Foreign Direct Investment) and ODA (Official Development Aid) were important elements in the economic relationship

As soon as Dr. Mahathir became Prime Minister, Japan assumed even more importance to Malaysia. As early as in the mid-70s when he was Deputy Prime Minister, Dr. Mahathir made frequent visits to Japan, most of them unofficial. During these visits he had established close relationships with several important Japanese entrepreneurs, businessmen and thinkers. He was greatly influenced by Japan's impressive success, by their work ethics and by their creative and management skills. He wanted Malaysia to learn from Japan. Six months after becoming Prime Minister in 1982 he embarked on his Look East Policy.

He was much less enthusiastic about the west and believed that nothing useful could be learned from them. In typical Mahathir style he said: "The Western nations have been labouring under an illusion. They believe in their own intellect and expertise and to them no one else can compete with them. And because of this they no longer work hard and instead take things easy. Through their unions, the western workers agitate for all sorts of benefits until there are western nations that pay more allowance to their unemployed than to those working. Thus many choose not to." This lop-sided argument was used to buttress his Look East Policy, according to one or two of his cabinet colleagues I talked to. To Dr. Mahathir Japan became the logical and obvious alternative, whose work ethics, discipline, dedication and loyalty would serve as a model for Malaysia. It was a policy not hatched in haste but given careful and deliberate consideration aimed at learning the secret behind the Japanese, and later also the Korean, success stories. Dr. Mahathir 'pursued this policy with intellectual vigour and political sense of urgency'[109] despite cynical remarks by some members of his Cabinet who expressed serious reservations in private about this new policy. Japan, of course, welcomed the policy.

Soon hundreds of students and trainees were attached to universities and institutions of higher learning and to technical and vocational institutions in the major cities in Japan. Hundreds more did short study tours of Japanese industries and corporations. All these people returned home with new knowledge and skills. Thousands have benefitted and the Look East Policy continues to receive encouragement and support from the Japanese Government.

In other ways the love affair shortly became rather one-sided. In 1983, Dr. Mahathir sought a multi-billion Yen loan to finance a number of key industrial projects, which would transform Malaysia into an industrialised country, including the iron and steel plant in Terengganu and the Proton car project. Two years later, the Yen strengthened dramatically against the Ringgit, tripling the size of this debt. This was because of pressure from the United States to lower its trade deficit with a number of the leading economies by weakening the exchange rate of the US dollar. In 1985, Germany, France, Britain and Japan signed an agreement, referred to as the Plaza Accords, to do just this at the Plaza Hotel, New York.

The main target was Japan. The Yen was revalued by 300 percent and Malaysia's debt correspondingly went up by 300 percent. This had dramatic negative effects on Malaysia's economy. We were left with a 'hugely inflated debt burden'.[110] This seriously undermined the industrialisation strategy and threw out of gear future plans. It was one-eyed but understandable that Malaysia saw itself as victimised by a conspiracy of the big powers.

The silver lining behind this dark cloud, if any, was that more and more Japanese companies started to move their operations to countries like Malaysia in order to circumvent high production costs in their own country. This helped somewhat to cushion the impact on Malaysia of the Yen revaluation.

From the very beginning of my stay in 1986 it became my urgent task to find some kind of solution, even if temporary, to lessen this horrendous debt burden. My calls on Gaimusho,[111] the Vice-Finance Minister, Toyoo Gyoten, MITI,[112] and other relevant agencies of the Japanese government, did not produce any positive response. The corporate leaders whom I met were equally unresponsive. I remember that Dr. Mahathir, on one of his many unofficial visits to Japan, met Prime Minister Takashita privately and discussed the massive problems Malaysia was facing. When I asked him how the meeting had gone he said that Takashita had said "*muzukashii*" (Japanese for 'difficult'). That, I felt, summed up the indifference of the Japanese at the highest level.

This problem stayed with us and was brought up during the discussions when Prime Minister Takashita paid an official visit to Malaysia in early May 1989. The matter was discussed at some length at the official meeting of the two delegations with Dr. Mahathir laying out a number of options in order to find a way to ease the debt burden. He pointed out that the loan repayments to the Japanese government had increased by a staggering 79.5 percent. He put forward a number of requests in a desperate effort to get Malaysia out of this financial trap, emphasising that Malaysia was justified in making these requests. Prime Minister Takashita confessed that this question was the one that troubled him most in the relations between Japan and Malaysia. But he said that he was not able to do anything about it. The meeting ended on a negative note.

Another effect of the very strong Japanese economy during the latter half of the '80s, this time affecting Japan in general and Tokyo in particular, was the tremendous increase in real estate prices. We heard about residential homes which increased so much in value that their owners could not afford to continue to live in them. It became impossible for them to pay their property taxes. Malaysia owned two such attractive lots of land in Tokyo. One was located in Shibuya and the other in Hon-Komagome.

Shibuya is an inner-city community in the west of Tokyo and this is where Malaysia's embassy is located. It was a pleasant part of Tokyo where business companies and private enterprises established offices but it also offered good shopping and excellent restaurants. Several other countries had chosen this part of Tokyo for their embassies and residences.

Hon-Komagome, where Malaysia had the Ambassador's residence, is located in northern Tokyo, between Ueno and Ikebukuro. It was a quiet neighbourhood with private houses surrounded by small gardens. On both sides of the residence we were neighbour to a girls' school. Our building was quite big by any standards and even more so by Japanese standards. We had a lovely garden across which one could look over to the beautiful Rikugien Park. It was always pleasant and soothing to return there after a day's work.

However, commuting between the residence and the chancery[113] was a nightmare due to the peak hour traffic jams, which seemed only to get worse over time. At the best of times the journey would take from 45 minutes to one hour in one direction. At worst there was no way of telling when you would arrive.

Considering that real estate prices had sky-rocketed during the latter part of the '80s it seemed prudent to look into the possibility of selling the residence and establishing a new one closer to the chancery.

The girls' school had already approached us to buy our property in order to establish one contiguous school complex. I presented the idea to the Ministry and it was studied by various agencies at home. They decided that we should sell the Hon-Komagome property and use the proceeds to build a new residence and chancery on the existing property in Shibuya. The Shibuya plot of land was large enough to accommodate both. The project was approved and work began during my term of office.

It was during the process of realising the project that I ran into all sorts of problems, both in Tokyo and, more seriously, at home in Malaysia. There was competition for the contract to build and strings were being pulled. This political interference only stopped when the Cabinet appointed a committee of three cabinet ministers, headed by the Finance Minister, to decide on the way forward. Even after that a complaint was lodged by one of the parties who had bid for the project accusing me of irregularities. I was cleared of these accusations as soon as the investigation started.

In Tokyo I had to deal with the objections raised by the neighbours in Shibuya. The proceeds from the sale of the residence were enough to finance also the purchase of a piece of land in a residential area close to the embassy where an apartment building could be built to accommodate our diplomatic officers and their families. Considering how expensive Tokyo rentals had become, an apartment building owned by Malaysia would produce further savings. However, the building we had in mind would be higher than many of the surrounding houses and we immediately received objections. I visited the six or so neighbours to explain to them the project and finally an amicable solution was reached. The contractor agreed to send them and their wives on a one week all-paid visit to Malaysia.

The whole project—a new embassy, a new residence and the addition of an apartment block—was completed in the fall of 1992, and was officially opened by the Prime Minister. By that time I was already back in Kuala Lumpur, but I was pleased to have been invited to Tokyo to see the successful result of all the negotiations, struggles and headaches we had endured in 1988 and 1989.

Living in Japan was a fascinating experience for me and my wife. To familiarise us with the country, the Foreign Ministry organised trips for us to different places. We spent a few days in Okinawa, the southernmost major island with an almost subtropical climate. As a Malaysian I did not think I could get very impressed by orchids, but I had never seen orchids as magnificent as the ones in the Tropical Dream Centre in the Ocean Expo Park. Another aspect of being from Malaysia is that I am not an expert on ice or snow, and could not imagine how it could be possible to create huge art works from such perishable material. A journey to Hokkaido proved that it was possible.

Wherever we went the reception was polite, warm and welcoming. Interesting programmes were prepared in detail, and we were treated to the most delicious meals, the presentation of which was like pieces of art. For me to talk about food in Japan would be to overwhelm with superlatives so I shall not go into that subject here. Suffice to say that I am an absolute fan of it. However, an occasional dish might need getting used to.

My wife and I were once invited to stay in a Japanese home in Shikoku. It was a traditional Japanese house. We slept on *futons*, Japanese mattresses, which were placed directly on the *tatami* mats covering the floor of our sleeping quarters. The bath was spacious with room for several to bathe at the same time. The family had prepared a very elaborate evening meal in our honour and had invited relatives and friends from the village. The atmosphere was warm, funny and boisterous.

It was easy to understand that a lot of effort had gone into the preparations for the meal and only the very finest and freshest ingredients were used. Dish after dish came, each delicious and beautifully presented. There was fish, raw and prepared, vegetables, pickled and fresh and, at the end, a raw chicken on a sculptured piece of ice. It was freshly slaughtered and had been cut up into small morsels with yellow drops of chicken fat still hanging on to them. I have always prided myself as being adventurous in food, but suddenly I did not feel so adventurous. We were told it had been the finest specimen in their chicken coop and it was now in front of me as a special treat. There was no way not to eat it; it was served with a dipping sauce and offered first of all to me. I hoped the host and his family did not notice how much I struggled. Their kindness and hospitality was unsurpassed. I made sure, however, that this special treat never crossed my culinary path again.

During the time I was in Japan, Emperor Hirohito was on the throne. Although already in his late 80s he continued his tradition of receiving the diplomatic corps at a magnificent lunch every New Year's day and also on his birthday. It was also on those days that the Imperial Palace grounds were opened for the public to visit. It was an honour to participate in these lunches. The elegance and utter simplicity of the palace, both inside and outside, never failed to impress us. We were ushered in to pay our respects to the Emperor who would then withdraw while we continued to a hall where long tables had been set up.

The lunches, for both events, would be served in a *bento* box, which, for this occasion, would be a red and black lacquered box with separate compartments for different kinds of food. The box itself would be wrapped in a *furoshiki*, a decorative cloth, which made it easy to take the *bento* box home, which was the intention. Another item on the table, also meant as a memento, was an imperial *sake* cup. It was made of the thinnest, white porcelain and decorated with the imperial chrysanthemum in gold. I have now five of these *sake* cups to remember these special occasions by.

One occasion that must remain as a rare honour for me and my wife was when we were invited to lunch with the Emperor. It was the practice of the Royal Household to invite three ambassadorial couples at a time to have the privilege, once during their stay, to join the Emperor for lunch.

In 1989, Crown Prince Akihito hosted the New Year's Day reception. His father Emperor Hirohito was seriously ill and the atmosphere among the guests was sombre. On 7 January, just a week later, the Emperor died after having reigned for 62 years. According to Japanese tradition the Chrysanthemum Throne must not be empty so Crown Prince Akihito became the 125th Emperor in a ceremony, which took place in the Imperial Palace on the same day. The Japanese Cabinet called for a six-day official mourning period for Government agencies and a two-day mourning period for private companies and citizens. Displays of sadness could be seen all over Tokyo. Radio stations played only classical music and TV channels devoted their programmes to memories of Emperor Hirohito.

The Japanese Government announced that the state funeral would take place about 40 to 50 days later. I could only guess at the enormous preparations taking place during that interim to organise this rite according to formal Japanese traditions. Facilities in Tokyo were prepared to receive dignitaries from all over the world. HRH Sultan Azlan Shah, our Deputy King at the time, represented Malaysia.

We received detailed instructions from the Imperial Household regarding the programme, the venue and the dress code. The dress required was a morning coat. However, diplomatic protocol states that a country's national costume will always be considered appropriate if so chosen. Not being the owner of a morning coat, I decided on our national costume. But we now knew that the funeral would take place on 24 February, a time when Tokyo could be both chilly and wet, and that the guests would be in tents.

I indicated to Their Royal Highnesses that the Malay national costume, entirely in silk, might not be enough protection. As for myself I approached the fashionable Mitsukoshi Department Store to rent a morning coat. That was bound to fail. They had nothing in stock for my 192 cm tall body. However, considering the occasion, they took it upon themselves to make one in my size, which they would rent to me. I went back after the funeral to return the suit and pay for the rental, and to my utter surprise the manager told me that I could keep it. It was a very kind gesture, but I also suspect that they realised that it would be difficult to find a Japanese client for a coat of that size. This perfectly tailored suit came in handy for the garden party celebrating Emperor Akihito's enthronement in November 1990, when royalties and dignitaries from all over the world would return to Tokyo. I and my wife were invited to follow our King and Queen for this occasion.

Tokyo was a favourite spot for Malaysians—for those who could afford it. The Sultan of Johor, when King, made no less than four visits to Tokyo while I was there. His Majesty was an avid golfer, trying out various courses in and around Tokyo, and was always fascinated by the golfing equipment produced in Japan. Almost always when the King was in Tokyo, Prince Tokugawa, a Johor Dato', would be at the Okura Hotel, which was where His Majesty preferred to stay. Dato' Tokugawa was a surviving descendant of one of the branches of the Tokugawa clan. The Johor Royal House had a long history of close relationship with the Tokugawa family and continued to stay in touch with them.

All through the three years we stayed in Tokyo we were thoroughly spoiled by the Japanese. Whenever there was an event or a get-together we, as guests of their country, would receive an exquisite gift, most of the time some beautiful handicraft. I would like to be able to say we reciprocated, but there was no way to keep up with their generosity. For instance, we received tickets to the annual Grand Tournament of Sumo wrestling, which gave us the privileged seating in a *tatami* clad square meant for four people. A *bento* box filled with food, as well as beer and *sake*, were included. We were invited to dinners offered by corporate leaders, which took place in traditional Japanese settings where beautiful and highly skilled geishas entertained the guests. One summer the Imperial Hotel of Tokyo treated the ambassadors of those embassies who were their regular clients to a recreational long weekend in Karuizawa in the Japanese Alps.

I think that anybody who has had the privilege of spending some time in Japan is forever affected by that experience, and affected for the better. It was something we often discussed among ourselves in the diplomatic corps. This is not just because of the incredible generosity shown us. It is the impact of what is inherent in the Japanese society; the way they live by qualities of respect, politeness, kindness and helpfulness. Of course, there can be roughness here, too, but we hardly ever witnessed any. Neither did we meet with wilful carelessness or indifference vis-à-vis people, situations or things. There is so much character and beauty in the Japan that I came to know. That is the reason for the title of this chapter.

Japan was a unique experience. It also turned out to be the last country I was posted to as Ambassador. It is difficult for me to imagine any other country which would fascinate me as much. My three years in Japan were among the happiest in my life.

## Endnotes

108   The Shinto principle is the backbone of Japanese culture, code of ethics, fine arts, national structure and family.

109   Chandran Jeshurun, *op. cit.*, p. 173.

110   Chandran Jeshurun, *op. cit.*

111   Referring to the Japanese Foreign Ministry.

112   Japanese Ministry of International Trade and Industry.

113   The chancery is the office segment of the Embassy, the other is the Ambassador's residence. Together they constitute the Embassy.

# CHAPTER 10

# Secretary-General: Facing My Big Test

I became Secretary-General of the Foreign Ministry on 1 April, 1989. Despite it being April Fool's Day, I felt none of the misgivings I had had in some of my earlier postings. I was 52 years old; I had been salted and seasoned in Thailand, Germany, Singapore, United Nations, Vietnam, China and Japan as well as with organisations such as NAM, IOC and ASEAN.

Secretary-General is the highest professional post in the Foreign Service. I had not expected to get it. When I married Lena I assumed that having a foreign wife would automatically disqualify me from the top position. But I was chosen anyway.

Dr. Mahathir had already been Prime Minister for more than a decade. His brand of foreign policy—outspoken in defending the interests of the developing world, critical of the West—had already put Malaysia on the global map. My own diplomatic experience, mainly in Asia, had led me in the same direction. For practitioners of diplomacy like me this shift to a more aggressive policy was refreshing. As some critics were quick to point out, we were 'punching above our weight'.

Dr. Mahathir's hopes and aspirations for Malaysia had extended to other developing countries. He directed his attention particularly to the problems of underdevelopment and poverty, South-South cooperation, US unilateralism on key issues of international security, the *unequal treaty*, as he rightly called it, on Antarctica and the lack of democracy and transparency in UN decision-making processes, especially in the Security Council.

His active and direct involvement in Malaysia's foreign policy and the strong stand he took on many issues kept the Foreign Ministry on its toes virtually 365 days a year. He imposed on Wisma Putra additional responsibilities and with these, enormous pressure to deliver on commitments made. In Dr. Mahathir's hands our nation's diplomatic profile and confidence grew, and mine grew with it.

So without even taking the month's leave that is normal between postings, I launched myself immediately into organising two of the largest Third World events that Malaysia has hosted to date. The first was the Commonwealth Heads of Government Meeting (CHOGM) held for the first time in Malaysia in 1989. The second was the G-15,[114] a group of the 15 stronger economies in the developing world, held in early 1990. These two events would require all the attention and manpower that the Ministry could muster.

CHOGM was my first big test and how I handled the preparations would, I reckoned, determine my future at the Ministry. It was in 1987 at the Vancouver CHOGM that Malaysia made a bid to host the 1989 CHOGM in Kuala Lumpur. Malaysia had invited Commonwealth Third World heads before, after the first CHOGM in Singapore in 1971. Not many came and even fewer were impressed. As Director-General of ASEAN then, I was inexplicably put in charge of the programme. But back then Kuala Lumpur was still a sleepy backwater and we had nothing much to show beyond rubber trees and tin dredges.

Thus by bringing all the Commonwealth leaders to CHOGM

in 1989, Dr. Mahathir believed we had now plenty to show, a whole array of developments that would demonstrate what a Third World country could achieve. Dr. Mahathir had not attended several previous CHOGMs and so had minimal contact with many African and Pacific leaders. We thought it was also time that they took their measure of him.

CHOGM, a biennial meeting of Commonwealth Heads of Government, consists of former British colonies together with Britain, Canada, Australia and New Zealand, in all a total of more than 50 states. The British Queen is the Head of the Commonwealth and by tradition declares the meeting officially opened.

Preparations were already in full swing when I returned. There were two aspects to the preparations. One was the substantive matters, which were to be included in the agenda and on which Malaysia wanted to put its stamp and make its views count. And these had to be completed in time for all members to study and come prepared for discussion.

The second aspect was the administration and protocol. The physical efforts which go into organising a meeting of this scale are enormous, as are the manpower requirements, and, of course, the administrative work to make it all come together. Yeop Adlan Che Rose was appointed the Organising Secretary for the Conference. Later Hashim Taib[115] was pulled from his posting abroad to help him. It is not for me to tell here about the hardships, problems and frustrations they encountered, but it is worth mentioning that they had to coordinate a dozen ministries and departments, from the PM's Office, the Palace and the Police to the Ministries of Immigration, Information, Health and Works, as well as the Military, in a national effort to see CHOGM through successfully.

The preparations for a meeting of this kind involve, among much else, reception at arrival and departure points, transportation, accommodation, medical facilities, food including special requests, security, special programmes for accompanying spouses, and arrangements for almost daily press briefings. A sub-committee was created for each of these activities. Carcosa,[116] the Government Guest House, was being upgraded to receive Queen Elizabeth II. So was the airport in Langkawi where the Retreat talks would be held, and the final touches had to be made to complete the Pelangi Hotel for the Heads and their spouses while in Langkawi.

The main committee for these activities was chaired by the Foreign Minister Dato' Abu Hassan and I was part of it. Dr. Mahathir was hands-on, as usual, and insisted on being regularly updated.

Dr. Siti Hasmah, the wife of the Prime Minister, was equally hands-on with regard to the ladies' programme. She was personally following the upgrading and renovation of Carcosa. She was ably supported by Dato' Zakiah Hanum, Director-General of the National Archives, who was the overall coordinator of the activities for the accompanying wives. The programme included cultural shows, excursions and sightseeing and each one involved a *makan*[117] to give the guests an opportunity to sample the different dishes of Malaysia. The energy with which both Dr. Siti Hasmah and Dato' Zakiah went about their roles was outstanding and contributed in no small measure to the overall success of the Kuala Lumpur CHOGM.

I call the protocol and logistics non-substantive matters but they are, in fact, the backbone for a meeting of this scale. Any glitches in the arrangements would offend the delegates and would certainly have a bearing on the substantive work at the Meeting itself. And certainly, Malaysia's reputation as an efficient and sensitive host would be at risk. We even staged dry runs of the separate Heads' itinerary and their wives' programme, to be sure that they would arrive back at their joint events on time.

It is tradition that the Secretary-General of the Commonwealth provides the first draft of the agenda. He then sends it to the Heads of Government for their input. Some of the ideas are carried forward from earlier CHOGMs, others relate to current political and economic developments that impact the Commonwealth. I had several meetings with the Prime Minister on the Commonwealth Secretariat draft in order to find out his thoughts and views and to reach an agreement on Malaysia's stand on these issues. We were also determined to include some issues of our own in the Langkawi Declaration.[118]

My main duty, besides being in charge overall, was to prepare the documents pertaining to these substantive matters. Ambassador Dato' Abdul Majid Mohamed, the Deputy Secretary-General, was the key man assisting me in this and Ambassador Dato' Renji Sathiah was temporarily brought back from his post overseas to help with the compilation of our positions and to deal with the press.

A month before the Meeting I travelled to London and on 5 September, 1989 addressed a seminar at the Commonwealth Trust. This seminar provided me with the opportunity to explain 'aspects of Malaysian foreign policy' and gave me the added opportunity to inform the seminar of Malaysia's new interest in the Commonwealth. I told them that Kuala Lumpur "would prefer less talk and more action".[119]

Two issues stood out as the foci for the CHOGM meeting. Whether the meeting was a success or a failure would depend upon the outcome of these issues. One was the issue on the environment, and the other was the effort to bring about the final dismantling of apartheid in South Africa. The normal practice was that the Secretariat would be entrusted to provide the working papers.

On the Langkawi Declaration on the Environment, which was the centrepiece of Kuala Lumpur CHOGM, Malaysia took the unusual step of preparing the draft. There were two reasons for this. This was firstly to demonstrate our commitment, and secondly to provide a draft into which we could include our own thoughts. Our draft was based on the discussions I had had with the Prime Minister, and which in principle he had approved. The Secretariat, as is its duty, had also prepared its own draft on the environment, which was submitted to us to study. After some discussions Dr. Mahathir agreed that our draft should form the basis for the discussion on the environment at CHOGM.

I now had to get the Secretariat to agree to this. I travelled twice to London to press our draft and also to go through other issues on the agenda. Shridath Ramphal, the Secretary-General of the Commonwealth, did not seem happy with our proposal. He took it up with Dr. Mahathir on his visit to Kuala Lumpur before CHOGM to discuss preparations. The Prime Minister stood his ground and insisted that the Malaysian draft be used.

The outcome was that the Langkawi Declaration on the Environment 1989 states: "The responsibility for ensuring a better environment should be equitably shared and the ability of developing countries to respond be taken into account." And "Environment concerns should not be used to introduce a new form of conditionality, nor as a pretext for creating unjustified barriers to trade."[120]

The Kuala Lumpur Statement on 'Southern Africa: The Way Ahead' called for the intensification of efforts against the South African white regime and condemned the Pretoria government for its illegal action to destabilise Mozambique and Namibia. It also stated that the Committee of Foreign Ministers established by the Okanagan Statement[121] should continue to do its work under the Canadian Secretary of State for External Affairs. Malaysia was added as a member of the Committee. Britain became the only member that did not subscribe to the Statement, which showed clearly where its sentiments lay.

Tunku Abdul Rahman, the first Prime Minister, had already in the 1960s seen to it that Malaysia was at the forefront of all anti-apartheid initiatives. He pursued it with such vigour that it ruffled the feathers of the white Commonwealth members, particularly of Britain.

We continued to push Malaysia's abhorrence of apartheid at a number of Commonwealth meetings. It was the hope that the final steps would be taken to dismantle apartheid once and for all so that South Africa, which had been suspended from the Commonwealth, could be welcomed back into the club again.

There was strong optimism that this would happen soon. Many countries in anticipation of the change were breaking the sanctions imposed by the Commonwealth and initiating economic and trade relations with the (white) Pretoria regime. There were some in Malaysia, too, who wanted to jump the gun, especially since others, including Singapore, were doing so. I strongly argued that we just could not do so as we would be seen as betraying the trust placed in us by Nelson Mandela and the African National Congress (ANC). From the time of Tunku Abdul Rahman, we had supported their struggle and there was no turning back now. The fact that Dr. Mahathir was a member of the High Level Committee of Eminent Persons to monitor the dismantling of apartheid would make it impossible for Malaysia to renege on its commitments. The momentum for change was already building up. Apartheid's days were numbered. We should not move in for short-term benefits at the expense of long-term gains. Dr. Mahathir agreed with the position I put forward and that silenced the advocates of an early establishment of trade ties, including the Minister of Primary Industry Dato' Lim Kheng Yaik.[122]

Kuala Lumpur CHOGM also saw the appointment of a new

Secretary-General. The Secretary-General of the Commonwealth is elected for a five-year term at a CHOGM meeting. The incumbent Shridath Ramphal from Guyana, was coming close to the end of his third term. He was a very dynamic and articulate person and had some support to get an extension. His stewardship of the Commonwealth was recognised and greatly appreciated, but the feeling of some, Dr. Mahathir included, was that a change was needed.

Aspiring to take over the Secretary-Generalship of the Commonwealth was Ramphal's deputy of many years, Chief Emeka Anyaoku from Nigeria. Chief Anyaoku had the support of the African and Asian Commonwealth countries. There was another interested party in the person of Malcolm Frazer, the former Australian Prime Minister.

Kuala Lumpur CHOGM was log jammed on the appointment. If the delegates left for the Langkawi retreat without a decision it could cramp discussions there. So I took it upon myself to recommend that a straw vote be taken as a last resort, so as to prevent the issue from being carried on to Langkawi. After the leaders' last executive session in Kuala Lumpur, Dr. Mahathir told me that Chief Anyaoku had been elected. He never told me if the decision was taken by a straw vote and in the excitement of having a solution I forgot to ask.

The decision regarding the newly elected Secretary-General was announced right away to the media. Dr. Mahathir was on the stage, flanked by Shridath Ramphal and me. It was the first decision taken by the Heads at the meeting in KL and, of course, there was excitement among the journalists and media people. One of them asked me if I was happy to be elected. I could only reply, "I am happy to be Secretary-General of the Ministry of Foreign Affairs of Malaysia, not of the Commonwealth." It was not the first time I had been mistaken for someone else.

In his book *Malaysia: Fifty Years of Diplomacy 1957–2007*, Chandran Jeshurun wrote that it was the consensus that the Kuala Lumpur CHOGM 'ranked among the most productive' in the series. "It was without question Mahathir's moment of glory."[123] But there was no respite for me. As soon as CHOGM was over I had to start the preparatory work for the G-15 Conference which comprised the more advanced economies in the developing world. The idea came up in the corridors of the Summit of the Non-Aligned Movement in Belgrade in September 1989. It was Shridath Ramphal who flagged the idea that the more advanced developing countries should get their act together and foster cooperation between themselves in matters of investment, trade and technology.

In UN jargon, these countries were referred to collectively as the 'South'. The rationale for the proposal was to strengthen the bargaining position of the more advanced developing countries in international negotiations. The developed West had its act together and usually got their way in these international forums. Shridath Ramphal (later Knighted by the Queen) discussed this idea with Dr. Mahathir who was immediately enthusiastic and impulsively committed Malaysia to hosting the Inaugural Summit.

There was a general consensus that developing countries were weak in international negotiations. Their lack of coordination and the absence of any common positions always left them at the losing end. The idea of the G-15 was to try to galvanise some common bargaining positions. It was also hoped that G-15 could explore and enhance direct trade and investment and so reduce its economic dependence on the developed countries. It was felt that this dependence was the root cause of the unequal terms of world trade.

The preparatory work for the G-15 Summit was more difficult

than CHOGM. Although there were more than 50 countries in the Commonwealth, at least all the leaders spoke English. For the G-15 we required a platoon of Arabic, English, French and Spanish interpreters and every document had to be translated four ways. Then there was also the absence of a coordinating Secretariat and Malaysia had to use its own resources to fill this role.

But most of all it was very difficult to find common ground. These 15 countries had very different levels of economic development and very different priorities Some were still highly dependent on their ex-colonial masters or their giant neighbours and were afraid of toppling the applecart by embracing yet to be tested South-South cooperation.

Setting the agenda was a nightmare. Even fixing a date seemed impossible. We called several preliminary meetings in Geneva to settle on common issues for Kuala Lumpur. These meetings were energy sapping and tedious. Delegates argued endlessly, often over quite minor differences. The Latin American countries were most lukewarm and I had a tough time dealing with them. This kind of endless bickering was what made the Third World caucus so ineffective and that was exactly what we were trying to change! But we finally pulled together an agenda. But could we get a date? We had settled on 1–3 June, 1990. However, at the one but final preparatory meeting in Geneva there were indications that many Heads of Government, because of timing or other reasons, would not be able to attend. Some wanted a change of date. Only eight countries had committed themselves and one of them was Indonesia. President Suharto's presence was important to us so I telephoned Dr. Mahathir who was on holiday in Europe. He agreed there should be no change of dates. The Summit was finally held from 1–3 June, 1990.

At the Summit itself the senior officials broke up into two groups, one chaired by the Secretary-General of Ministry of Primary Industry Wong Kam Choon on economic matters, the other on political matters chaired by me. In the last two days of the Summit the Heads of Government went to Genting Highlands for their Retreat. Like CHOGM, this was meant to encourage informal and free-flowing discussions. Meanwhile, back in Kuala Lumpur, officials of the G-15 worked long hours to reach consensus on the draft Communique. I was greatly relieved that we managed to complete it in time for the Heads to read it before their final meeting.

I was even more relieved when there was little debate on the documents presented. President Diouf of Senegal said that he had been briefed by his officials that the committees had worked hard and had covered all the positions, so he moved that the Communique be adopted without debate. He was immediately supported by another Head of State, whose name escapes me. As Secretary of the Summit I quickly whispered to Dr. Mahathir that he should move for the adoption of the draft. He accepted my suggestion, and the Kuala Lumpur Communique was adopted without change.[124]

At the Kuala Lumpur Summit only eight of the 15 Heads of Government attended, the rest were deputised by Foreign Ministers. Nonetheless, the Kuala Lumpur Summit laid the groundwork for future action. Some of the key issues on which we did find a common platform were to push for the completion of the Uruguay Round and to call for the elimination of trade distorting subsidies for agriculture. All shared a concern for controlling the production and illegal trade in narcotic drugs and protecting the environment. This first G-15 meeting called for a group of experts to formulate strategies to deal with the burden of external debt. It also established a Committee to coordinate G-15 positions and issues of major concern to the group at the forthcoming Rio Summit.

To strengthen South-South exchanges the Summit set up SITDEC (South Investment Trade and Technology Data Exchange Centre). Finally the Summit agreed to hold its Summit meeting annually. To organise this the Foreign Ministers of Malaysia, Venezuela and Senegal formed a Steering Committee to coordinate work until the next Summit in Caracas, and the following in Dakar. This was the Troika, which was later institutionalised to coordinate the work of G-15.

The subsequent Summit in Caracas was a follow-up on the action plan, which had been endorsed in Kuala Lumpur and basically covered the same ground again. Caracas adopted the Statute for SITDEC and endorsed the working draft agreement on Multilateral Payments Arrangements proposed by the Expert Group Meeting in Kuala Lumpur. Malaysia was entrusted with implementing the arrangement on a pilot basis. The Dakar Summit saw an intensification of South-South cooperation in a number of areas including food production, energy and medicine.

The difficulties I encountered in this attempt to bring only 15 'South' countries together really opened my eyes and made me understand why, for most of the 20th century and still to this day, the developed countries can dominate the world and steer most economic benefits to themselves. They can always exploit the divisiveness and timidity of Third World leaders.

With the successful hosting of CHOGM and G-15, I felt I had passed the test.

### Endnotes

114  The Group of 15 (G-15) was established at the Ninth Non-Aligned Movement Summit Meeting in Belgrade, Yugoslavia in September 1989. This informal forum was set up to foster cooperation and provide input for other international groups, such as the World Trade Organisation and the Group of Eight. It is composed of countries from the Caribbean, South America, Africa and Asia with a common goal of enhanced growth and prosperity and on cooperation among developing countries in the areas of investment,

trade and technology. The membership of the G-15 has expanded to 17 countries, but the name has remained unchanged. Chile, Iran and Kenya have joined since the start and Yugoslavia is no longer part of the group.

115    Yeop Adlan Che Rose and Hashim Taib were both capable senior career diplomats.

116    The former official government Guest House that has been turned into a boutique hotel. The building was the Official Residence of colonial Governors before Independence and subsequently, until the '80s, the Residence of the British High Commissioner (Ambassador).

117    A meal.

118    That is the declaration of the meeting on contemporary issues of global concern adopted by the Conference.

119    Chandran Jeshurun, *op. cit.*, p. 199.

120    Commonwealth Secretariat: Langkawi Declaration on the Environment 1989.

121    Adopted at Nassau CHOGM 1985 and reaffirmed at Vancouver CHOGM 1987.

122    Upon his retirement from politics, he was honoured with the title Tun. He passed away on 22 December, 2012.

123    Chandran Jeshurun, *op. cit.*, p. 200.

124    It was expected that the final session would drag on with comments and quibbles over the draft. I had advised Dr. Mahathir, the Chairman, that if an opportunity arose for him to move on quickly he should seize it and bring about an early conclusion. Indeed within the hour we were out of the meeting. The ease of the process surprised most of those who were present, including veteran Tan Sri Ghazali Shafie who was present as an observer. He told me he had expected the Conference to last all night.

# CHAPTER 11

# ASEAN: A Vision Fulfilled

My return to Kuala Lumpur from Tokyo in 1989 coincided with a growing awareness among members of ASEAN that the organisation had to be more alive to the unfolding political developments in the region and even beyond. Although ASEAN was always at the frontline of Malaysia's multilateral diplomacy, by the late '80s we were not satisfied with an organisation that only focused on events taking place in our own region. We wanted a regional grouping, which was strong enough and well organised enough to promote its interests in the global arena.

We needed to expand ASEAN to include all ten countries of Southeast Asia. We needed to strengthen and revamp the Secretariat. We began to seriously give our attention to global peace and security, and how to address conflict in the region in that context. This was the thinking that gave rise to the ASEAN Regional Forum (ARF),[125] which brought ASEAN together with all the Pacific powers, Europe and the Indian sub-continent for regular formal dialogues on current issues. But I am getting ahead of myself. It would take another four years of active diplomacy to pull off the first ARF meeting in 1994.

My first year in the job ended with the euphoria of the fall of the Berlin Wall on 9 November, 1989, which changed everything. One by one the East European countries, the communist regimes of Eastern Europe, broke loose and moved towards determining their own destinies. Within a year, the Soviet Union itself collapsed. Poland was the first on 5 April, 1990, when Solidarity (the trade union at the forefront of opposing the regime) was legalised; Hungary on 27 June when the border restriction to Austria was discarded and Czechoslovakia's Velvet Revolution of mass demonstrations forced the regime's capitulation on 24 November. Romania, Albania, Bulgaria, the Baltic States, and the Central Asian republics were to follow suit over the next two years.

This systemic change in the global political landscape had profound implications for Asia, in particular Southeast Asia. The question on everyone's mind was what now for the Indo-Chinese countries? And for Southeast Asia as a whole? It was too early to make any sensible predictions. But there was a real concern in ASEAN capitals that the populism sweeping Eastern Europe could bring disruption and conflict if it surfaced in Asia. That is why the ASEAN take on the 1989 Tiananmen protests was so very different from the reactions in the West.

Western governments and the international (read western) media were loud in their condemnation of the Chinese government for what was seen as a harsh and even brutal repression of popular expression by students clamouring for a more open society. But the Chinese clampdown was greeted in most ASEAN capitals with a sense of relief. Whatever happened in China would cast a long shadow over Southeast Asia and indeed the whole region, but we needed a stable and prosperous China to lead the region into the 1990s.

Now that I was back in Kuala Lumpur it was a question of following through the regional implications of the collapse of communism in Europe. Central to ASEAN's demand was the Vietnamese withdrawal from Cambodia, leading to Cambodia's self-determination. Indonesian diplomacy played a pivotal role in the process towards the withdrawal of the Vietnamese, initiated by Foreign Minister Mokhtar Kusumaadmaja and later by his successor Ali Alatas. By 1986 ASEAN had officially accepted Indonesia to act as the ASEAN interlocutor on this issue with Vietnam.

The breakthrough came in July 1987 when Vietnam accepted the idea of an informal meeting between the Khmer parties, to which other concerned countries would be invited. This was the so-called 'cocktail party' formula.[126] This led to the first Jakarta Informal Meeting in July 1988, at which the issue of the Vietnamese invasion and occupation of Cambodia—the external question—was decoupled from the Khmer 'civil war'—the internal question. The second Jakarta Informal Meeting took place in February 1989 after a change of government in Thailand had radically shifted Bangkok's policy toward a quick negotiated settlement. The second Jakarta meeting, chaired by Alatas, at which Vietnam accepted the notion of an 'international control mechanism' for Cambodia, was followed by escalating diplomatic activity—efforts that finally led to the 1989 and 1991 Paris International Peace Conference on Cambodia[127] co-chaired by Indonesia and France.

But it was Tengku Ahmad Rithauddeen, the Malaysian Foreign Minister (1975–81 and 1984–86), who had first suggested a *proximity* meeting. Following Vietnam's invasion of Cambodia in 1979 ASEAN decided that he[128] should lead an ASEAN delegation to talk to Hanoi and Phnom Penh. In his yet-to-be published notes extended to me Tengku Ahmad Rithauddeen jotted:

'…To resolve the issue, I had introduced what was then known as 'Proximity Talks'. … The rationale to have Proximity Talks is that the two warring parties should be able to sit down and negotiate the issues that can be discussed and solve the problems between them. It is most fundamental that opportunities be made for the two warring parties to sit down to solve the issues that would bring about the solving of Cambodian problems…

So, I devised a plan under which a third party (an independent and honest broker, as it were) would first meet with one of the parties, and then meet with the other…

Coming back to Proximity Talks the modality was this: "You come to a meeting but you don't sit at the same table. The meetings would be fixed for two or three days. When they come to the meeting, they would first meet with the moderator, or peace maker. We would meet the Cambodian leaders (Khmer Rouge) first, in the morning. Then in the afternoon, we would meet the Hun Sen group together with the invading Vietnamese armed forces. The venue would be a neutral place, like Jakarta." That was my proposal.

However, it was difficult to get consensus within ASEAN… my proposal was not accepted. After my term as Foreign Minister, ASEAN pursued this matter. After nearly ten years, the Cambodian warring parties went to France for the Paris Peace talks. In my view, what was accepted by Paris was no different from the modality proposed by me. Initially, the Proximity Talks proposal did not achieve the expected result. However, after I left the Foreign Ministry, ASEAN leaders pursued the Proximity Talks proposal at a meeting in Jakarta. ASEAN leaders subsequently participated in the 1991 Paris Peace talks where the Cambodian problems were finally resolved, leading to a ceasefire, repatriation of displaced Cambodians and a free election…'[129]

Tengku Ahmad Rithauddeen's approach was the basis of the Jakarta Informal Meetings, which began in 1988. The elements he put forward in his proposal subsequently became the basis of discussion in Paris when representatives of 18 countries, the four Cambodian parties, and the UN Secretary-General met from 30 July to 30 August, 1989 in an effort to negotiate a comprehensive settlement. They hoped to achieve those objectives seen as crucial to the future of post-occupation Cambodia, namely a verified withdrawal of the remaining Vietnamese occupation troops and genuine self-determination for the Cambodian people.

By the time I arrived back in Kuala Lumpur the following year the process was already in its third meeting. ASEAN senior officials were not directly involved but at each meeting were briefed at the end of the day by their Indonesian counterpart.

This confidence-building among all parties by Indonesia paved the way for the Paris International Peace Conference on Cambodia of 1989/1991. Together with some senior officials from Wisma Putra, I accompanied the Foreign Minister Dato' Abu Hassan to Paris where the conference was jointly chaired by France and Indonesia. Malaysia was elected to chair a Working Committee, and as I was not able to commit my time to the entire Conference which lasted for close to one month, Ambassador Zainal Ibrahim, a senior member of the delegation, took over Malaysia's chairmanship of the committee.

Although at the end of the first session in 1989 the Conference did not produce any final settlement, it nevertheless did lead to the final solution of the problem when the challenge was taken up by the Five Permanent Members of the United Nations Security Council that for this purpose included Australia, Indonesia and Japan. Agreement was subsequently reached on the Framework for a Comprehensive Political Settlement of the Cambodian Conflict, which spelt out transitional and military arrangements to administer the country before the elections, which would be held under the auspices of the UN, with human rights protection and international guarantees. It also provided for repatriation of the displaced Khmers along the border with Thailand, and to disarm and demobilise the factional armies.

The Paris Agreement was endorsed by the UN. After more than a decade the guns fell silent and peace finally returned to Cambodia. One of the most intractable problems confronting ASEAN was finally solved. When I first assumed office as Secretary-General of the Foreign Ministry, the ASEAN members still comprised the five founding countries— Malaysia, Thailand, Indonesia, the Philippines and Singapore—and also Brunei, which joined ASEAN on 8 January, 1984. Subsequently ASEAN expanded to ten members and took a more assertive role in global relations. On 28 July, 1995, Vietnam became the seventh member; Laos and Myanmar joined two years later on 23 July, 1997 followed by Cambodia on 30 April, 1999.[130]

The need for regional cooperation among countries within the Southeast Asian region was already recognised soon after our independence. In 1961 the Association of Southeast Asia (ASA) was formed, comprising Malaysia, the Philippines and Thailand. Although ASA's focus was economic cooperation and political non-interference it could not survive the tensions brought about by the Indonesian Konfrontasi and the Philippines' claim to Sabah.

Equally stillborn was MAPHILINDO, which was Sukarno's attempt to bring together the people of Malay stock in Malaya, Philippines and Indonesia and forestall the establishment of Malaysia. Sukarno saw the formation of Malaysia as a British imperialist plot, or rather a plot to frustrate his dream of a Greater Indonesia, Indonesia Raya. Precisely because of its racist basis the idea was unacceptable. It was only after

Sukarno's fall and the abandonment of armed conflict with Malaysia that it became possible to form a regional organisation which would last. ASEAN, which has for more than 40 years been the centrepiece of Malaysia's foreign policy, was formed on 8 August, 1967 with the signing of The Bangkok Declaration. On 27 November, 1971, the Foreign Ministers of the five ASEAN founding members signed the declaration on peace, freedom and neutrality, better known as the Kuala Lumpur Declaration of 1971.

In terms of political cooperation, one of ASEAN's major developments came out of the first ASEAN Summit in Bali in February 1976. This was a most timely meeting considering the changes in the geopolitics of the region. The United States had pulled out, Vietnam had been reunited and new governments were in place in Phnom Penh and Vientiane. At the inaugural Bali summit, ASEAN leaders signed three major documents: the Treaty of Amity and Cooperation in Southeast Asia (TAC), the Declaration of ASEAN Concord and the Agreement Establishing the ASEAN Secretariat.

But 20 years later it had become clear that ASEAN's decision-making was weakened by some of the arrangements made at the Bali Summit. The Secretariat was headed by a Secretary-General, whose post rotated among ASEAN members every two years, in alphabetical order. He was supported by a Standing Committee, which was also rotated among the member capitals every two years. This structure stymied effective response to the growing number of challenges and issues facing ASEAN. Making prompt decisions as events unfolded would require a less cumbersome mechanism.

An ASEAN committee headed by Tan Sri Ghazali Shafie (assisted by Nordin Sopiee, head of ISIS)[131] was formed to restructure ASEAN. It was to take into account the views of the members and make the necessary recommendations to the Foreign Ministers' Meeting. I remember that after having visited all the ASEAN countries, Tan Sri Ghazali Shafie and Nordin Sopiee met me at Wisma Putra, Kuala Lumpur, their last stop. Having chaired the high level committee to restructure the Commonwealth Secretariat,[132] I strongly put forward my views on how the ASEAN Secretariat should evolve.

I recommended that first and foremost the Secretary-General be given more recognition by investing him with ministerial rank so that he was on par with the foreign ministers. He should serve for five years. He should be recognised as the Secretary-General of ASEAN and not as Secretary-General of ASEAN Secretariat. I pushed for him to be supported by at least two Deputies, one to head the political division and the other, economic and functional cooperation. The Committee, headed by Tan Sri Ghazali Shafie, made recommendations along these lines with inputs from other members. They were accepted and Ajit Singh, at that time the Director-General of ASEAN Malaysia, was elected in January 1993, the first Secretary-General under the newly restructured ASEAN Secretariat.

Ajit Singh's appointment was a result of a trade-off between Malaysia and the Philippines. In order to secure Malaysia's candidature, I reached a gentleman's agreement with my Philippines counterpart that Malaysia would support their declaration on the South China Sea and in return they would withdraw their candidature for this term. The Philippines were keen to get full ASEAN support for a code of conduct[133] to manage the competing claims to parts of the South China Sea. So we got our ASEAN Secretary-General in the person of Ajit Singh, and the Philippines got their declaration at the Foreign Ministers' Meeting in Manila in July 1992. Nothing was in black and white but it was, as I said, a gentleman's agreement.

Five years later Ajit wanted to have his term extended. He approached Dr. Mahathir to request government support. Dr. Mahathir did not consult me on this. I only came to know about it when Dr. Mahathir mentioned that he had not agreed to Ajit's request. I was relieved as otherwise we would be reneging on our earlier agreement with the Philippines. And so Ajit left and he was replaced by the Philippines candidate Rodolfo Severino Jr., a distinguished diplomat who had been my counterpart.

It was during this time that the momentum for the enlargement of ASEAN membership began to build. The intense diplomatic efforts by existing ASEAN members at building confidence and giving assurances of friendship and of cooperation with Hanoi following the end of the Vietnam War began to bear fruit. It was not difficult, in my mind, for Vietnam to embrace ASEAN. In ASEAN it would have a security shield in their centuries-old uneasy relationship with China, which on several occasions had led to open conflicts. The situation in Laos and Cambodia was also stabilising, although still clearly under communist leadership. But what form of Government they chose for themselves was none of our business. We needed only to win over Myanmar to complete the 'ideal' membership of ten.

It was in this spirit that we went about resolving the thorny details of expanding ASEAN to include Cambodia, Laos, Myanmar and Vietnam. As it happened, Malaysia was holding the Chairmanship of ASEAN at that time and it fell on me to travel to the other capitals to inform them of our desire to welcome them into ASEAN and to explore their readiness and timing to join the grouping.

It was appropriate that Malaysia should be leading this mission. Malaysia had been at the front edge among ASEAN states recognising the Indo-Chinese states and, under the Mahathir Government, in openly calling for their inclusion in the regional zone of peace and neutrality. It was the decision by ASEAN to invite Myanmar that provoked the most controversy. From the ASEAN point of view the inclusion of Myanmar was a logical extension of the policy to create a strong regional body with a proven ability to peacefully resolve conflicts between its members. Ten was also better than six as ASEAN, with increasing aggressiveness, defended its interests against the forces of globalisation.

There was, however, criticism worldwide, but the strongest opposition came from the EU countries. After I retired they continued to voice their objection to the point that they would not engage ASEAN in the ASEAN-EU bilateral meetings if Myanmar was seated as a member. ASEAN stood its ground. I found the EU stand highly hypocritical, given the skeletons in their own closet, especially genocide in Bosnia-Herzegovina and Kosovo and sectarian violence in Northern Ireland.[134]

The ASEAN approach, as I said at the time, was to win over Myanmar under a policy of 'constructive engagement'. This, rather than isolating Myanmar, was more likely to ensure regional peace. I pointed out that we in ASEAN had never used human rights issues as a bargaining instrument, and non-interference in each other's internal affairs was fundamental, without which ASEAN would have fractured long ago. Myanmar, finally, became a member of ASEAN in July 1997. I had already retired by then, but on the eve of Myanmar joining ASEAN, speaking about Malaysia in the context of global politics at Universiti Kebangsaan Malaysia (UKM) in March 1997, I said that "… on Myanmar, Malaysia is aware that certain sections of the international community have serious concerns about the denial of democracy in the country. But there are also several other countries that do not practise democracy. Yet, these countries enjoy good relations with the same group of countries that are finding fault with Myanmar. We believe that ASEAN should continue to pursue its 'constructive engagement' policy with regard to the present ruling government. ASEAN looks forward to Myanmar joining the organisation, in line with its overall objective of embracing all the countries of Southeast Asia in this regional grouping, turning our region into a cohesive family of ten, and into one of prosperity and of plenty."[135]

Of course, there are those today who would argue that, in this age of rapid globalisation and inter-relatedness of countries and cultures, this sort of non-interference is no longer viable or even valid. I would answer that this is a question which the ASEAN nations, if they need to, can ask themselves, and then also answer themselves. Their answer will likely follow along the lines of the continued relevance of the values of non-interference and neutrality implicit in the Zone of Peace, Freedom and Neutrality (ZOPFAN).

Although ZOPFAN was a Cold War construct, and in that sense submerged under subsequent ASEAN agreements, its argument in favour of neutrality and non-interference continues to be viable today. It encapsulates ASEAN's underlying philosophy on the conduct of relations between and among themselves and also in the conduct of its relations with others. The goal of this philosophy was the defence and protection of peace and stability in the region.

In this tumble of events involving ASEAN in the 1990s, ASEAN was making its own policies according to a sharper perception of its own interests. It was also a time when the international political environment was becoming more conducive to building bridges between ASEAN and the global powers. Despite occasional hostile reactions to specific issues, ASEAN was a group whose political aspirations had to be acknowledged. This was the background to the formation of the

ASEAN Regional Forum (ARF) where political issues could be discussed with both regional and global powers.

Malaysia was then holding the chairmanship of the ASEAN Standing Committee and, as decided at the SOM (Senior Officials Meeting), I was entrusted to travel to the Soviet Union (as it still was called although in its dying days) and to China to invite these two countries to participate in the ARF and, in the case of China, to be invited as a dialogue partner. They readily agreed. Subsequently in 2011 Chinese Premier Wen Jiabao expressed China's gratitude that Malaysia had proposed to ASEAN to begin dialogue with China, as has been already mentioned earlier. Both these two countries welcomed the invitation and today are part of the ARF. It was a significant breakthrough for ASEAN to involve the global powers in its pursuit of political stability and security.

Since the formation of the ARF, ASEAN has taken on a different character. It has become more interested in and aware of the political developments within the larger region of East Asia and beyond.

There were differences of views and hard fought arguments over both the issues of enlarging ASEAN and the institutionalisation of the ARF, but all was done in the spirit of ASEAN fraternity and resolved without much sleep loss! This less confrontational approach and more avuncular conduct went a long way to set the mood at meetings within ASEAN and also with its dialogue partners.

Even with China, the United States and Japan there was a friendly tone in the discussions, at least during my time. I was particularly aware of the reciprocal pleasant and friendly dispositions of the Chinese Vice-Minister of Foreign Affairs Tang Jiaxuan[136] and of US Under Secretary of State Vincent Lord and also US Secretary of State James Baker when discussing relations with us, which is something that makes me happy to remember. It was through all these frequent meetings and contacts that ASEAN had with the dialogue partners in the ARF and others that our knowledge and understanding grew deeper over the years and helped to resolve conflicting issues and interests.

The only problem we found at the time was the relationship between ASEAN and the EU; with this I mean specifically the European Union officials in Luxembourg in connection with the meeting there in 1993–94. Somehow there was a big gap between us. Discussions dragged along never moving from what seemed to be irreconcilable positions. Personally, I found that the EU was trying to impose their values and viewpoints on us. It seemed to have slipped their minds that ASEAN is another 'sovereign' organisation, just as the EU is, and we were all there representing our respective sovereign nations. The EU officials were, at that meeting, quite arrogant and even rude.

There were a couple of incidents that I remember. One was my being refused entry to a lunch in my honour, and the other was when we, having agreed to meet the EU officials after their breakfast at an agreed upon time, had to wait for these officials to leisurely finish eating without a hint of them offering us even a cup of coffee.

Kishore Mahbubani does not spare words when he describes this attitude in his book *The New Asian Hemisphere*:[137]

'This European tendency to treat non-European cultures and societies with disdain and condescension has become deeply rooted in the European psyche. In 1993–1994 I attended a meeting of ASEAN and EU Senior officials in Luxembourg. The ASEAN team was led by Tan Sri Ahmad Kamil Jaafar, a distinguished Malaysian diplomat. The Luxembourg hosts invited us to lunch. Just about when Tan Sri Kamil was about to greet his Luxembourg hosts, a young Luxembourg official asked him (in the presence and earshot of Tan Sri Kamil's Luxembourg counterpart) whether he had brought along his invitation. Since he had not done so, he was refused entry to the lunch at which he was supposed to be the guest of honor.

To understand the psychological impact of this incredible rudeness, remember the famous incident of Mahatma Gandhi being thrown out of a South African first-class train compartment even though he had a first-class ticket. It was a clear demonstration that Asians were meant to be second-class citizens. To be refused entry to a lunch at which one was supposed to be the guest of honor was more than a slight. The ease with which the Luxembourg officials delivered the insult revealed the disdain the European officials had for Asians.'

That may have been the action of a functionary. But it happened again at the highest level of EU leadership. This was at the first ASEM (Asia-Europe Meeting) Summit in Bangkok. Helmut Kohl, the German Chancellor, had asked for a meeting with Dr. Mahathir and I entrusted the Malaysian Embassy to inform the Germans that since this was a request from Chancellor Kohl, the meeting should be conducted at the hotel where Dr. Mahathir was staying. I remember that Dr. Mahathir had, in one of his relaxed moments, told me that when attending the Rio Summit Chancellor Kohl had asked to meet Dr. Mahathir but contrary to diplomatic decorum he had asked that Dr. Mahathir meet him at the hotel where Kohl was staying. Dr. Mahathir told me he had to travel some distance to meet the German Chancellor. This time in Bangkok when told that the meeting would be held at Dr. Mahathir's hotel, word came back quickly that because of Kohl's busy schedule he would not now be able to meet the Prime Minister. Was this again an example of the deep-rooted psyche of the master race? I wonder!

Now back to the unfinished business with the EU in Luxembourg. I told them crisply, with no attempt to be polite, that if they were so insistent on driving home their point, and insistent on their irreconcilable positions, they could keep their views to themselves. We would be quite happy to go home without an agreement in hand. After this meeting there was a change in the leadership of the EU delegation. The Luxembourg Government holding the EU Presidency at that time replaced their leader. We noticed a change in the EU attitude, which enabled the two sides to agree on a joint communiqué.

Today, it appears that the subject of ASEAN has become one not just of regional cooperation but also of *regional identity*. It is the question of regional identity which has become more problematic, and this can be clearly seen in the whole story of the East Asia Economic Community (EAEC) idea, an idea that metamorphosed into an ASEAN project to which I was deeply committed. One of my biggest disappointments in office was the failure of the EAEC. It later developed into the ASEAN Plus Three[138] but that only happened after I had retired. During my time, the EAEC idea produced serious problems for Malaysia in trying to sell the proposal to our ASEAN partners.

The idea of EAEC was doomed from the start. The Ministry of Foreign Affairs was not privy to any discussions on it; nor were the other ASEAN members. It was Dr. Mahathir's idea that there be a collaborative group comprising ASEAN plus China, Japan and Korea to strengthen their bargaining position on trade issues and counter the economic hegemony of the West, especially in the face of the lack of progress on the Uruguay Round of GATT negotiations. When Dr. Mahathir sprung this idea for an EAEC on us, he did so in a wholly surprising context—the occasion was a welcoming dinner in honour of visiting Chinese Premier Li Peng in Kuala Lumpur. On this night of 10 December, 1990, Dr. Mahathir spoke of the EAEC in the context of the rivalry over world trade and the protectionism of the US and Europe.[139] But on this same occasion Dr. Mahathir also made the proposal for the ASEAN Plus Three,[140] although what garnered more attention was his shock announcement about the EAEC. It caught us all by surprise, as it did our neighbours, particularly Indonesia.

Like the others in ASEAN, the Indonesians felt slighted at not having had any forewarning let alone consultation about an idea which not only affected them directly but which was now, suddenly, declared in a public forum in the presence of a foreign leader outside the ASEAN fold. We had such a difficult time with the fallout and had to expend a lot of diplomatic energy in trying to get our friends in ASEAN to accept the idea.

Sometimes I wonder if this unhappiness was because of the idea itself or simply the manner in which it was presented to them. I always return to the conclusion that it was both that killed the chances of the EAEC. I do not believe Dr. Mahathir intended to sideline the others in ASEAN by making his shock announcement but the fact remains that he did not consult anyone beforehand. Quiet prior legwork was not Dr. Mahathir's style. He was his impulsive self again, a trait of which I had been forewarned about when I assumed my post in Kuala Lumpur. Indonesia found itself under pressure and saw its usual leadership role threatened and the ASEAN Secretariat in Jakarta as being undermined. Any move that would submerge the Secretariat and its role would not receive support from them.

The United States immediately opposed the idea of an East Asia trade bloc which would challenge their domination of the Pacific region.

This put the other ASEAN countries on the back foot. Singapore, which hosted the APEC[141] Secretariat, felt uncomfortable with the proposal as it did not include the United States, Australia and New Zealand. Japan, a country that cannot say no to the US and South Korea, having been reminded of the blood debt it owed the United States, rejected the idea. In their case, it was not just how the idea was announced but the exclusion of the non-Asian states of the Pacific Rim which fuelled their rejection. It came down to a clash between an Asian identity with its implications of confrontation with the West, and a more inclusive Pacific identity.

Meanwhile, I had a rough time getting the ASEAN Senior Officials on board and had tried hard to convince Ali Alatas, the Foreign Minister of Indonesia, and Wong Kan Seng, the Foreign Minister of Singapore. I finally spoke to the two Foreign Ministers directly as my efforts at the Senior Officials Meeting of ASEAN were getting nowhere. Finally, at the ASEAN Summit in Singapore in January 1992, Ali Alatas spoke to me and told me that in his informal consultations among his colleagues that included the Singapore Foreign Minister, they had come to the conclusion that they could accept EAEC as a caucus but not a community. This was two days before the Summit.

I flew home to discuss this with Dr. Mahathir and pleaded that our only option was to accept this formula. In all my discussions on the subject of EAEC, the positions of the other members were very definite. All we had succeeded in doing was to mute their rejection and unhappiness into a lukewarm but polite acceptance of a watered down EAEC. In a state of pique Dr. Mahathir angrily stated some time later that, "In East Asia we are told that we may not call ourselves East Asians as Europeans call themselves Europeans and Americans call themselves Americans. We are told that we must call ourselves Pacific people and align with people who are partly pacific, but more American, Atlantic and European. We may not have an identity that is not permitted, nor may we work together on the basis of that identity."[142]

Not surprisingly, it was soon after he had said this that he did not attend the APEC Seattle Summit, prompting that notorious remark from Prime Minister Paul Keating of Australia,[143] which ignited even further the flames of animosity engulfing regional politics at the time. Perhaps this is why, later in 1993, although ASEAN accepted that the EAEC be housed within APEC, there was no room for Australia and New Zealand within it. Later when ASEAN abandoned the EAEC idea completely in favour of ASEAN Plus Three, which was also mooted by Dr. Mahathir at the same time as the EAEC, this was formed also without Australia and New Zealand. As if to soften the blow, the EAS (East Asian Summit)[144] was put in place which includes these two countries and others.

Matters concerning the EAEC finally came to a head one day when I was in Ipoh having a game of golf—it was a game between Wisma Putra and the diplomatic corps with the King leading our team. Soon after the game I was approached by a senior police officer in Ipoh with the news that the Prime Minister wanted to see me immediately—in fact, that very same evening at Sri Perdana, his official residence. Since it was already 4.00 p.m., I did not have time to wonder what urgent matter could be at hand. I simply had a quick shower, got into my car and told my driver to drive at breakneck speed. Which he did. I got there just in time and found a small group, including the Minister of International Trade and Industry Datuk Seri Rafidah Aziz and Tan Sri Halim Ali, the Deputy Secretary-General of Wisma Putra, already assembled there.

Dr. Mahathir started the meeting by telling us that since we were not making much progress with the EAEC, he had decided to drop the whole idea. That was another bombshell, almost as big as the one he dropped when he first sprung the idea. I saw gestures of agreement with the Prime Minister and felt that they were even relieved that finally we were done with the EAEC. I personally believed that the concept of East Asians getting together to handle our problems in this part of the world was a workable idea. It was an indigenous response to the economic and financial challenges we faced and we should not allow ourselves to be dictated to by outside powers as to what we could or could not do.

I completely understood Dr. Mahathir's vision for the EAEC to be a community, much like the EU, that could hold its own in the world and grow in economic and financial strength. I really wanted to see the EAEC idea through and so I spoke frankly with Dr. Mahathir about my views. Surprisingly, he then agreed not to drop the idea after all, and so he didn't. Not for a while, anyway, but it gradually died out on its own in the end.

These then are my recollections of the many years of fruitful and most satisfying dealings I had in ASEAN and of the pleasurable times I spent with my ASEAN colleagues. Some of them, like Bhirabongse Kasemsri, Kasem Kasemsri, Arsa Sarasin, Thep Devakul, Vithya Vejajiva and Pracha Gunakasem of Thailand, and Peter Chan, K. Kesavapany (who later was appointed Singapore High Commissioner to Malaysia) and Kishore Mahbubani of Singapore, were already old friends from my earlier postings. Likewise, Brunei's Lim Jock Seng, who now sits in the Foreign Ministry as Second Minister of Foreign Affairs and Trade. Sastrohandoyo Wiryono and later his successor, Izhar Ibrahim of Indonesia, and Rod Severino of the Philippines all became, in the course of our regular SOM meetings, good friends.

The friendly atmosphere that evolved at these meetings made it possible to talk openly and frankly and reach agreements on issues even in informal discussions over a good meal. This was extremely helpful during those times when it was necessary to reach consensus quickly as a group when dealing with, for example, ASEAN-EU, APEC, ASEM and dialogue partners. This practice must be upheld as sacrosanct.

In particular the subject of who belongs in ASEAN, begun during my time in the Foreign Ministry but continuing long after I left and lingering until today, has turned from a question of what defines South-East Asia to what defines East Asia, and further, what defines the Asia Pacific region. The subject of ASEAN expansion is an old topic which our founding fathers were aware of, from Tunku Abdul Rahman to Tun Abdul Razak and Tun Dr. Ismail, who in 1966 already spoke of looking forward to a regional association embracing all the countries of Southeast Asia. "We cannot survive for long as independent peoples—Burmese, Thais, Indonesians, Laotians, Vietnamese, Malaysians, Cambodians, Singaporeans and Filipinos—unless we also think and act as South-East Asians."[145]

Today, because of globalisation and many other factors, the boundaries are being pushed even further from what might geographically define us—we are now not only talking about Southeast Asia but about East Asia and about the Asia Pacific region as a whole. Doubtless, this is something that will be talked about for years to come as the search for an effective regional strategy becomes even more tightly woven into the search for a regional identity.

* I have purposely not touched on the economic work or economic discussions that took place in ASEAN. This was not under the domain of the Foreign Ministry but of the Ministry of Trade and Industry (MITI). But it would not be justifiable if I did not mention the impressive developments that took place in the area of ASEAN cooperation. All the discussions on the economic aspects were handled by the MITI Minister and the Secretary-General. I

*was not involved with their work but from time to time received briefings by the Secretary-General of MITI. It is worth putting on record that the Common Effective Preferential Tariff (CEPT) led to the ASEAN Free Trade Area (AFTA) signed in Singapore on 28 January, 1992. The progress in economic integration was impressive and the hope for an ASEAN Economic Community (AEC) by 2015 remains strong and attainable.*

*At the ASEAN Summit in Bangkok in December 1995 the ASEAN Framework Agreement on Trade Services was adopted and in the meantime ASEAN has signed free trade agreements with the following countries: Korea, Japan, Australia, New Zealand and India. By January 2010, the ASEAN-China Free Trade Area (ACFTA) was already in force.*

## Endnotes

125   Wikipedia: The ASEAN Regional Forum (ARF) is a formal dialogue in the Asia Pacific region. ARF met for the first time in 1994. As of July 2007, it is consisted of 27 participants. ARF objectives are to foster dialogue and consultation, and promote confidence-building and preventive diplomacy in the region. The current participants in the ARF are as follows: all the ASEAN members, Australia, Bangladesh, Canada, the People's Republic of China, the European Union, India, Japan, North Korea, South Korea, Mongolia, New Zealand, Pakistan, Papua New Guinea, Russia, East Timor, United States and Sri Lanka. The ARF is a key forum and provides a setting in which members can discuss regional security issues and develop measures to enhance peace and security in the region.

126   The July 1987 Mochtar-Nguyen Co Thach (Vietnam's Minister of Foreign Affairs) communiqué.

127   There were two sessions of this Conference from 30 July to 30 August, 1989 and the other from 21 to 23 October, 1991.

128   As Chairman of the ASEAN Standing Committee then.

129   The 1979 Senior Officials meeting decided that he should lead an ASEAN delegation to Hanoi to discuss resolving the problem caused by the Vietnamese invasion of Cambodia and the installation of their favoured regime.

130   Laos and Myanmar were admitted as members of ASEAN at the 30th ASEAN Ministerial Meeting in Malaysia in July 1997. At that time, Cambodia enjoyed Observer status, with a view to eventual membership, which happened two years later.

131   Formerly Director-General of Malaysia's Institute for Strategic and International Studies, ISIS.

132   Following the decision of Kuala Lumpur CHOGM a Committee to restructure the Commonwealth Secretariat was set up to draw up recommendations for consideration at the next CHOGM. I chaired the Committee of Officials to work out the framework and scope of restructuring.

133   See following chapter on ASEAN Code of Conduct.

134   See Chandran Jeshurun, *op. cit.*, p. 290.

135   As Special Envoy of the Prime Minister, I was presenting a paper at a seminar organised by the university.

136    Tang Jiaxuan (born 17 January, 1938) was Vice-Minister of Foreign Affairs from 1993 to 1998 and Minister of Foreign Affairs from 1998 to 2003, after various diplomatic postings.

137    Kishore Mahbubani, *The New Asian Hemisphere*, New York, Public Affairs, 2008.

138    ASEAN Plus Three (APT) is a forum comprising ASEAN and China, Japan and South Korea. Leaders consult on a wide range of issues. The group's significance and importance was strengthened by the Asian Financial Crisis. In response to the crisis, ASEAN closely cooperated with China, Japan and the Republic of Korea. Since the implementation of the Joint Statement on East Asia Cooperation in 1999 at the Manila Summit, APT finance ministers have been holding periodic consultations. ASEAN Plus Three, in establishing the Chiang Mai Initiative, has been credited as forming the basis for financial stability in Asia, the lack of such stability being a contributing factor to the Asian Financial Crisis.

139    See Chandran Jeshurun, *op. cit.*, pp. 231–236.

140    See Johan Savaranamuttu, *op. cit.*, p. 192.

141    Asia-Pacific Economic Cooperation (APEC) is a forum for 21 Pacific Rim states that seeks to promote economic cooperation in the Asia-Pacific region. It was established in 1989 in response to the growing interdependence of Asia-Pacific economies and the advent of regional economic blocs (e.g. the European Union) in other parts of the world.

142    See Johan Savaranamuttu, *op. cit.*, p.192.

143    In December 1993, Keating was involved in a diplomatic incident over his description of Dr. Mahathir bin Mohamad as 'recalcitrant' when Dr. Mahathir refused to attend the 1993 APEC Summit. Dr. Mahathir demanded an apology from Keating, and threatened to reduce diplomatic and trade ties with Australia. Some Malaysian officials talked of launching a 'Buy Australian Last' campaign. Keating eventually apologised to Mahathir over the remark.

144    The East Asian Summit (EAS) is a forum held annually by leaders of, initially, 16 countries in the East Asian region. Membership expanded to 18 countries including the United States and Russia at the Sixth EAS in 2011. EAS meetings are held after the annual ASEAN leaders' meetings. The first summit was held in Kuala Lumpur on 14 December, 2005. The decision to hold the EAS was reached during the 2004 ASEAN Plus Three summit  and the initial 16 members were determined at the ASEAN Plus Three Ministerial Meeting held in Laos at the end of July 2005. China has stated its preference for both EAS and ASEAN Plus Three to exist side-by-side.

145    See Ooi Kee Beng, *op. cit.*, pp. 168–69.

My daughter Yuhanis (left) and son Tariq in their childhood years.

My father Mohamad Jaafar bin Haji Shamsuddin and mother Hajah Satariah binte Haji Abaid

With Razali at the MCKK fancy-dress football. We won the first prize as toddy-sellers.

Penang combined school football team, 1955/1956. I am standing at the back, fourth from the left.

MCKK 1st XV All Blacks rugby team, 1958. I am seated at the front row, second from the left. On my right is Mr. N. J. Ryan, who later became Headmaster and on the extreme right is Mr. Bryan Baird.

With Pathet Lao soldiers outside of Vientiene. Circa 1977.

With Prime Minister Pham Van Dong at his office, prior to his visit to ASEAN countries, 1978.

Visiting the Vietnamese Refugee Camp in Thailand, 1981.

Meeting with Premier Zhao Ziyang at Zhongnanhai, Beijing.

With the Foreign Minister of China, Wu Xuqian, at his office in Beijing.

At a dinner hosted by King Norodom Sihanouk and Queen Monique at their 40-room palace in Pyongyang.

With Zainal Abidin, the First Secretary, on my right at one of North Korea's most important monuments, the 60-metre-high bronze statue of Kim Il Sung, Pyongyang.

Receiving Prince and Princess Hitachi of Japan, together with my wife Lena, at a Malaysian function held at the Imperial Hotel, Tokyo.

With Dr. Mahathir Mohamad at the G-15 Summit in Kuala Lumpur, 1990.

Beseiged by press and media personnel during the G-15 Summit.

Meeting with Vice-Foreign Minister of China, Tang Jiaxuan, to invite China to be a dialogue partner of ASEAN, late 1991.

Audience with King Norodom Sihanouk at his palace in Phnom Penh, 1995.

# CHAPTER 12

# Territorial Disputes

Years of interactive diplomacy within ASEAN had established a sense of belonging to a large family. Above all, regular meetings, in particular among the senior officials at my level, had created an atmosphere of deep abiding friendship. This made it so much easier to discuss sensitive bilateral issues.

As in human relationships, in relations between neighbouring countries it is always those closest to us with whom we share more common interests, and correspondingly more areas where mutuality of interests will overlap, either for the better or as points of contention. It is the latter that will invoke the need for resolution whenever they arise. Between nations this would desirably be conducted through peaceful negotiations rather than acrimonious squabbles, as some neighbouring states have resorted to. Ancient and modern history is filled with bitter and violent disputes, many a time spilling over to full scale wars, in attempts to resolve conflicts between neighbouring states. But here I shall record a few episodes of the peaceful resolution of disputes, or incipient disputes, with Malaysia's immediate neighbours that occurred during my time as Secretary-General of the Foreign Ministry.

Malaysia shares common boundaries with most of the ASEAN

countries and has had territorial disputes with several of them. Three of these involved territorial disputes over sovereignty of islands. One involved an overlapping territorial claim. One concerned the overlapping continental shelf limit. And one—the most irritating and dangerous—involved a claim to one state of Malaysia.

But in all matters involving territorial disputes Malaysia had always pursued a peaceful resolution of the contested claims. This usually involved a long series of bilateral and personal meetings with the leaders and officials of the countries concerned before we were able to reach agreement on resolution.

The disputes we had over ownership of the islands of Pulau Ligitan and Pulau Sipadan with Indonesia and over Pulau Batu Puteh with Singapore were finally settled by referring them to the International Court of Justice (ICJ) and seeking its adjudication. We reached agreement to settle the disputes through the ICJ in 1994 and 1998 after failing to reach a settlement bilaterally.

As all the parties to the disputes were not signatories to the Statutes of the ICJ, the precondition for the ICJ to hear the case(s) required the litigants to conclude a Special Agreement on the disputes and to accept the decision of the Court as binding and final.

The negotiations with Indonesia for the Special Agreement involved two meetings, in January 1997 in Kuala Lumpur and in April 1997 in Bandung. The Special Agreement was signed on 31 May, 1997 by the two Foreign Ministers—Datuk Seri Abdullah Badawi for Malaysia and Ali Alatas for Indonesia.

The negotiations for the Special Agreement with Singapore took a longer time and the two sides only reached agreement in 1998. Because of Malaysia's pre-occupation with the pending case of Pulau Ligitan and Pulau Sipadan with Indonesia at the ICJ, it was mutually agreed to defer presenting the dispute for international adjudication until the case with Indonesia was settled. This was to last five years until 2003 when the Special Agreement was finally signed by both parties by the respective Ministers of Foreign Affairs.

My own part in these negotiations involved the preceding stages. Indonesia first challenged Malaysia's sovereignty over Pulau Ligitan and Pulau Sipadan in 1969 when it disputed our sovereignty of the two islands during negotiations on the delimitation of the continental shelf boundary; while in the case of Pulau Batu Puteh the dispute came about following Singapore's protest against the inclusion of the island in the map, entitled 'Territorial Waters and Continental Shelf Boundaries of Malaysia' published by Malaysia in 1979. The disputes dragged on till the early 1990s when I led the Malaysian delegation in three rounds of formal talks with Indonesian officials. At about the same time, in February 1992, Singapore officially submitted to Malaysia its Memorandum in support of its claim and in June the same year we officially responded with our own Memorandum. In Singapore's case the drawn out dispute, which was raised on several occasions between the leaders of the two countries,[146] tended to undermine further an already prickly relationship.

In the negotiation process, the first earnest meeting with Indonesia was held in Jakarta in 1992 where as leader of the Malaysian delegation, I had to face my good friend and counterpart at Indonesia's Department of Foreign Affairs Director-General Wiryono, who led the Indonesian team. As this was a serious issue involving territorial sovereignty the meeting from the beginning assumed a serious note, although the underlying friendship and respect I held for Director-General Wiryono and he for me held fast. Between 1992 and 1994 we had three rounds of talks to resolve the issue but without success.

During the period that interspersed these meetings there was some distracting interference by self-proclaimed 'friends of Malaysia and Indonesia', perhaps well-intended, who claimed to be close to the two leaders and who offered impractical solutions. It was also reported to me that a senior Malaysian Cabinet Minister had insulted our competence by suggesting to President Suharto that since there were two islands to the dispute perhaps the two countries should take ownership of one each! I was sure that President Suharto would have mockingly smiled at this simplistic idea. Unfortunately, I was not able to verify this story. In any case, at the final exploratory meeting in Jakarta, Indonesia informally raised the proposal that we use the ASEAN High Council as a mechanism for mediation. I rejected the idea outright on the simple grounds that almost all the members of the High Council would be from ASEAN, and every one of them had a claim on parts of Malaysia![147]

Prior to this, at one of the meetings in Jakarta, one of the members of the Indonesian delegation informed me that if this dispute was left unresolved the military might feel compelled to pressure President Suharto to 'take steps' that would be regretted by both countries. I saw this as a veiled threat and pointedly asked him if this meant that a second Konfrontasi was an option. And again while I was flying to Langkawi from Kuala Lumpur with members of the Indonesian Presidential delegation to be on hand to receive President Suharto on his visit there in 1994, one of the senior Indonesian diplomats whispered to me that Deplu (Indonesian Department of Foreign Affairs) was under tremendous pressure from the military to push the claim, much against the position of Deplu, who saw its weakness.

At my third and last meeting with the Indonesians I had reached the conclusion that we were heading nowhere and I contacted Tan Sri Halim Ali, Deputy Secretary-General, to ask him to convey my proposal to the Prime Minister to seek his approval that we refer the case to the International Court of Justice. Word came back almost immediately, while I was still in Jakarta, that the Prime Minister had agreed to the suggestion. Indonesia agreed to my proposal and the process of consultations towards this end thus got underway.

Shortly after my third and last meeting in Jakarta, on the occasion of President Suharto's visit to Langkawi in September 1994, as part of the annual bilateral meetings between leaders of the two countries, the two leaders decided to appoint Deputy Prime Minister Anwar Ibrahim and Secretaris Negara (State Secretary) Moerdiono as their personal representatives to continue the discussion. These two met four times between 1994 and 1996 and at the final meeting in June 1996 agreed to recommend to their respective leaders that the issue be referred to the ICJ. Three months into my retirement, I learned that the two leaders, officially agreed in October 1996 to refer the case to the ICJ.[148]

In the case of Singapore, following its submission of the Memorandum in 1992 and our counter submission that followed, the two sides settled down to the first round of talks in 1993. I led the Malaysian delegation and leading the Singapore side was Sivakant Tiwari, a senior legal counsel from Singapore's Attorney-General's Chambers. At this talk Singapore said, for the first time, that it was not only disputing ownership of Pulau Batu Puteh but also two other adjoining maritime features, Middle Rocks and South Ledge. This at once complicated the issue and I told them that I had no mandate to discuss Middle Rocks and South Ledge, which according to Kadir Mohamed 'was the main factor which closed the possibility of reaching any form of bilateral solution'.[149] Thus at the subsequent second round of talks held in 1994, I concluded that the two sides were not going to reach any meaningful conclusion as neither could convince the other. Having sensed the futility of any further discussion, in my final remarks I said, quoting a Javanese saying, "*Ono ning ora ono, ora ono ning ono.*" which roughly translates as "What you don't have you think you have and what you think you have you don't have". Finally, as with Indonesia, the leaders of the two countries agreed to refer the dispute to the ICJ.

In preparation for the submission to the ICJ, Malaysia engaged the services of two eminent and distinguished members of the international law fraternity. They were Professor Sir Elihu Lauterpacht and Professor James Crawford, both of Cambridge University. I met them at their University and discussed their participation. I did, however, encounter strong reservations by our own legal fraternity as to the necessity and wisdom of hiring them. Indeed I had a hard time getting my way around this. The Attorney-General felt that our own legal experts were adequately qualified to handle the matter without involving foreigners. I stood my ground on both occasions and pointed out that nothing must be left to chance when it came to the question of the territorial integrity of our country. I did get my way and was greatly relieved when the Prime Minister Dr. Mahathir agreed to my line of thinking and further gave me backing when he said that there was to be only one leader of the team in both cases with Indonesia and Singapore and that was to be me.

Meanwhile, our team set about preparing the grounds for the negotiations. On the ground working closely with Lt. General Maulob Muamin, the head of Malaysian Military Intelligence, we had put in place our 'fishermen' to monitor the regular visits and arrivals of Indonesian 'tourists' to Pulau Sipadan. And while the dispute was under negotiation, tourists were not stopped from visiting the island of Sipadan and we continued to promote the island as a tourist destination. My Indonesian counterpart, Wiryono had on several occasions protested that while the islands were in dispute and negotiations being held nothing should be done to give the impression of ownership of the islands. I politely retorted that the two islands had always been Malaysian and until otherwise decided we would carry on as always. He was going through the motion of protesting and my polite but firm response was also reaffirming our stand, and there was tacit mutual acceptance of our respective positions.

As for Singapore, the issue of Pulau Batu Puteh was added to my brief when I attended a meeting on the subject called by the Prime Minister, I believe in 1992. Attending that meeting were senior representatives of the Attorney-General's Chambers, including the Attorney-General himself, the Prime Minister's Department, the Department of Mapping and so on. It was suggested by the Attorney-General that since our case did not appear to be strong enough to challenge Singapore's position we should fence our negotiation with Singapore on the basis of getting Singapore to agree to Malaysia retaining traditional fishing rights in and around Pulau Batu Puteh. I did not agree to standing down before getting to know the issue thoroughly. Hence I pleaded with the Prime Minister that since Wisma Putra had already begun serious and extensive research on the historical and documentary evidence surrounding Pulau Batu Puteh that he should give the Ministry a year to complete its work and only then decide on how to proceed to the next step. Having obtained the Prime Minister's consent, Wisma Putra began to look at all the historical and documentary evidence available locally and also in the archives of other countries that had had contact with Malaysia in the 19th and early 20th centuries. We had input from relevant branches of the Government and we again engaged the expert services of Professor Sir Elihu Lauterpacht and Professor James Crawford. After all that, we came to the conclusion that our case was not as weak as earlier feared! Since Malaysia had a case, the Prime Minister gave his approval to begin official negotiations with Singapore in 1993.

Both disputes dragged on beyond my time as Secretary-General. The Indonesian claim was finally settled on 17 December, 2002, and on 23 May, 2008 the case of Pulau Batu Puteh was settled with Singapore. In both instances, Tan Sri Abdul Kadir Mohamed, who subsequently became the Secretary-General of the Foreign Ministry, took over the leadership of Malaysia's negotiating team and ably steered both litigations through the ICJ.[150]

The ICJ ruled by a majority of 16 to 1 that the sovereignty of Pulau Ligitan and Pulau Sipadan belonged to Malaysia. It was conclusive, final and binding. As Chandran Jeshurun wrote, "The verdict of the ICJ was a vindication of the professionalism of the Ministry (of Foreign Affairs) and served to raise its profile as fully capable of defending the national interest at the international level."[151]

And, regarding the dispute with Singapore, the ICJ's judgement was:

- Found by 12 votes to four that sovereignty over Pedra Branca/Pulau Batu Puteh belongs to the Republic of Singapore;
- Found by 15 votes to one that sovereignty of Middle Rocks belongs to Malaysia;
- Found by 15 votes to one that sovereignty of South Ledge belongs to the State in the territorial waters of which it is located.

Consequently, to quote Abdul Kadir Mohamed, "Malaysians may never want to look upon the decisions of the Court as any form of consolation prize for Malaysia. But United Nations Convention on the Law of the Sea would confirm that the Court's decision to award sovereignty over Middle Rocks to Malaysia—which should consequently include South Ledge as well—has given Malaysia an equal standing with Singapore in that part of the Singapore Straits near BP (Pulau Batu Puteh)."[152]

Meanwhile, in parallel with the above disputes with Indonesia and Singapore, we also had territorial issues pending resolutions with Brunei, Thailand and Vietnam. With Brunei, there was the unresolved territorial claim over Limbang. With Thailand there remained the unsettled business of completing the border demarcation and with Vietnam that of the overlapping continental shelf limit.

The joint border demarcation exercise with Thailand had commenced in the mid-1970s but ratification of final demarcations had stalled and this prevented progress on demarcation of the maritime boundaries as well. The problem rested with the Thai constitutional requirement to refer the packages of agreements to Parliament. Although this was the right process to take as it involved the territorial integrity of the country, it was well nigh impossible to get this unwieldy process through speedily. We did, however, in 1979 reach agreement, only as an interim measure, to establish the Malaysia-Thailand Joint Development Area to jointly exploit the resources in the seabed claimed by the two countries. But this interim measure did not eliminate the legal basis of the claims by the two countries.

As the Under Secretary of Southeast Asia at Wisma Putra from 1976 to 1977, I was somewhat involved at the early stages of the negotiations. A Memorandum was signed by the two countries in February of that year. In May 1990 an agreement was reached in Kuala Lumpur to form a Joint Development Authority with a permanent secretariat to be housed in Kuala Lumpur to manage the exploration and exploitation of natural resources. Years later, after my retirement, I was appointed one of the Joint Chairmen of the Joint Development Authority in 1996. With this agreement the two countries began in earnest to exploit the maritime resources in what is now known as the joint development area in the Gulf of Thailand, the area disputed by both countries pending final settlement. This enabled both countries to benefit even before resolution of the dispute.

The dispute with Vietnam came about as a result of the overlapping continental shelf in the Gulf of Thailand. Each country uses a different baseline to calculate the equidistant line for demarcating their respective claims to the continental shelf.[153] In the discussion with Vietnam I used the example of the arrangement we had reached with Thailand with regard to overlapping claims; i.e. to put aside the legal aspects until final settlement, but meanwhile agree to jointly exploit the maritime resources in the area in dispute. This understanding was reached in June 1992 after a series of meetings I had with my Vietnamese counterpart, Vice-Minister of Foreign Affairs Vo Quan. We agreed to apply the joint development principle using the Malaysia-Thai Joint Development as a model. Following this agreement, PETRONAS and Petrovietnam, the two national petroleum companies, began negotiations on a commercial arrangement based on the principle of equality of rights and obligations.

As for Brunei, the issue fell on my lap when Brunei shifted the responsibility of the handling of the dispute with Malaysia sometime in 1993 from its Attorney-General to the Foreign Ministry and we accordingly reciprocated. I then found myself entrusted to handle the issue with Brunei's Permanent Secretary Lim Jock Seng[154] leading the Brunei side. The preliminary and early meetings I had were conducted in a less structured manner and were marked by utmost friendship. They indeed turned out to be meetings of gentlemen, a true example of what inherent goodwill between two nations and their officials can do to ease the negotiating process.

By the time negotiations were in full swing I had retired, but the friendship and trust ensured that the dialogue continued in the same vein,[155] reflecting the long cultural ties between the two countries. The dispute was finally settled with the Exchange of Letters in Bandar Seri Begawan between Prime Minister Abdullah Badawi and Sultan Hassanal

Bolkiah on 16 March, 2009. The agreement reached at the highest level reflected the deep friendship and respect between the two leaders. This essentially settled the boundary issues and demarcated the common border between the two countries. according to five historical agreements of which two directly involved Limbang.

There was yet one more territorial claim that Malaysia had had to live with for as long as Malaysia had existed. The matter emerged in 1962 when President Diasdado Macapagal, the father of President Gloria Arroyo Macapagal, not only laid claim to Sabah but embedded it in the Philippines constitution in 1969 (Republic Act 5546). The basis of the claim was bizarre enough. In 1962 the Philippines government signed an agreement between itself and one Mohammed Esmail Kiram, who claimed descendency from the defunct Sultan of Sulu.[156] Mohammed Esmail thereupon ceded the territory of North Borneo to the Philippines.

Malaysia knew this was a politically fabricated issue for domestic expedience. Malaysia, Thailand and Indonesia all made several attempts to assist the Philippines to drop its claim amicably and honourably. These initiatives failed. Wisma Putra has always maintained, after a thorough study, that the Philippines did not have any legal or historical basis whatsoever to support their claim to Sabah. Finally at the ICJ hearing between Indonesia and Malaysia on the case of Pulau Ligitan and Pulau Sipadan in 2001/02, the Philippines attempted to resurrect its claim through a request for intervention. According to Abdul Kadir Mohamed this intervention "began as an irritant and a distraction to the proceedings between the two parties to the dispute—Malaysia and Indonesia. In the end the Philippines not only failed in its bid to intervene but lost substantial ground—diplomatically and legally—in its attempt to resurrect the Philippines claim to Sabah."[157] Perhaps after all these years wise heads should prevail to remove this stone in the shoe of ASEAN relations. But Philippines domestic politics is too imbedded with political expediency for any leader to have the strength to get the claim out of the way. It will thus remain a thorn in otherwise harmonious bilateral relations with Malaysia. The issue lingered on all through my time in office and, until today, without the resolution we were able to achieve in all the other inter-ASEAN cases.

By the time I left office there was another conflict arising, far more dangerous because it was partly outside the ASEAN framework of conflict resolution. This was in the South China Sea, specifically the Paracels and the Spratlys. The countries contesting ownership of parts of the two groups of islands are Vietnam, the Philippines, Brunei and Malaysia, but with the addition, outside the framework, of China; China (and Taiwan) laid claim to large areas of the South China Sea.

Malaysia had laid claim to and today controls Terumbu Ubi (Ardasler Reef), Terumbu Mantanani (Marineles Reef) and Terumbu (now Pulau) Layang-Layang (Swallow Reef). Dr Mahathir states in his book[158] that Tun Hussein Onn, when he was Prime Minister, was against occupying Amboyna Cay and ousting the Vietnamese troops. In order not to confront Vietnam he decided not to claim Amboyna Cay. Confrontation with Vietnam was thus avoided. When Dr. Mahathir became Prime Minister he decided to take steps to secure our claim on Terumbu Layang-Layang. Sometime in the early 1990s he called for a high-level meeting of senior government officials from relevant ministries and departments including top military brass. From the Ministry of Foreign Affairs' side we had done our homework and came prepared to put forward our views.

Dr. Mahathir began the discussion by explaining his view that Layang-Layang was a *terumbu* (an atoll) and it belonged to Malaysia. He went on along this line of logic for close to ten minutes, and when at the end of it he asked for comments I stood up beside him, with maps in hand, to explain that while we agree that we should lay claim to the *terumbu,* our position would be strengthened if the *terumbu* became an *island.*[159] We had prepared three maps, which I opened up in front of him to show the three options available to us. I pointed out that the atoll was outside our territorial waters but within our continental shelf limit. I ended my presentation by recommending that we claim the atoll and take option three, which was to turn the *terumbu* into an *island.* To turn it into an island it must have life and economic activities. These were features necessary to make it an island.

Dr. Mahathir was listening closely—as were the others, stunned into disbelief at my boldness in challenging the Prime Minister in full view of this line-up of senior officials. I explained further that we could not just call it an island—we would have to transform it into one. All he said was, "Okay, I accept your view." and he got up and left the meeting. He was visibly upset at being challenged. But to his credit, Dr. Mahathir took it up and immediately instructed the navy to begin work to transform the *terumbu* into an island. He took an active interest in its development and soon enough it began to show features of an island. Meanwhile, other features or atolls, numbering close to ten, claimed by Malaysia, remained in dispute.

The disputes in the South China Sea, centred on the Spratly group of islands, have the potential of destabilising the security and stability of the region as a whole and must not be allowed to spiral out of control. At the time of writing, the spat between China and the Philippines on Scarborough Shoal had not as yet slid into open conflict but if not checked both China and the Philippines might be forced into actions that they may regret. The likely involvement of outside powers cannot be ruled out. Already the United States has reached agreement to place their marines in Darwin, Australia, and the American nuclear submarine *USS North Carolina* appeared at Subic Bay, a move strongly criticised by China. The Philippines, in the meantime was beginning to upgrade its naval force. This nervous situation could escalate further.

The ASEAN Code of Conduct (COC) is a set of guidelines agreed by ASEAN to handle disputes and prevent conflicts in the South China Sea. A series of meetings between ASEAN and China, that had stretched over many years, failed to bring the two sides any nearer to reaching a mutually acceptable agreement on the framework. At the time of writing the ASEAN Summit in Phnom Penh was still unable to reach any consensus, first among ASEAN members, then ASEAN with China. Disagreements reportedly flared up between the Philippines and host Cambodia on how to deal with China. This clearly illustrates how tenuous the ASEAN consensus is on handling China in an effort to reach agreement on the COC. When Surin Pitsuwan, the ASEAN Secretary-General, reportedly suggested that China begin discussions on the COC, aimed at easing tension, the Chinese played down the suggestion. As things go the COC would seem a distant goal—a bridge too far!

ASEAN's strength is in its numbers and in its history of peaceful resolution of disputes. But the Chinese have a long held position that disputes be resolved through bilateral negotiations only. Since all the relationships between China and individual ASEAN members are unequal, will China bully its way to achieve its goals? The South China Sea is a regional issue and ASEAN must play a role in its solution. Although it is difficult to build political trust on all sides when the temperature is rising so sharply, failure to do so will threaten peace and stability not only in the region but further afield.

# Endnotes

146   For a chronology of this, refer to Kadir Mohamed, *Malaysia's Territorial Disputes: The Case of Pulau Batu Puteh, Middle Rocks and South Ledge at The International Court of Justice*, Malaysia, Institute of Diplomacy and International Relations, 2009, pp. 2–3.

147   This was before Vietnam, Laos, Cambodia and Myanmar joined ASEAN.

148   This was then followed by further discussions to reach a special agreement for the two sides to submit to the ICJ as was required for non-signatories to the Statutes of the ICJ. This was agreed and signed in May 1997 by the respective Foreign Ministers and then it was followed by three submissions of written pleadings by the parties in 1999, 2000 and 2001. The final step was the Oral Hearings at the ICJ in The Hague held from 3–12 June, 2002. See Kadir Mohamed, *op. cit.*, pp. 36–39.

149   Ibid, p. 3.

150   See Kadir Mohamed, *op. cit.*

151   Chandran Jeshurun, *op. cit.*, p. 269.

152   Kadir Mohamed, *op. cit.*, p. 25.

153   Furthermore both Malaysia and Vietnam are also involved in the multi-national claims over some of the Spratly Islands and the adjacent waters that also involve China, the Philippines and Taiwan.

154   Later honoured with the title Pehin and appointed Second Minister of Foreign Affairs and Trade. Pehin is the title of a very high order and is not awarded through the annual award, but through special ceremonies carried out once every several years. The awards are only for those who have served the Sultan well.

155   In the exercise to demarcate their common border it was agreed that the watershed principle be used to fill in the gaps. This essentially reaffirms the current de facto boundary without major deviation. Malaysia subsequently said, however, the Limbang Question will be settled when the survey and demarcation of the boundary between the two countries is completed.

156   The Sultanate of Sulu as an international entity disappeared in 1878 when it was conquered by Spain and ceased as an entity in 1936 when the United States abolished the sultanate entirely upon the death of the last Sultan. No subsequent international treaty between successive colonial powers had recognised the territory of Sabah (then known as North Borneo) as forming part of the Philippines. It was instead recognised as British North Borneo, which became the state of Sabah in Malaysia. To quote Judge Franck of the ICJ, "the Philippines claim to Sabah had become a purely historical matter because whatever the basis, it had been overtaken by the exercise of self-determination by the people of Sabah in 1963." See Kadir Mohamed, *op. cit.*

157   For more historical details, see Kadir Mohamed, *op. cit.*, pp. 44–50.

158   Mahathir Mohamad, *A Doctor in the House*, Malaysia, MPH Group Publishing Sdn. Bhd., 2011, p. 344.

159   At the beginning, the Prime Minister and those present strongly insisted on referring to the cluster using the historical and popular Malay term '*terumbu*', meaning 'atoll' when translated to English, resisting my suggestion that it be referred to as '*pulau*', meaning 'island'. But I pressed home the point that substantively these two words carried considerable differences. An atoll could not be recognised as land justifying territorial waters demarcation and we could stand to lose out in marking our sea boundary.

# CHAPTER 13

# The Betrayal of Bosnia-Herzegovina

*"...faith in modern civilisation is fast diminishing. We can put a man on the moon. We can examine stars light-years away, we can achieve instant contact with every part of the world, we can build intelligent machines and many more wonders. But we are still quite uncivilised, for when it comes to killing each other, we are worse than animals."*[160]

So much has already been said and written about Bosnia-Herzegovina and the brutal and tragic war that took place there during the first part of the '90s that a repetition is not needed. This was a conflict that assaulted every civilised norm and standard of the international community as it stood on the cusp of the millennium. I would like to reflect on, and relate, precisely how it was that our small country took several giant leaps into unknown territory, a territory somewhere between accepted universal principles and where only chaos and injustice reigned. This was a territory where universal principles like non-interference and the peaceful settlement of disputes no longer applied. In such a region of anarchy, whether real or philosophical, how should nations act?

The universal principles just mentioned may well be enshrined in the United Nations Charter. Yet, these same principles are often unattainable ideals. The Bosnian conflict showed the world just how empty, even irrelevant, its idealism had become for successful foreign policy. Prime Minister Dr. Mahathir, in the quote above, expressed concern over what he saw was the *de-civilisation* of the human race. US President Bill Clinton had earlier summed up his attitude on Bosnia when he said: "I don't think anybody suggests that if there is a hiccup here or there or a conflict here and there that the United States is going to send troops."[161] His Secretary of State James Baker went one better when he explained US inaction by saying, "We don't have a dog in that fight."

The Bosnian war strenuously tested the practical application of two fundamental universal principles—that of peaceful settlement of disputes, and that of non-interference in the affairs of sovereign states. Both principles had established the very foundations of the United Nations itself. Its Charter also clearly states, in Article 51, 'the right of nations to defend themselves'. Yet these principles, throughout the years of the Bosnian conflict, remained utterly elusive.

When it became clear that the practical application of what we thought were universally accepted norms was discarded in favour of harsh *balance of power* considerations, Malaysia stood firmly in support of establishing those timeless values which respect both individual and human rights to justice and fairness on the one hand, and nations' right to sovereignty and freedom on the other.

Some nations, however, preferred to abide by the UN Charter only in words or when it suited their own purpose, hiding behind a false screen of neutrality—a lot of effort was made to do absolutely nothing.[162] This was not neutrality; this was hypocrisy. We argued for a proactive diplomacy that would admit that the United Nations could not, in this instance, remain neutral because that would mean treating victims and aggressors alike. In 1994 I said, "While many people in the world seem ready to let the Serbs determine the fate of Bosnia, we in Malaysia should not despair because our Bosnian friends have refused to succumb. We should never be a party to those looking for excuses to do nothing, or to put it differently, to do everything in order to do nothing, and fall into a mental trap that nothing can be done about Bosnia-Herzergovina."

The false screen of neutrality maintained by most of the powers of the West displayed a deliberately perverse reasoning that only served to consciously drive the conflict in Bosnia into a deeper depth of genocide, although the term used was 'ethnic cleansing'. Dr. Mahathir correctly said that ethnic cleansing in this instance was just a euphemism for genocide.[163] Several United Nations Security Council resolutions authorised the use of force by its troops in Bosnia, notably UN Security Council Resolution 836, which gave explicit authority to UNPROFOR[164] to respond to bombardments against the *safe havens* by any of the parties.

As we know, no protection for the safe havens was forthcoming because the Western powers insisted that the UN should remain 'neutral'. I argued then that this was perversity of the highest order, to tell the world that the Bosnians could not be protected because the lives of UNPROFOR troops would be endangered. It was clear that it was the permanent members of the Security Council who were responsible for making the peacekeeping rules that put United Nations soldiers into a situation that dishonoured both themselves and their mandate under the UN.

It is not my intention here to look into the details of the injustices committed under the name of greater peace during the Bosnian conflict.

As I said, evidence of all this has been revealed and copiously written about elsewhere. My interest here is to ask the question: what happens when diplomacy fails? Among the most dismal failures of diplomacy was the United Nations' arms embargo upon the former Yugoslavia which most of the Western powers, especially Britain and France, insisted be applied to the breakaway states of Bosnia and Croatia.

This left almost all the military equipment of the former Yugoslavia in the hands of Serbia—and Croatia and Bosnia with almost nothing with which to defend themselves. The British and French, using the form of twisted logic prevalent throughout the crisis, insisted that lifting the embargo would unleash a bloodbath and prolong the war, in spite of the fact that there was already a bloodbath with no end in sight. Among the Western countries, the United States and Germany favoured lifting the embargo but actually did nothing in the light of British and French objections.

In the case of the Bosnian war, decisions were made in the name of the international community, but actually by only a handful of nations. They imposed a fundamentally unjust policy upon a nation, which had only recently been recognised as independent and sovereign.[165] The Bosnian conflict became a vigorous test of the concept of international responsibility. When the international community's traditional instrument for accountability, namely the UN, failed to live up to its mandate, what or who was left to bring those responsible for injustice to account?[166]

In December of 1994, at the very height of the conflict, I said: "It is a sad commentary on the concept of international responsibility when the question of whether Serb advances should be halted is being weighed against considerations of whether the cohesion of NATO will be affected. It would seem a conclusion has been reached that the possible obliteration of a nation state named Bosnia-Herzegovina is a small price to pay for the preservation of NATO's integrity...."[167] Malaysia was concerned with what it understood to be a clear rejection of the universally accepted rules of fair play in favour of establishing the security of and the balance of power in Europe via a strong Serbia.[168]

Our rejection of this breach of the rules of fairness and respect for the sovereignty—and very survival—of this new nation was at the heart of our involvement in helping the Bosnians, much more than just the religious factor. Malaysia's parliamentary members, including the opposition, were all united in condemning the double standards shown by the West in dealing with the Bosnian issue. Having said this we do not deny the religious factor, or the fact that the Bosnian or Kosovo conflicts were a result of the deliberate persecution and premeditated extermination of Muslims from Slav lands. Muslim Slavs were considered by ultra-nationalists to have betrayed Christianity by becoming 'Turkified'.[169]

We could not and did not accept that one nation should be allowed to obliterate another sovereign state. Our opposition to acts of aggression by one state on another was amply demonstrated in past cases where we made our decisions clear for others to see.

The biggest obstacle in those early days of the war was, as mentioned earlier, the arms embargo imposed upon all of the former republics of Yugoslavia by UN Security Council Resolution 713 adopted on 25 September, 1991. Bosnia-Herzegovina were therefore deprived of any way of arming themselves. Serbia had inherited the lion's share of the arsenal of the former Yugoslav National Army (JNA). By extension the Serbs in Bosnia could fall back on assistance from Serbia, and indeed Serbia was supplying arms, both light and heavy, to them and JNA forces were also involved in the war. The Croatian army, the other breakaway state from Yugoslavia, while in need of arms, did not find it too difficult to get them in through its long coastline.

The Bosnian government lobbied hard to have the embargo lifted but was opposed by the United Kingdom, France and Russia. Despite efforts by the US and Germany to lift the arms embargo they failed to persuade Britain, whose British Foreign Secretary Douglas Hurd argued that lifting the embargo would only prolong the war.[170] The imposition of the embargo led to an acute military imbalance. Was this, then, a quick way to remove Bosnia-Herzegovina from the map of Europe, and was there then a hidden motive behind this move by the British government? The Western powers were closing their eyes to the genocide happening daily in their backyard. They found it convenient, as pointed out by Professor Michael Sells,[171] to deny that there was genocide because to do so would obligate them to take action as required by the United Nations Convention on the Prevention and Punishment of the Crime of Genocide.

It was against this backdrop of western inaction and self-imposed paralysis that I was called some time towards the end of 1992 by the Prime Minister, to say that Malaysia had to move quickly to assist the Bosnians. I then held discussions with Tan Sri Ghazali Shafie,[172] Dr. Baharom Azhar of the Prime Minister's Department, and General Maulub Maamin, Head of Military Intelligence. Joining me from Wisma Putra was Kadir Mohammad, Head of Policy Planning and my Special Assistant Zulkephli Mohd. Noor. A plan of action was drawn up and put in place, ready to be implemented. It was named 'Project Scarecrow'.

Our initial strategy was to explore whether we could get the support of some Muslim countries in the Middle East, particularly the Magreb[173] countries and Muslim countries of Central Asia, which had recently freed themselves from the Soviet Union. Bosnia was already exploring the possibility of aid from Saudi Arabia and one or two Gulf States.

Tan Sri Ghazali Shafie undertook to travel as a Special Envoy of the Prime Minister to Egypt and a couple of other countries. To our disappointment he failed to get to meet President Hosni Mubarak, and his discussions in Cairo were less than encouraging. My visit took me to Kyrgystan, Uzbekistan, Turkmenistan, and Kazakhstan. My discussions were equally disappointing. The Central Asian republics which had only recently re-established themselves as independent states were not in a position, nor in the mood, to assist or support our effort in any form, even diplomatically. I understood their priorities. Despite my disappointment, one positive outcome of my visit was that we made our first contacts with these newly re-established republics, which would lead to further development of mutually beneficial economic and trade relations in the following years.

The disappointment with a lack of clear support from the Muslim countries that we approached meant that we had to rethink our strategy. We identified two areas on which we would focus, firstly on a diplomatic offensive in the west, and secondly on the question of providing military assistance. In the first instance I travelled to New York and with the help of Razali Ismail, our Permanent Representative to the UN, and Muhamed Sacirbey, the Permanent Representative of Bosnia-Herzegovina, I met with some top media people in New York. In Washington I met a handful of senators and staffers, and before we left Razali and I conducted a televised press conference.

All this was part of our effort to drive home the glaring military imbalance, which left the victims, the Bosnians, at the mercy of the aggressors, the Serbs. We had hoped that our efforts would stir their conscience into action. I also managed to get the Prime Minister's approval to organise two international forums, one in Bonn and the other in London, to which some European parliamentarians and US senators were invited. In Germany, we were assisted by a group of activists sympathetic to the Bosnian plight. Dr. Haris Silajdzic[174] and some other Bosnian ministers, as well as Tan Sri Ghazali Shafie, attended the two forums.

While the forums were being planned and organised, on the ground we took actions which included pasting of posters depicting pictures of atrocities committed by the Serbs at some of the key locations in and around the UN Headquarters in Geneva. A few people were *recruited* to demonstrate near the main entrance of the UN Headquarters in Geneva.

In the meantime the OIC contact group met from time to time to keep abreast of the situation, but apart from issuing communiqués, nothing else came out of it. When I met Dr. Haris Silajdzic and President Alija Izetbegovic[175] at one of these meetings in Geneva they pleaded for assistance, either in cash or materials, and asked me if Malaysia could also provide the leadership to persuade some Muslim countries to come to their assistance.

Without prior consultation and instruction from the Prime Minister, but knowing how strongly he felt about the one-sided situation in Bosnia-Herzegovina, I committed myself to this fresh request and informed President Alija Izetbegovic that we would do so. I subsequently discussed this new development with the Prime Minister who gave me his strong and unreserved support. We moved quickly to implement the plan.

Our first shipment of light weapons was held up in Cyprus for almost a week, sometime in July/August 1993 creating great anxiety among us. Finally the ship set sail for Istanbul. Istanbul was from time to time used as a base for the onward transshipment of weapons and other forms of assistance by the OIC countries.

It was also at one of the meetings that Dr. Haris Silajdzic suggested that Malaysia work with Pakistan. He added that his sister Sadjedeh, who was Bosnian Ambassador to Pakistan, would be happy to assist me with some introductions. My relationship with those whom I met in Islamabad and with whom I worked on getting assistance to Bosnia developed into an enduring friendship. By the time we were discussing with Pakistan on military assistance, Brunei had come on board and its generous contribution fortified our joint effort.

Except for a narrow opening to the Adriatic Sea, Bosnia is almost landlocked. In the early days, we tried to figure out the best way for our assistance to reach Bosnia, and decided as a first step to go through Croatia. The Croatian government was also at this time at war with the Serbs and now aligned itself with the Bosniacs. But they too were in need of military supplies and in order to meet their needs, their Government imposed a 30 percent levy, or tax, on all supplies going through Croatia to Bosnia. I needed to do something about this and travelled to Zagreb on several occasions to meet with Prime Minister Nikica Valentic, and later his successor, Prime Minister Zlatko Matesa in order to get them to waive the tax.

The result of my efforts was that a few shipments were exempted from this tax, but on most occasions we had no choice but to comply. Our assistance, and similar assistance from others, now began to reach its destination. However, despite my pleading, Croatia continued to strictly maintain its position that no heavy weapons were allowed to pass through. Confronted with this problem, we resorted to using our Bosnian contacts in Istanbul working at the same time with the Turkish authorities.

The support received from Malaysia and other OIC countries began to have an impact in halting the Serb advances and gave the Bosnians breathing space to regroup and time to consolidate their defences. Dr. Haris Silajdzic, when I met him some time towards the end of the war, swore by the effectiveness of the Pakistani anti-tank guns, the *Green*

*Arrow/Baktiar Shiken*. Working closely with the people in Pakistan and also my good friend Lim Jock Seng from Brunei,[176] we began to supply the Bosnian army with more of these lethal weapons.

These anti-tank guns, according to Dr. Haris Silajdzic, stopped the marauding Serb tanks from entering Sarajevo, and in the fighting in Bihac, a UN *safe haven* in the northwest of the country, the Serbs' advance was rolled back due to the new supplies of weapons they received from OIC countries. A sad note for me about Bihac was to receive the news that the Foreign Minister Irfan Ljubijankac, with whom I was working closely, had died on 28 May, 1995 when the helicopter he was in was brought down by Serb fire.

Gun-running was not a job I was ever trained for, but it became part of my many-sided responsibilities as Secretary-General. I made my first visit to Sarajevo in the early years of the war. It was the beginning of winter when we arrived in Zagreb, cold and tired after a long flight. After a short rest we were briefed by Colonel Hashim Hussein,[177] Commander of MALBAT[178] of UNPROFOR. According to Colonel Hashim, there were reports, well before MALBAT arrived in Bosnia, that our soldiers were made up of headhunters, and "that after killing our enemies we would decapitate them and their skulls would be shrunk and stuck on the loft of our houses for display". That, he believed, put a scare into the Serbs. Or so he said.

The next morning we left for the airport and on arrival were told that the UN aircraft was not able to take us as it was fully loaded. We were told that another UN aircraft leaving at two in the afternoon would, with luck, take us to Sarajevo. My 11.00 a.m. appointments with Prime Minister Dr. Haris Silajdzic and subsequently President Alija Izetbegovic had to be rescheduled. Was it a blessing that we missed that flight? Because at about 11.05 that morning the Serbs fired two wire-guided rockets at the entrance of the Presidency through which I was supposed to be escorted for my appointments.

Not only had I been lucky that day. My Bosnian counterpart precisely at that time stepped inside to hang up his coat. Was it by divine intervention that our lives were spared? I recalled that many years ago, as a young diplomat with time on my hands, I visited a numerologist and subsequently a soothsayer in Kuala Lumpur. They both told me that there was always someone protecting me. If I missed my appointment for whatever reason I had to look at this misfortune as someone trying to prevent me from serious harm. How uncanny I thought.

Taking the 2.00 p.m. flight we left for Sarajevo. As the aircraft was making its descent we were advised to remove our flak jackets and sit on them as the Serbs in the hills below, surrounding three sides of the airport, would usually take pot shots at UN aircraft during landing and take-off. At the airport, we were bunkered in until, as luck would have it, an Armoured Personnnel Carrier (APC) came to the airport on some errands and would be returning to Sarajevo almost immediately. In we scrambled. It was a relief to be moving, but along the way the APC came under sniper fire and the sound of bullets hitting the armour of the APC sent shivers down our spines, particularly those who, for the first time, found themselves in a war zone. I was thinking hard about the Kuala Lumpur soothsayers.

It was almost dark when we reached the Holiday Inn, which no longer resembled a hotel. It was cold, damp and dim. The lobby was a cavernous freezing space where one felt anything could happen. The building had been badly scarred by the war and so had our rooms. The windowpanes were long gone and were replaced by plastic sheets, and behind the plastic sheets there was no view to enjoy. The destruction of the city was obvious all around.

One sight in particular assaulted my eyes, a spectre of twisted metal and concrete that had been the headquarters of the daily newspaper *Oslobodenje*, whose brave journalists toiled in the basement to produce a newspaper issue every single day. It was here in Sarajevo that I learned for the first time how sleeping can be a frightening experience. We had to sleep fully dressed with our flak jackets on and our faces covered at all times with the blue UN helmets.

During my brief visit, which was my first to Sarajevo but not the last as I had to make a few more trips there during the war years, I met and had discussions with Prime Minister Dr. Haris Silajdzic. We talked about continued material support and also how we could involve more OIC countries. Dr. Haris Silajdzic thanked me for the assistance already received by them and told me monetary assistance would also be welcomed as they had their own contacts to source materials from. President Alija Izetbegovic whom I met after the meeting with Dr. Haris Silajdzic requested that we should look at other options, one of which was to get the OIC contact group to work towards committing themselves to seriously supporting the Bosnian government war effort. This I promised him. On the ground I was working closely with Hassan Cengih[179] to coordinate our operations, and on the diplomatic front with Bosnian Ambassador Mustafa Bjadich at the UN in Geneva.

Leaving Sarajevo for the airport and returning to Zagreb was another harrowing journey. Again there was no APC for us and again we had to scramble into one that came to collect someone else. It was an Egyptian APC and after some pleading the driver agreed to include us. In a desperate attempt, my Special Assistant Zulkephli opened his passport to show a valid visa for Egypt making sure that 'Malaysia' was clearly visible to the Egyptian soldier. That simple act did the trick. Along the way we were stopped several times but to our relief they turned out to be UN checkpoints. It was the same morning that a young Serb girl was killed by sniper fire at the grounds where we had been standing waiting for an APC.

Again on the way back we missed the morning flight, and again we found ourselves bunkered at the airport. Sarajevo airport was manned by a French contingent under the command of Lt. Col. Gary Coward. He took pity on us and invited us to a three-course lunch with them. We enjoyed a meal with red and white wine, followed by dessert and a tray of assorted cheeses. As we walked towards the aircraft I joked with him that if I were his enemy I would mount my offensive during lunch. We thanked him, however, profusely for his generosity and kindness.

As the war continued and escalated, I became increasingly disenchanted, and even angry, at the OIC contact group.[180] They issued ineffectual communiqués which did not help the Bosnians on the ground nor had any impact on the international community. I was determined to get things moving and before the January 1994 Foreign Ministers Meeting of the contact group I spoke to the Foreign Minister who was already in Geneva to attend the contact group meeting, to call for an expanded meeting of the group that would include the Defence Ministers and Defence Chiefs. There was now, by mid-1990s, a growing resolve I sensed among them to be directly involved in a more sustained effort to provide military aid to Bosnia.

Malaysia's proposal as put forward by Foreign Minister Abdullah Badawi was accepted at a meeting held in Geneva in January 1994. The following year on Friday, 21 July, 1995, the OIC declared in Geneva that it no longer recognised the UN arms embargo. Proclaiming it to be 'invalid' the Group announced it was ready to send military aid to help the Bosnian government against the Serbs. Dr. Mahathir openly accused the UN and NATO of "allowing the slaughtering of Bosnians by the Serbs".[181]

The expanded contact group meeting was then held in Kuala

Lumpur from 11 to 14 September, 1995 and was named 'A Special Meeting on Bosnia-Herzegovina of the OIC Contact Group and Troop Contributing Countries to UNPROFOR'. This meeting would be one of Project Scarecrow's most important contributions to our efforts to assist Bosnia. For the first time in the history of the OIC a meeting was organised when all foreign and defence ministers were present as well as the chiefs of the armed forces of the OIC contact group. The participating countries were Bangladesh, Bosnia-Herzegovina, Croatia, Egypt, Indonesia, Iran, Jordan, Kuwait, Malaysia, Morocco, Pakistan, Qatar, Saudi Arabia, Senegal and Turkey. Also present was the OIC Secretary-General. The meeting assessed the latest developments in Bosnia-Herzegovina and charted a common position on the question of future military aid to its government.[182]

At the time I had only stated that officials were 'all of one mind' as to how to approach the situation, then and in the future, but I was pressed to explain what I meant by that. I referred to the important decision of 21 July, 1995 made by the OIC on the arms embargo, saying that it was now "time for concrete proposals". I said that this "should be more focused... and should direct itself toward helping Bosnia as it faces not only the situation on the ground but also as it faces the other factions at the conference table".

It was, I said, just as vital to deal with this problem at the conference table. By now the OIC had already reached a point of united resolve and decided that all efforts should be made to strengthen the Bosnian government without making any further compromises. I told the media that we were looking at various 'options', telling the press that "we want the Bosnian government to be strong enough to face the Serbs. As you know, the Serbs have a massive collection of heavy weapons while the Bosnian army is not that well-equipped". It was also agreed during the meeting to establish the Assistance Mobilisation Group (AMG).[183] The AMG met on several occasions in Turkey, Iran and Bosnia to map out its action plan, and the final meeting of the AMG took place in Sarajevo just before the Dayton Agreement.

It was, however, not until the OIC declaration of 21 July, 1995 that there was a public statement admitting to the breach of the UN arms embargo. Before that date the official stand of the OIC was that it recognised the arms ban. It was the decision of the September 1995 Kuala Lumpur Meeting to ignore the embargo that brought matters into the open. Analysts were then all too aware of our substantial military presence in Bosnia as well as the fact that our standpoint was shared by many of the other Muslim-majority governments.[184]

We do believe that our actions created an impact because by early September there was a concerted effort by the West to find a solution to the war. On September 1995, for the first time since the beginning of the war, the foreign ministers of Bosnia, Croatia and Serbia met to lay the foundation for future peace talks. They agreed to recognise each other's borders, something they had not done since the former Yugoslavia fell apart. Indeed, Serbia and Croatia had earlier conspired to dismember Bosnia-Herzegovina.

Also unlike the earlier unacceptable Vance-Owen Plan,[185] they now agreed to keep Bosnia intact, dividing the land almost equally between the Bosnian Serbs and a Muslim-Croat alliance. All this was agreed upon in Geneva amid NATO air-strikes against the Serbs, which only stopped when the Serbs removed their heavy weapons from around Sarajevo. We insisted that these air-strikes should continue—on the day following the milestone agreement reached in Geneva. I told the press that we felt NATO air-strikes were necessary not as an indication of war but rather "as an instrument of peace".

In the worst massacre of the Bosnian war, Radko Mladić[186] entered Srebrenica in 1995 and systematically slaughtered more than 8,000 Muslim men and boys, while UN troops stood by. It was tragic that at the worst time of the war the UN had the worst Secretary-General in history. On New Year's Day in 1993, for example, Boutros Boutros Ghali was roundly criticised for his remarks in Sarajevo; while surrounded by the almost total destruction of the city, he said he could think of ten other places on earth that were worse than Sarajevo.[187]

Enforcing the UN arms embargo to prevent the supply of arms to Bosnia-Herzegovina was to me truly hypocritical. I cannot help but suspect that the stance of some European countries, while faultlessly principled, was meant to produce a weakened state. And the fact that Bosnia-Herzegovina was a Muslim country was perhaps to them a consideration.

The help that was offered by Malaysia and others in the contact group was critical to enable the Bosnian forces to finally stand their ground against Serb forces. And that gave them at least the minimal ability to meaningfully negotiate a peaceful settlement. Coupled with the change of attitude of one or two members of the international community, and the more even-handed role by the US towards the later phase of the conflict as an arbiter to the peace process, Bosnia-Herzegovina finally secured the peace accord on 21 November, 1995.

The Dayton Peace Agreement brought an end to the slaughter of the Bosnians by the Serbs. Richard Holbrook, the American diplomat who brokered the agreement admitted that there were a number of serious flaws in the Agreement. The most serious was that it "left two opposing armies in one country, one for the Serbs and one for the Croat-Muslim Federation"; and the second was "to allow the Serb portion of Bosnia to retain the name Republika Srbska". Holbrook later also admitted that he could have pushed harder.[188] The question that came to my mind when the agreement was signed was whether the seeds of a future war had now been sown into the agreement. Years later I asked Prime Minister Dr. Haris Silajdzic why Bosnia had succumbed to this pressure, and he said that they could not possibly continue the war. "The country was devastated and too many lives had been sacrificed and many more would have been killed if the war had continued." It could also be that they were under tremendous pressure by the Americans to accept the Agreement as it was.

The tragic path of massacre and genocide was not even initiated by the Bosnians. As Yugoslavia began to disintegrate, both Slovenia[189] and Croatia[190] voted overwhelmingly to become sovereign and independent states. The Yugoslav National Army went to war with both of them. From that point on it was Hobson's choice for Bosnia-Herzegovina, it either had to seek independence or else it would be left in a rump Yugoslavia under Serbia's domination.[191]

In the words of President Alija Izetbegovic: "After Slovenia and Croatia left Yugoslavia, Bosnia and we, the Bosnian people together with our country, found ourselves at a crossroads: one left in an incomplete Yugoslavia, which meant a state federation with Serbia and Montenegro, ruled by the Milosevic/Karadzic; the other led to independence. There was no third option. War and dying could not be avoided because we were weaker and the aggressor would not negotiate. We could choose to be slaves..."[192]

Bosnia-Herzegovina chose not to be slaves. For this they paid a heavy price.

# Endnotes

160   Extract from Dr. Mahathir Mohamad's Keynote Address at the international conference organised by Just World Trust (JUST) in December 1994 in Kuala Lumpur with the theme 'Rethink Human Rights'. Proceedings of the conference were published in a publication entitled *Human Wrongs: Reflections on Western Global Dominance and its Impact upon Human Rights*, Penang, JUST, 1996.

161   America adopted a lackadaisical attitude to the Balkan conflict under the Bush (Sr.) administration. See Peter Ronayne, *Never Again? The United States and the Prevention and Punishment of Genocide since the Holocaust*, Boston, Rowman & Littlefield, 2001, p. 115. Even Clinton himself, although ultimately the arbiter of the Dayton Peace Agreement, had said as late as February 1994 that "Until those folks get tired of killing each other over there, bad things will continue to happen." (See ABC special, 'While America Watched — the Bosnia Tragedy', 30 March, 1994.) The Bosnia conflict was viewed as a sectarian or ethnic affair outside of big power interests rather than as a tragedy involving the perpetration of crimes against humanity.

162   See my article entitled 'The Betrayal of Bosnia-Herzegovina by the Champions of Human Rights' in *Human Wrongs: Reflections on Western Global Dominance and its Impact upon Human Rights*, Penang, JUST, 1996. p. 133.

163   Noel Malcom's seminal work on the conflict articulately debunks the myths of ethnic and religious strife as causing the Bosnian conflict, holding the West and its misguided strategies in the war accountable for Bosnia's destruction. See his book *Bosnia: A Short History*, London, MacMillan, 1994.

164   The United Nations Protection Force (UNPROFOR) was the first United Nations peacekeeping force in Croatia and in Bosnia-Herzegovina during the Yugoslav wars. It was created by UN Security Council resolution 743 on 21 February, 1992.

165   Bosnia-Herzegovina declared its sovereignty in October 1991 followed by a referendum for independence from Yugoslavia in February and March 1992. Bosnia-Herzegovina declared independence shortly afterwards, on 1 May. Bosnian independence was recognised by the United States and the European Union on 6 April and on 22 May, 1992 it became a member of the UN. On 6 April, 1992, open warfare began and Bosnian Serbs began their siege of Sarajevo which ended only with the Agreement signed in Dayton in December 1995.

166   Madeleine Albright, Secretary of State under US President Clinton, argues in her book *The Mighty and the Almighty*, that Americans have a duty to bring perpetrators of injustice to account. Whether it was actually carried out is, of course, highly debatable.

167   Kamil Jaafar, *op. cit.*, p. 134.

168   Sir Malcolm Rifkind, as Britain's Defence Secretary until July 1995 and thereafter as Foreign Secretary, was a principal architect of Britain's disastrous policy towards Bosnia. Britain obstructed all meaningful intervention to halt Serbian aggression and genocide in Bosnia, notably by staunchly upholding the UN arms embargo that seriously restricted Bosnia's ability to defend itself. He now expresses regret over what he says was "the most serious mistake made by the UN". Indeed, we can agree in this instance with Holbrooke when he spoke of "the greatest collective failure" with regard to how the West handled the former Yugoslavia. See Richard Holbrooke, *To End A War*, New York, The Modern Library, 1999, p. 21.

169   See Michael A. Sells, *The Bridge Betrayed — Religion and Genocide in Bosnia*, London, London University Press, 1996.

170   See preceding footnote on Sir Malcolm Rifkind.

171   Michael A. Sells, *op. cit.*

172   He had by then retired, his last political portfolio being Minister of Foreign Affairs.

173   The Maghreb refers to countries in the region of Northwest Africa, west of Egypt, that includes Morocco, Algeria, Tunisia, and Libya, Mauritania, and the disputed territory of Western Sahara.

174   From 1990 to 1993 he served as the Foreign Minister of Bosnia-Hezergovina and as the Prime Minister from 1993 to 1996.

175   President of Bosnia-Herzegovina 1990 to 1996; 1996 to 2000 member of the Bosnian-Herzegovinian Presidency.

176   Brunei's financial contribution was significant.

177   Colonel Hashim was, on his return home, promoted to General and appointed Chief of Army.

178   Malaysian Battalion.

179   Hassan Cengih was later appointed Deputy Minister of Defence, but was removed after the Dayton Agreement, at the insistence of the United States who had accused him of injecting Mujahiddeen fighters into the Bosnian war. He remains a good friend to this day.

180   The Contact group consisted of eight countries, Egypt, Iran, Malaysia, Morocco, Pakistan, Saudi Arabia, Senegal and Turkey.

181   See the article in *The New York Times* by Michael Richardson entitled 'Malaysia Says It Will Send Arms to Bosnians', published on Monday, July 24, 1995.

182   Indonesia, Bangladesh and Jordan were not part of the eight-nation contact group but attended in Kuala Lumpur as troop contributing countries. Qatar was also present as an observer. Brunei was a low-profile but extremely helpful partner to us in aiding the Bosnian cause.

183   The AMG had two components: the political committee of which I chaired and the military committee chaired by the Chief of the Malaysian Defence Forces, General Ismail Hj. Omar. I also chaired the Committee of the Whole.

184   Reuters reported that the Geneva declaration by the OIC contact group stated that Islamic states that already had troops with the UN in Bosnia would leave them there, perhaps beefed up, if the UN Protection Force pulled out.

185   In early January 1993, the UN Special Envoy Cyrus Vance and EC representative Lord Owen began negotiating a peace proposal with Bosnia's warring factions. The proposal, which became known as the Vance-Owen Peace Plan, involved the division of Bosnia into ten semi-autonomous regions which virtually divided the country on ethnic lines. This received the backing of the UN. The plan was rejected by all parties to the conflict. On 18 June, Lord Owen declared that the plan was 'dead'.

186   Ratko Mladić (born 12 March, 1942) is a Bosnian Serb who came to prominence in the Yugoslav Wars, initially as a high-ranking officer of the Yugoslav People's Army and subsequently as the Chief of Staff of the Army of the Republika Srpska (the Bosnian Serb Army) in the Bosnian War of 1992–1995. In 1995, he was indicted by the International Criminal Tribunal for the former Yugoslavia (ICTY) for genocide, war crimes and crimes against humanity. As the top military general with command responsibility, Mladić was accused by the ICTY of being responsible for the 1992–1995 siege of Sarajevo and the Srebrenica massacre—the largest mass murder in Europe since World War II.

187   Richard Holbrook, *op. cit.*, p. 69.

188   Ibid.

189   Wikipedia: On 23 December, 1990, more than 88 percent of the electorate voted for a sovereign and independent Slovenia. On 25 June, Slovenia became independent through the passage of appropriate legal documents. On 27 June in the early morning, the Yugoslav People's Army dispatched its forces to prevent further measures for the establishment of a new country, which led to the Ten-Day War. On 7 July, the Brijuni Agreement was signed that sealed Slovenia's independence. The European Union recognised Slovenia as an independent state on 15 January 1992, and the United Nations accepted it as a member on 22 May, 1992.

190   In June 1991, Croatia declared independence from the Yugoslav which came into effect on 8 October of the same year. On 15 January, 1992, Croatia gained diplomatic recognition from the European Union and subsequently the United Nations. The war effectively ended in 1995.

191   From Noel Malcolm's book *A Short History of Bosnia-Herzegovina*, quoted in Alija Izetbegovic, *Inescapable Questions: Autobiographical Notes*, Islamic Foundation, Limited, 2003, p. 9.

192   Extract from a speech by Alija Izetbegovic on 3 March, 2000 at an SDA Party (the Muslim Party for Democratic Action) pre-election meeting in Sarajevo. See ibid., p. 440.

# CHAPTER 14

# The Ghost of Gazimestan[193]

The war in Bosnia-Herzegovina had hardly ended when Ismet Hamiti, a Kosovar and a senior official of the International Telecommunication Union, got in touch with us through my Special Assistant, appealing for our assistance. He had heard of our involvement in Bosnia-Herzergovina and now wanted us to help out in Kosovo. This was early 1995. He had been keeping up with developments in Kosovo and was concerned with what was happening to the Kosovars at the hands of the local Serbs and the Serbian National Army (JNA). They desperately needed assistance and he hoped we would respond to their cry for help. Milosevic had unleashed his security forces to rid Kosovo of ethnic Albanians. One more act of genocide. We could not refuse. And so we found ourselves in another war and in another country but looking into the faces of the same perpetrators of genocide.

Historically a province within Serbia, Kosovo had been autonomous, having its own schools and its own language. However, in 1989 the Yugoslav President Slobodan Milosevic revoked this autonomy, setting in motion the chain of events which led to open conflict between Serbia and Kosovo nationalists. Milosevic's first objective was to purge Albanian Kosovars, who comprised the majority of the population,[194] from almost all public positions, particularly from the police force. With its former autonomy revoked the first non-communist party in Kosovo came into being. The Democratic League of Kosovo (LDK) elected Ibrahim Rugova its president on 23 December, 1989. The LDK directly challenged the ruling communist regime using a policy of non-violence, boycotting Serbian and Federal elections and creating a parallel administration of hospitals, schools and taxation for the ethnic Albanian population. In 1992 and in 1998 Rugova was elected President of the self-styled 'Republic of Kosovo', which was not recognised by Belgrade.

However, Rugova's strategy of peaceful resistance was not supported by many and the country was split into those who believed in non-violence and those who felt that force was the only option to achieve independence. Rugova came under strong criticism, particularly when Kosovo was excluded from the Dayton Peace Agreement ending the conflict in Bosnia-Herzegovina. Many Kosovars feared that this could be a sign that Kosovo had little chance of western support for its independence aspirations. In 1997 the Kosovo Liberation Army (KLA) was established and began to carry out its own campaign of harassment and attacks on the JNA (Yugoslav National Army) and the local Serb population. Within a year of its establishment the KLA had grown into a full-scale army capable of challenging, or at least resisting, the JNA.

It was in such a scenario of internal tensions and external threat that we went into Kosovo. Our visit was arranged by Ismet Hamiti. How to get there and whom to meet was all organised by him. I went with an open mind wanting to get acquainted with the leaders of all parties and to understand their aspirations and hopes and what they needed to attain their goals. It was in January 1999, at the height of winter, when we flew into Skopje, the capital of Macedonia, and took a taxi to the Macedonian/Kosovo border. There, waiting on the Kosovo side, was an ice-cream van ready to drive us to Pristina, the capital. It was a three-hour journey and from the small misty windows of the van we could see the destruction of farmlands, houses and buildings, and occasionally entire villages. This was genocide all over again unleashed by Milosevic.

We did not feel safe, and anything could happen to us along the way as there was no security escort. But we arrived in Pristina in one piece and stayed in a hotel without any heating. It was freezing. We put on all the clothes we had all the time, sleeping in them and sitting down for meals in them. I remember thinking to myself, as I arrived in Pristina, that just outside it lay the plain of Gazimestan. This was where Milosovic made his infamous declaration in 1989 to celebrate the 600th anniversary of the Battle of Kosovo, saying, ominously, that "after six centuries we are again engaged in battles and quarrels. They are not armed battles, but this cannot be excluded yet."[195] He was referring to the battle in 1389 when the Serb army, led by Prince Lazar, was defeated by the Ottoman forces. Prince Lazar died in that battle. It was at the height of political tension in Yugoslavia that Slobodan Milosevic stood on the plain of Gazimestan and unleashed the full force of Christo-Slavic ideology, thereby resurrecting 'the curse of Kosovo' and with it the ghost of Gazimestan.[196] He was determined to settle the score and once and for all solve the problem of Kosovo.

I met first with Ibrahim Rugova and Hashim Thaci, who later became Prime Minister, and then with members of the inner circle of the KLA. I also met Ramush Haradinaj, who also rose to become Prime Minister and was considered a national hero by the Kosovars for his role during the war. With these leaders I discussed both the political and military situation and the form of assistance they required, determining what their immediate and long-term priorities were. My discussions were exploratory in nature.

It was during this my first visit that I began to understand the internal tensions among the leaders and how these tensions and conflicts were being played out. My meeting with the military leaders was more productive and concrete and I learned of the assistance they badly needed. I told them that I would discuss their requirements with my government as soon as I returned home.

Ibrahim Rugova requested me to carry his gift to Dr. Mahathir, which was a stone supposedly from the mines in Mitrovica in the north of the country and was part of his own collection. It was his practice to do this in order to show his gratitude. It was also said that the size of the stone would show the level of his appreciation. This stone was slightly bigger than a tennis ball.

As with our journey into the country we travelled out of it to Macedonia without any security escort, finding this time a regular van to rent. It took us safely to the border where we had to load our luggage into a rickety wheelbarrow belonging to a young boy working hard to earn some precious money. With his help we worked our way through deep snow to the border checkpoint. A long queue of desperate people was already formed, all trying to reach the safety of Macedonia. The queue posed a problem for us because we had a flight to catch in Skopje. We had very little option but to bribe our way through. This involved guards and the immigration authorities on both sides of the border. We made our way to the airport in time and out of Macedonia to catch our flight home.

Back at home Zulkephli Mohd. Noor, my Special Assistant, was contacted by Izmet Hamiti again. This time Hamiti wanted to meet me personally. We met in Bangkok and Izmet Hamiti presented a wish list of the KLA. Having decided that what was required was within our means to help, I told him that I would need the approval of the Prime Minister. This was not difficult for me to obtain as the Prime Minister was as keen and committed on Kosovo as he had been on Bosnia. I called Izmet Hamiti later to tell him the good news, and also to inform him that we were planning to make a second trip to Pristina. Hamiti promised to assist in the arrangements of my second visit and this time he was in Pristina to receive us.

Assistance to Kosovo took the form of non-lethal communication equipment, including field radios to help facilitate communications among military commanders allowing them to coordinate their operations and also to reach the command control at Pristina. Again with the approval of the Prime Minister we brought in about 30 Kosovars to Kuala Lumpur for training in various fields.

My second visit was planned for 4 to 6 October, 1999. It was preceded by my meeting on 2 September, 1999 in Frankfurt with Dr. Buja Bukoshi, a former elected Prime Minister. He expressed happiness about our planned visit and briefed me on the politics within the leadership. He encouraged me to speak forcefully with the leaders about staying united.

Following this meeting with Dr. Bukoshi I flew from Rome to Pristina, courtesy of the UN. There in Pristina I met again, among the leaders, Dr. Ibrahim Rugova and Hashim Thaci, the self-styled Prime Minister of the provisional government. His readiness to settle for an autonomous Kosovo within Yugoslavia was strongly opposed by the other leaders. He established himself as Prime Minister of the provisional government, which was not recognised by the other leaders. I also met General Agim Ceku, who became the principal commander of a more structured KLA. I met up again with Dr. Bukoshi. I took the opportunity of being there to have a discussion with the representative of Dr. Bernhard Koucher, the civilian administrator of the United Nations Mission in Kosovo (UNMIK).

My visit came about after the failure of the Rambouillet Accords, a proposed peace agreement between Yugoslavia and Kosovo Albanians brokered by NATO. The Accord would in effect lead to the establishment of an independent Kosovo. To many western observers the Accord was heavily weighted against Yugoslavia. Yugoslavia and the Serb faction rejected the Accord and refused to sign the draft agreement as they found the terms unacceptable. Following the failure of Rambouilliet and the continued fighting between the JNA and the KLA, NATO followed through its earlier threat by bombing Serbia between 24 March and 10 June, 1999. Though I had retired by then as Secretary-General of the Foreign Ministry I was appointed Special Envoy of the Prime Minister and still took a keen interest in developments in the Balkans. The NATO bombing brought about the withdrawal of the Yugoslav army from Kosovo and resulted in Milosevic agreeing to a foreign military presence there.[197]

What became clear to me in my discussion with the leaders was that now that the war had ended the immediate task was to begin the reconstruction of the country and to move steadily towards peace and stability. However, the hatred towards the Serbs was deep. Atrocities committed by the Serb paramilitary supported by the JNA and Serb civilians were deliberate and calculated and were perceived by the Kosovars as an attempt at systematic ethnic cleansing. Many of them informed me that it was not possible at this early stage to put a stop to acts of revenge as almost all families had been victims of Serb atrocities.

The internal tensions also became clearer to me when both Dr. Rugova and Dr. Bukoshi expressed strong negative views of Hashim Thaci saying that Hashim Thaci's 'Kalashnikov politics' would work against the aspirations of Kosovo. Hashim Thaci was moving towards eliminating those who opposed him. He was regarded a thug by many

I talked to. But without exception all the factions agreed on one goal—independence. Independence, however, failed to achieve a united Kosovo based on ethnic integration. The Government continues to this day to wrestle with the issue caused by the Serb population in the north not recognising nor accepting the independence of Kosovo and not wanting to be part of Kosovo. In my meeting with UNMIK representatives they too admitted this reality. UNMIK[198] admittedly failed in its reconciliation and in their reconstruction effort. They expressed resignation to these failures on their part.

Our assistance to Kosovo was brought to a close as soon as the war ended. Malaysia became the first Asian country to open a liaison office in Kosovo in 2000, marking the beginning of formal relations. In 2008, Kosovo declared its independence and Malaysia extended diplomatic recognition on 30 October of the same year. With independence, the ghost of Gazimestan was finally exorcised from Kosovo.

## Endnotes

[193]   Gazimestan is the name of a monument commemorating the historical Battle of Kosovo, in 1389, between the army led by Serbian Prince Lazar Hrebeljanocic, and the invading army of the Ottoman Army, situated about six to seven kilometres north-northeast of the actual battlefield, known as Kosovo Field, about five kilometers northwest of modern-day Pristina. The monument was built in 1953 by the Federal Republic of Yugoslavia. It is in the shape of a medieval tower. The name originates from the Ottoman Turkish word '*gazi*', meaning 'hero', which in turn is a loanword from Arabic. Thus, in a portmanteau with the Serbian word '*mesto*', meaning 'place', Gazimestan's meaning becomes 'Place of Heroes'. The Battle of Kosovo is particularly important to Serbian history, tradition and national identity, even though they lost it.

[194]   Wikileaks: More than 80 percent of the population in Kosovo are of Albanian descent and are Muslims. The proportion of Albanians was below 70 percent until 1961, but increased to 81.6 percent in 1991.

[195]   See Alija Izetbegovic, *op. cit.*

[196]   See also Michael A. Sells, *op. cit.*

[197]   See Wikipedia on Kosovo War.

[198]   United Nations Mission in Kosovo.

# CHAPTER 15

# Somalia: Descent Into Anarchy[199]

*"The world can provide short-term humanitarian aid to Somalia, but it cannot rebuild a nation that appears set on a path of self-destruction."*[200]

Dealing with the problem of Somalia was another extraordinary assignment. From 1993 to 1994, MALBAT (Malaysian Battalion) served in Somalia under the United Nations Operation. In January 1994, Lt. Gen. Aboo Samah was appointed Commander of UNOSOM[201] II forces. Having seen the destruction and sufferings of the country and the people, he explored the possibility of Malaysia providing a helping hand. In mid-1995, about four months after the termination of UNOSOM II, I discussed with General Maulub, the Chief of Military Intelligence, the possibility of Malaysia playing a role in Somalia. General Maulub had earlier discussed this possibility with General Aboo Samah. Having decided that we should help I presented our idea to the Prime Minister who readily gave his approval, especially in the light of the fact that Mohamed Farrah Aidid, leader of the Somali National Alliance, and Ali Mahdi Mohamed, leader of United Somali Congress, had written to him requesting Malaysia's involvement in their country's conflict.

Having received his instruction I set our plan in motion. This became known as 'Operation Morning Glory'. It was an effort outside the IGAD[202] process or any other efforts by concerned African states.

Again I was travelling to a country torn by war which had descended into almost total anarchy. The warring between the two leaders had brought about near total chaos and untold misery to the people on both sides of the divide. Here I was trying to negotiate with two rebel factions within a country that had, literally, no institution of any sort or government authority in place. The leaders I had to deal with were warlords and a law unto themselves. They both exercised authority through force of arms and organised gangs in their respective areas.

In 1970, Siad Barre had proclaimed a socialist state that paved the way for closer relations with the Soviet Union. He ruled over what is now Somalia, a country that was a result of a merger of a former British colony and an Italian colony. Siad Barre had imprisoned Farrah Aidid, his one-time army general, his Ambassador to India, and finally his intelligence chief, on suspicion of plotting a coup against him. It was Farrah Aidid's clan that in the end overthrew Siad Barre's government.

This triggered a fierce and brutal struggle for leadership and control of the country by various factions and between Mohamed Farrah Aidid and Ali Mahdi Mohamed. It marked the beginning of a civil war that attempts by other governments in the region failed to stop. Clan-based warlords took control, the two most powerful among them being the clan belonging to Farrah Aidid on the one hand, and Ali Mahdi on the other. Ironically they were of the same clan but of different sub-clans. There were also other minor warlords who kept shifting their allegiance from one to the other.

It was against this chaotic backdrop that, on 24 March, 1995, I landed in Mogadishu. We chartered a five-seater single engine aircraft, commonly referred to as a bush aircraft, to fly from Nairobi to Mogadishu. This kind of aircraft does not have any toilet facility and so the plastic bags and empty bottles came in handy during the three-hour flight. One of our strict conditions was that both of the two opposing clans must be on hand to receive our team. This was to ensure our neutrality—and our safety. We landed on a makeshift airstrip near the beach not far from Mogadishu and drove over bumpy sand dunes towards the city. We were escorted by heavily armed militia from the two warring factions, two in front and two in the rear in their technicals—pick-up trucks mounted with heavy machine guns and full of heavily armed militia equipped with AK47 assault rifles and rocket propelled grenades (RPGs). We arrived in the city without incident.

Mogadishu was divided into two zones by the 'Green Line', each zone dominated by its respective rival faction. Ali Mahdi had lodged himself in the north and Farrah Aidid had taken control of the south. The city had been devastated by years of war. Buildings and houses were in total ruins. People were deprived of almost every little belonging they once had. They lived under a few branches stuck into the ground covered with plastic sheets. Some cowered in parts of bombed-out buildings that were still standing.

It was one of the worst scenes I have ever encountered in my life. This horror of a city reflected the intensity and brutality of war played out in the streets. Years of fighting between rival clans, coupled with famine and lack of medical facilities, had led to close to one million deaths, according to a BBC report. The country was descending into the worst famine it had ever experienced with two million people at risk of dying of starvation. The spectre of death for so many brought about 'Operation Restore Hope',[203] a joint UN/US humanitarian effort. This was long before we got involved.

The next day we were escorted to meet Farrah Aidid, crossing the Green Line, the shifting boundary between the two factions, into territories under his control. Our escort was made up of two technicals, one in front and one in the rear, with two other pick-ups carrying fully armed militia. The scene along the way was ghostly and the people we saw were all carrying AK47 assault rifles and some carried RPGs (rocket propelled grenade). There was no way for us to identify which faction they belonged to.

Farrah Aidid received me and my team warmly with boys and girls lining the path leading to his residence which was also his headquarters. He was pleasant enough and was prepared to listen to the proposal we carried with us. The discussion was held after a luncheon and was attended by Aidid's senior aides as well a representative from Ali Mahdi's faction. I explained to him that I had come to Mogadishu to convey the decision of the Prime Minister of Malaysia to offer assistance to Somalia. I said that the Prime Minister was committed to offer what help we could to ease the humanitarian situation and to bring about national reconciliation. Aidid replied that the process of national reconciliation was progressing smoothly. He sounded optimistic. But I stressed our offer was contingent on both parties' agreement. I told him that I would bring this up with Ali Mahdi the next day.

He presented me with two books, *Muhammad, His Life, Based on Early Sources* by Martin Lings and *The Preferred Future Development in Somalia*, edited by him and Satya Pal Ruhela. It seemed to me that the only positive thing about the meeting was an excellent lunch of grilled lamb. Somalia is one of the suppliers of live goats to Saudi Arabia for the *korban* (offering) during the *haj* period.

Before I took leave he pulled me aside and apologised for the attack on our troops in Mogadishu,[204] in which one Malaysian soldier died.

He said that when the Malaysian APC (Armoured Personnel Carrier) was travelling at speed it was difficult for his militia to differentiate the Malaysian flag from the American flag. I was not sure if I could believe him. But then it is not difficult to mistake a Malaysian flag for an American one. It had happened before.

Subsequently, I also met Ali Mahdi and went over the same ground as I did with Farrah Aidid, calling him to put aside their enmity and committing to work towards a semblance of peace in Somalia. Farrah Aidid's representative was also present.

Ali Mahdi, unlike Farrah Aidid, seemed initially unsure of our stand with regard to the two parties. Our only interest, I told him, was to find a way to stabilise the country so that we could move in with humanitarian assistance. I told both the leaders that we were sincere in our commitment and that we would endeavour to get other countries to join this effort. Specifically, I told them that as a start we might look into getting the Mogadishu airport and seaport functioning again to facilitate assistance getting into the country. Ali Mahdi stressed the point that political reconciliation was key to solving the problem of Somalia and acknowledged that without external help reconciliation would be difficult to achieve. When the discussion was moved to another room, this time without the presence of Farrah Aidid's representative, he confided in me that the problem of Somalia was the problem of one man, Farrah Aidid. On the opening of the airport and the seaport he would only support it if the revenue derived from them was split on a 50-50 basis.

We left Mogadishu for Nairobi after four days. The aircraft had returned to pick us up. By the time we arrived in Nairobi we were simply exhausted. In Nairobi both before we went to Mogadishu and after our return, I had discussions with the UNDP representative Erling Dessau. Dessau clarified that although the UNOSOM mandate had ended on

31 March, 1995, UNDP would stay close to the situation in Somalia as it still had projects in several parts of the country. It was for security reasons that they left but as soon as some normalcy returned they would be ready to go back.

We realised that Malaysia's role in facilitating this was important for organisations such as the UNDP. I told Dessau that the right approach must be adopted and that the keyword was patience. Anger over UNOSOM and anything UN was still widespread, and I reminded him that UNDP, or any other UN agency, should not do anything to undermine the delicate process undertaken by Malaysia.

The report I scrambled together upon my return to Kuala Lumpur stated that the key to any progress lay with Farrah Aidid who was conducting himself from a position of strength while Ali Mahdi was desperate to have external assistance to bolster his position. It also stated, that "the sensitivity of the two leaders would be factors that must be taken into consideration if this delicate exercise is to lead anywhere". There was a wide gap between the leaders, politically and in leadership style.

Over the next few months we kept in touch with our contact person in Mogadishu, Abdurraman Ali Osman. On receiving some hopeful news from him we went back for a second visit. By this time, in March 1996, about a year after our first visit, Farrah Aidid had set up his headquarters in Baidoa situated in the south about 260 miles from Mogadishu. We flew directly from Nairobi to Baidoa to meet him, and the next day to Mogadishu to meet with Ali Mahdi. The two leaders agreed in principle to come to Kuala Lumpur. I was encouraged by this positive response.

It was at this meeting in Baidoa that, as a parting gift, Farrah Aidid presented me with a walking stick. This walking stick, he said, had kept him from harm, and he told me how he had eluded the US rangers who were hunting for him and they came nowhere near to capturing him.[205]

Farrah Aidid had led an attack on the UN Peace Keeping force that resulted in the death of 24 Pakistani soldiers. In response the UN sanctioned a manhunt for Farrah Aidid. In what became known as the Battle of Mogadishu the US sent in their Army Rangers and Delta Force to capture him. In this operation 18 American soldiers were killed. In the same battle one Blackhawk helicopter was brought down, an incident that was to inspire the Hollywood movie called *Blackhawk Down*. This was the walking stick, he stressed, which had protected him and he hoped it would also protect me. One month later Farrah Aidid was shot and died a week later from his wounds.[206] The walking stick is still protecting me.

Farrah Aidid's death did not change the situation on the ground. Our contact person Abdurraman Ali Osman met with the factions in Nairobi in March, and reported that things were calm and looked promising. Hussein Aidid had replaced his father and made it clear that the Sodere Agreement,[207] brokered by the Ethiopian government and IGAD, was a failure and he rejected it. He alleged that the Sodere Agreement had sidelined him and his forces. Ali Mahdi and the respected elder Ali Ugas from the north of Mogadishu, who was the deputy president of the National Salvation Council (NSC) and the Somali National Alliance (SNA) and formerly mayor of the city, also rejected the Sodere Agreement. Ali Ugas and Ali Mahdi wanted Hussein Aidid to be given a role in the peace negotiations otherwise there would be no peace.

On the way to Mogadishu I met with Osman Ali Ato[208] in Nairobi on 21 March who informed me that Ali Mahdi could not return to Nairobi to meet with me. But I spoke with Ali Mahdi later over the phone. Osman Ali Ato informed me that he was not happy with my planned visit to Mogadishu. He felt that the visit, taking place at this time, would undermine the work of the National Salvation Council, which had been given the role to decide the future of Somalia. Osman Ali Ato told me frankly that my planned discussions with Ali Mahdi and Hussein Aidid in Somalia, done outside the NSC, could be seen as undermining the Council. For this reason he wanted me to postpone my visit to Mogadishu and instead begin discussions with the NSC. I had to refuse his suggestion insisting that arrangements had already been made and I could not cancel the visit. I gave my assurance to Osman Ali Ato that my visit to Mogadishu was intended to get the latest report on the situation there, telling him that I hoped that he would understand and not harbour negative feelings about our efforts.

That same day, 21 March, I met Ali Ugas at the rest house where we were staying in northern Mogadishu. I asked him what exactly he wanted from our involvement, telling him at the same time that if the fighting was to continue we would have to abandon our mission. Ali Ugas pleaded that Malaysia hang on and not let the Somalis down, telling me that my visit was a "*rahmah* (blessing) from Allah to give guidance to the people of Somalia in order that they understand the true meaning of unity and harmony".

To illustrate how convinced he was of this, and also his commitment to the opening of the airport and seaport, he invited the militia head, Chief Musasuede, who was in control of the airport, to attend the talks with me. This was unusual because Chief Musasuede was notoriously reclusive, never wanting to meet or speak with any foreign person. I was apparently the first. At the meeting Chief Musasuede assured me that the airport issue would be resolved soon. Ali Ugas expressed his confidence that peace would soon return to Somalia.

The following day, 22 March, we went to meet with Hussein Aidid at the office of 'the president'. I offered him my deep condolence on the death of his father Farrah Aidid. (Hussein had previously been Farrah

Aidid's security advisor.) He referred to the Sodere Agreement and complained that it did not reflect the Somali people's wishes and that he himself had not been informed in advance of its conditions, accusing Ethiopia of harbouring an agenda of its own.

I told Hussein Aidid that we hoped that the leadership issue could be resolved by the Somalis themselves. I also took this opportunity to tell him that the Prime Minister of Malaysia had instructed me to invite both him and Ali Mahdi to Kuala Lumpur, and to announce there, if both agreed, the opening of the airport and seaport. He readily agreed to the visit, giving me the assurance that both ports could be opened within three months after June 1997. I must admit that I left both meetings feeling that we were getting somewhere.

Hussein Aidid, as a person, appeared easier to deal with than his father and appeared more positive towards the peace process. He and Ali Ugas, in fact, shared similar views on how to arrive at peace. I got the impression that the peace process of the NSC would be achieved in the following three months.

I did succeed in getting both Hussein Aidid and Ali Mahdi to come to Kuala Lumpur. By then I believed that they were quite familiar with me and trusted our efforts to be honest and genuine. Looking back it was remarkable that they actually did come, arriving in Kuala Lumpur on 4 June, 1997 for a three-day visit. We had deliberately put them up in the same hotel in symbolic reference to their being united. I confirmed our decision to manage both the airport and seaport of Mogadishu on a temporary basis. I also told them that a contingent, made up of air force and army personnel, was in fact ready to be despatched to Somalia for this purpose.

On the political front Malaysia offered to assist in the reconciliation process by helping them stabilise an interim national assembly consisting of all factions. Both leaders reaffirmed their commitment to bring peace and stability back to Somalia. Just a week earlier both leaders had solemnly put their signatures on the Joint Agreement in Cairo laying out the principles of unity. On 6 June in Kuala Lumpur they piously initialled the broad framework of an agreement that we hammered out together.

Up to this point we had all been hesitantly optimistic that something could be done to help Somalia. However, it soon turned out that my Kenyan counterpart had been right when he told me that the factions would agree to any proposals put forward by those willing to help but when reaching home they would renege on their agreement. How true also in this instance! They failed to put aside their differences and went back to war. The Cairo Joint Agreement which called for the establishment of national reconciliation and the setting up of a transitional government was opposed by both Hussein Aidid and Ali Mahdi although they had previously signed it together.

That brought to a close Operation Morning Glory.

## Endnotes

199   Wikipedia: In 1969, Mohamad Siad Barre seized power and established the Somali Democratic Republic. In 1991, Barre's government collapsed as the Somali Civil War broke out. Since 1991, no central government has controlled the entirety of the country, despite several attempts to establish a unified central government. Without a central government, Somalia reverted to local forms of conflict resolution, civil, Islamic or customary law. The internationally recognised Transitional Federal Government controls only parts of the capital and some territory in the centre of the nation.

200   Peter Biles, BBC World Affairs correspondent in Africa.

201   United Nations Operation in Somalia I (UNOSOM) was a UN-sponsored effort to provide, facilitate, and secure humanitarian relief in Somalia, as well as to monitor the first UN-brokered ceasefire of the Somali Civil War conflict in the early 1990s.

202   The Intergovernmental Authority on Development (IGAD) is an eight-country regional development organisation in East Africa. Its headquarters are located in Djibouti.

203   Operation Restore Hope was a US initiative, charged with carrying out UN Security Council Resolution 794: to create a protected environment for conducting humanitarian operations in the southern half of Somalia.

204   He was referring to the Battle of Mogadishu in October 1993 in which one Malaysian soldier and one Pakistani died; seven Malaysians and two Pakistanis were wounded. They were part of UNOSOM troops in Somalia despatched to free US troops trapped by Somali militia fighters loyal to the self-proclaimed president Mohamed Farrah Aidid. It was the bloodiest battle involving US troops since the Vietnam War.

205   The Battle of Mogadishu in 1993, referred above, was an operation that was launched with the aim of capturing the leaders of the Habr Gidr clan, headed by warlord Mohamed Farrah Aidid. See above references to this.

206   On 24 July, 1996 Mohamed Farrah Aidid was wounded during a firefight between his militia and forces loyal to former Aidid allies Ali Mahdi Muhammad and Osman Ali Atto. Aidid suffered a fatal heart attack on 1 August, 1996, either during or after surgery to treat his wounds.

207   The Sodere Agreement was not effective because both of its sponsors, Ethiopia and Kenya, were perceived to have their own agendas and not be neutral mediators.

208   Osman Ali Atto is a former main financier of the Aidid faction, a multi-millionaire businessman. But in 1995 he split with Aidid and formed the SNA. Fighting between the forces of Osman Ali Atto and of General Aidid in South Mogadishu lead to 200 dead between April and June 1996 and 150 in July 1996. Aidid was wounded and died of his injuries on 1 August in that same year. His son Hussein Mohamed Farrah succeeded him. Osman Ali Ato then allied with Ali Mahdi Mohammed.

# CHAPTER 16

# Sudan: A Self-Inflicted Malady?

When I was instructed to look into the possibility of Malaysia playing a role in the search for peace in Sudan I was filled with excitement. It stirred my mind to look back into the history of Sudan. Through my days of having to study the history of the British empire, which was a must when we went to British colonial schools, I was fascinated by their political and military exploits. I remembered the Anglo-Egyptian Condominium a century ago, a construct to control and rule Sudan, which in its dying days turned out to be an Anglo-Egyptian pandemonium.

That was the context of the drama of General Gordon who was killed on the stairway of his palace a few yards from the mighty Nile by the forces of Mohamed Ahmad Al-Mahdi. This was poignantly romanticised in the Hollywood movie *Khartoum*. Khartoum is where the White Nile and the Blue Nile meet, and the merger of the two Niles would, to any mind, symbolise the unity of Sudan and its people. In reality, the opposite had always been the case.

The problem of Sudan centred on the questions of ethnicity and religion. Sudan is the largest country on the African continent, the most geographically diverse with mountain ranges that divide the arid and desert north from the swampy rainforest of the south. The Nile also splits the country between east and west. Ethnically it is even more diverse, with Arabs dominant in the Arab Muslim north and the Christian and animists the majority in the south, known as the black south. Internecine wars between the north and the south and east and west, lately in Darfur and Kordofan, have claimed close to two million lives. This includes those who died as a result of famine or from being repeatedly displaced as the war zones moved over them again and again.

The government in Khartoum is led by President Omar al-Bashir. President al-Bashir came to power when, on 30 June, 1989 with the support of Hassan al-Turabi's National Islamic Front (NIF), he replaced the government of Sadiq al-Mahdi's, the great-grandson of Ahmad al-Mahdi. Promoting himself to the rank of general, al-Bashir took over control of the country as President, Prime Minister and Chief of the Armed Forces, all rolled into one.

In a move to consolidate his control and stamp his authority, instigated by Hassan al-Turabi and the NIF, the government introduced public order police in 1993 to enforce *shariah* law, which resulted in the arrests of those breaking the law including both Muslims and non-Muslims in the south.

In the south Dr. John Garang led the Sudan People's Liberation Movement (SPLM) and its military arm, the Sudan People's Liberation Army (SPLA). Supporting the SPLM and the SPLA was a cross-section of African groups, Christian, animist and Muslim. The Darfuries in the west, who are African Muslims, were challenging what they regarded as Arab exploitation and imperialism.

Dr. John Garang was born to a poor family of the Dingka ethnic group. He had his early years of education in Tanzania, and through hard work managed to continue his tertiary education in the US. Although he was offered a chance to continue his studies there he chose to return to Tanzania and join the University of Dar-es-Salam. It was here that he met Yoweri Museveni, the future President of Uganda, who became his strong supporter in his struggle against the government in Khartoum. He waged almost 20 years of civil war.

To this day I am not quite sure how we came to be involved in the problem of Sudan. In an effort to bring an end to the civil war, President Nelson Mandela could have explored with Dr. Mahathir the possibility of Malaysia and South Africa playing a mediating role. The idea could have been brought up during Dr. Mahathir's visit to South Africa in mid-1994. I had a suspicion that President Mandela, knowing that we had excellent relations with Sudan and with President al-Bashir who, incidentally, had had a stint at the Royal Military College in Malaysia, had talked to Dr. Mahathir. Or was it the other way round? President al-Bashir, I believed, had also requested Malaysia to get involved as he saw Malaysia as an honest broker. The decision was made for Malaysia and South Africa to facilitate together the peace process in Sudan. At that stage I was not at all clear what our role should or could be.

With these thoughts in my mind and with instructions from the Prime Minister I went first to South Africa to meet up with the Deputy Foreign Minister Aziz Pahad. President Mandela, on his own, was already trying his hand at mediation even before the question of Malaysia's involvement was on the table. He was putting his enormous prestige to the test. We discussed a very rough programme of action and as a start, I decided to begin exploratory discussions with the Sudanese government.

Following these initial consultative meetings I flew to Khartoum in February 1997 accompanied by the same colleagues who had been working with me on Somalia. In Khartoum I met several senior officials and ministers. I called on President Omar al-Bashir and later had a long discussion with Hassan al-Turabi, the religious ideologue and leader of

NIF, who was credited with insisting that the *shariah* law be maintained throughout the country. I got nowhere with him. Hassan al-Turabi was a man given to presenting nothing else but an endless soliloquy. It was not possible to even get a word in sideways. A one-time ally of al-Bashir he later fell out with him and was imprisoned on al-Bashir's orders from March 2004 to June 2005. Prison was perhaps more suited to monologues. I was more successful, however, in getting my views across in my discussions with Osman al-Taha and President Omar al-Bashir. I also met other important personalities and my meetings with them turned out to be helpful in understanding the depths of their problem and their hopes for the future.

Responding to my visit and expressing appreciation of our efforts the Sudanese government dispatched their Minister of Federal Affairs to look at our system of federal government, which they might consider using as a model. In my meeting with President al-Bashir, and also his Foreign Minister, I tried to impress upon them the need to take into account the sensitivities of other religions and ethnic groups and that perhaps these sensitivities should guide their way forward. I also advised them to confine *shariah* law to the north and took the opportunity to inform them that Malaysia would be prepared to be involved in the economic and social development of Sudan.

Subsequently on one of my several visits to Sudan our government agreed to appoint an Honorary Consul to take care of Malaysia's interests there and to assist in any arrangements that needed to be made, including staying close to the leaders and, more importantly, monitor events as they happened. On 9 August, 1997 Mahmoud Abdelrahim was appointed Malaysia's first Honorary Consul in Sudan. He continued to serve Malaysia even after we opened our mission in Khartoum on 30 September, 1999.

I was in Europe in late August 1997 when I received instructions to proceed to Pretoria to represent Dr. Mahathir, who was not able to be there, as the meeting organised by President Mandela coincided with Malaysia's National Day celebration. The meeting was convened at the initiative of President Mandela and it included President Mugabe of Zimbabwe, President Museveni of Uganda and President Omar al-Bashir of Sudan. Absent from the meeting was President Arap Moi of Kenya. Dr. John Garang, of SPLM/SPLA did not attend. He was in South Africa from 27 to 29 August, 1997 and had already met with President Mandela. Despite President Mandela's best efforts, Dr. John Garang refused to meet with al-Bashir, insisting that he had to first sign the Declaration of Principles (DoP), agreed to at the IGAD meeting in Nairobi in 1994.

From the outset the atmospherics of the meeting were far from conducive and were dominated by a sense of mutual suspicion. When the idea for the meeting was first mooted by Pretoria, Sudan had insisted on Malaysia's participation. The meeting among the leaders also included Hassan al-Turabi. There was, however, no side meeting between President al-Bashir and President Musoveni. By mutual agreement with President Mandela I did not attend the meeting but was later briefed by him on the outcome. Separately I also met with President al-Bashir.

The meeting of the leaders established a broad framework that the leaders hoped would lead to a final solution. Basically the DoP would form the basis of the negotiations and the undertaking by Sudan not to impose *shariah* law throughout the country. They insisted, however, that Arabic must remain the national language. IGAD, it would seem, would be the main mechanism for a face-to-face negotiation between the government in Khartoum and SPLM/SPLA. Although the meeting was fraught with uncertainty, it did, in the end, produce a roadmap towards achieving peace in Sudan. Both President Mandela and President al-Bashir separately encouraged Malaysia to continue its efforts to broker a face-to-face meeting.

Back in Kuala Lumpur we finally established contact with Dr. John Garang's man, in the person of Dr. Chol Ding, a practising physician in London. After meeting him in London, and having discussed our plans, arrangements were made for us to have another talk with Dr. Chol Ding and his SPLM colleagues on 13 September in Nairobi before meeting with Dr. John Garang there. We were, however, subsequently told that Dr. John Garang was not able to return in time to Nairobi from Kampala.

Our being in Nairobi was not altogether wasted as an appointment to call on President Daniel Arap Moi of Kenya was already in place. This meeting was important in putting our efforts and those of South Africa into proper perspective. President Arap Moi was adamant that Kenya and the other IGAD countries saw any 'parallel initiative' as unwelcome and that it would risk scuttling the focus of the IGAD process.

I made it clear to him that it was not our intention to highjack the IGAD mediation process, and it had never been our intention to do so. The strong position that he expressed on behalf of the IGAD countries was emphasised and re-emphasised during my later travels to those countries. It also became clear to us during this meeting that he was very critical of President Mandela and his government in South Africa. He went so far as to say that his working relationship with President Mugabe of Zimbabwe was easier than that with President Mandela and that he felt President Mandela had not done enough to improve the lives of South African blacks. To him South Africa remained largely a 'white South Africa'.

At this point I could not help but remember that President Mandela had told me earlier that he was concerned about the "selfishness" of some African states and the "unwillingness" of their leaders to give up power, and he wondered if it was not time for President Arap Moi to step down. He also, in reference to President Arap Moi, criticised "the Swazi king for perpetuating an undemocratic system". President Arap Moi finally said that he had no difficulty with Malaysia in respect of advancing the search for a settlement in Sudan, and asked that we continue with our exploratory efforts.

I returned to Nairobi again on 25 September when I was assured that Dr. John Garang was ready to meet me. He quickly apologised for the inconvenience caused to me for having to visit Nairobi a second time. In thanking him for receiving me I handed him a letter from Dr. Mahathir with an invitation for him to visit Malaysia. He said it would perhaps be possible for him to do so the following year. In my conversation with him I again went over the same points that had been put forward to President Arap Moi earlier on and stressed that our intention was to contribute to the IGAD process and that we hoped that a peaceful solution could be achieved with justice and honour for all the Sudanese people. He informed me that when the question of Malaysia's involvement was first brought up to him he told President Mandela that he knew very little about Malaysia. But after getting the views of his people who had visited Malaysia he was now comfortable with our involvement and felt that Malaysia could be a 'partner of IGAD' in the peace process, just as some European countries were. But he rejected President al-Bashir's overtures for a parallel initiative for the IGAD process, which had been purposely misrepresented by the Sudanese government.

Regarding the SPLM/SPLA position on the settlement Dr. John Garang explained that his goal was not independence for the south but rather a unified secular state, one with power sharing among the main ethnic groups. He further explained that the profits from national resources of the country should be shared on an equitable basis. At the moment he maintained that the south was deprived of any benefits from the oil revenues although the oil resources were extracted from the south. He sounded bitter and angry especially as the south was in dire need of humanitarian and economic assistance. When referring to the oil exploration he asked me to convey to Dr. Mahathir that the SPLM/SPLA was aware of Malaysia's involvement and that they would not harm our investment or any of our people. I thanked him for this assurance.

Towards the end of my conversation with him I told him that I had conveyed our position to President al-Bashir that we would like to see the integrity of Sudan maintained but that *shariah* law should not be applied throughout a country as diverse as Sudan. On the economic side we shared, of course, Dr. John Garang's view that the country's resources should benefit all Sudanese. We also impressed upon him the need for Sudan to look into the federal system that we had adopted since independence, a system which has worked well for us. Indeed, I told him, the Sudanese Minister of Federal Affairs had visited Malaysia precisely in order to look at our model. Before I took leave I informed him that Malaysia had approved financial assistance to two SPLM/SPLA institutions. He assured me that the money would be well spent.

Following the meetings I had had with President Mandela, President Arap Moi and President al-Bashir I undertook a visit to IGAD member countries that included Uganda, Ethiopia, Eritrea and Djibouti, and made also new visits to Sudan and Kenya from 18 to 28 November, 1997. Basically it was another effort at explaining our position and encouraging them to press on with the peace process in Sudan, and also to settle their own bilateral problems. The leaders of Eritrea, Ethiopia and Uganda all stressed that the IGAD process was the only route to peace in Sudan—in other words, they did not want Malaysian intervention in the ongoing peace process.

I was pleased that Dr. Mahathir made an official visit to Sudan in May 1998. He was able to better understand the terrible political ramifications of the conflict. The country had been ravaged since independence and its economy pulverised. He also saw the enormous economic potential that was at the disposal of Sudan and the lucrative opportunities for cooperation between Malaysia and Sudan.

As Malaysia got itself more deeply involved in the peace process we began to see how complex, sensitive and perplexing the whole exercise was. Sudan had not known peace since independence in 1956. The situation was made worse by Sudan's neighbours who all felt they had a stake in the country. The Egyptians wanted a unified Sudan to protect the Nile; some of the African states had a stake in Sudan's dissolution. The complexities of the situation included a whole range of issues; security, control of economic resources, religion and state, and fear of arabization.

Yes, why, indeed, did we get ourselves involved? Our involvement would inevitably clash with the central position adopted by the IGAD countries. They did not welcome any other initiative particularly from outside the region. The IGAD process was already in place. The answer had to lie in the fact that Sudan had had serious problems with the IGAD countries. It suspected them of pushing their own strategic interests, while pretending to broker peace. President Yoweri Museveni of Uganda, a close friend and supporter of Dr. John Garang, had for many years been responsible for supplying arms to the SPLM/SPLA. Similarly Sudan had also implicated other IGAD countries in supplying arms to the south.

Given such a situation Sudan was compelled to look at other alternatives. It saw South Africa's and Malaysia's involvement as a parallel initiative that could morph into a more balanced negotiating process free of the bias of the other IGAD countries. But the agreement, finally, to direct negotiations between them and the SPLM/SPLA under the chairmanship of Kenya signalled the end of their attempt to wrest mediation away from IGAD. By that time the IGAD process, under the chairmanship of President Arap Moi, had assumed its own momentum, and Malaysia eased itself out.

On 9 January, 2005, long after I had gone into retirement, the Sudanese government and the SPLM signed a Comprehensive Peace Agreement in Nairobi. The Agreement provided for a referendum which was held in January 2011. South Sudan declared its independence in July of the same year. This finally brought to close one of the longest and bloodiest wars in Africa.

# CHAPTER 17

# Working with Prime Ministers: Personal Glimpses

A strange thing happened to me on my way back to Tokyo from Kuala Lumpur when I made a two-day stopover in Hong Kong. I was bemused when I heard the soothsayer say that in the job I was presently doing I would soon be number one. If number one meant the Secretary-General of the Ministry then for a number of reasons I could not believe it. However, soon after, in early 1989, when the Prime Minister visited Tokyo he indicated what was in store for me—I was to return home to take over the reins of the Foreign Ministry. This was confirmed later on when Dato' Abu Hassan, the Foreign Minister, visited Tokyo.

On 1 April, 1989 I received my letter of appointment, and it was not an April Fool's joke. My appointment, however, caused some unhappiness amongst a handful of my colleagues. It was an appointment which was unprecedented thus far in the practice of the Foreign Ministry. I would be replacing the incumbent who had been in the job for only six months. They pleaded with me to decline the appointment. When we joined the Foreign Service every one of us aspired one day to reach the very pinnacle of the service, so at this point I found myself in an ambivalent situation. I could understand only too well how my predecessor must have felt, and I could also understand the arguments behind the pleadings from some of my colleagues. But at the same time, I did not know how to, nor dare, go against the Prime Minister's decision. And I did not wish to. I was proud to have been selected for the position.

In a career of close to 34 years in the Foreign Service I went through the incumbency of four prime ministers, starting with the first, Tunku Abdul Rahman Putra. Tunku was like a father figure. Perhaps I felt so because at the time I was still a young diplomat learning the ropes. I used to meet Tunku in Bangkok and later in Singapore when he visited the two capitals. After three successive postings, the last being Singapore, I returned home and was attached to Tunku for almost six months to work with Dato' Ali Abdullah in setting up the Islamic Secretariat in late 1969. Together with Dato' Ali I spent some days with the Tunku in Karachi during the OIC Conference in December 1970 and subsequently in Jeddah to start up the Islamic Secretariat.

It was while we were in Jeddah that I was persuaded, despite my lame and unconvincing protestations, to join him in Mecca for the *umrah*. I was in the end happy that I went for the Tunku was given the rare honour of being taken into the *kaabah*. On the few occasions when I accompanied Dato' Ali Abdullah to see the Prime Minister at his office, part of which was also his residence, Tunku never failed to tell his wife how much I looked like my father. My father was keen on football and used to play the game with the Tunku when he was the District Officer in Kulim. This was as close as I would get to the Tunku.

At the time of our second Prime Minister Tun Abdul Razak, I was a mid-level diplomat and felt more at ease at that level. I worked closely with him on ASEAN matters, in particular the proposal for the establishment of ZOPFAN, and also on issues of the OIC and NAM. He was kind and generous in his attitude towards me. For example when there was a slight glitch in my handling of the ASEAN Foreign Ministers'

At Sarajevo airport with Tan Sri Kadir Mohamed, the Head of Policy Planning to my far right, and Zulkephli, my special assistant on my right.

Meeting with Prime Minister Dr. Haris Silajdzic at the Presidency during my first visit to Sarajevo. Also present were Tan Sri Kadir Mohamed and Ku Jaafar, Chargé d'Affaires, Malaysian Embassy Croatia.

Waiting for the Armoured Personnel Carrier at the Holiday Inn along 'Sniper Alley', Sarajevo. It was at this spot where a Serb girl was killed by Serb sniper fire from across the hill.

With President Alija Izetbegovic at his hotel suite in Geneva, discussing plans for assistance to Bosnia.

In discussion with Gen. Rasim Delic (third from left) and Ambassador Mustafa Bijedic of Bosnia-Herzegovina (fourth from left) at the OIC contact group meeting in Kuala Lumpur.

With President Ibrahim Rugova of Kosova in Pristina.

With Gen. Ramush Haradinaj. On my left is Lt. Gen. Maulub, Chief of Military Intelligence, Mindef.

With Ali Mahdi on my left, Lt. Gen. Maulub (centre) and Hussein Aidid (far right) in my office, 1997.

Meeting with Ali Mahdi at his residence in Mogadishu.

This was how the Somalis lived, 1995.

Exchanging of gifts with Farrah Aidid in Baidoa, 1996. The walking stick, his gift to me, is still in my possession.

Meeting with President Omar al-Bashir of Sudan, circa 1997.

With Dr. John Garang, Chairman/Commander of SPLM/SPLA at his residence on the outskirts of Nairobi, Kenya.

On the road to Baghdad.

Laying the wreath at the Martyrs' Tomb in Baghdad.

meeting in Kuala Lumpur to launch ZOPFAN on 27 November, 1971 he did not seem angry and in fact joked about it with me.

He had on occasion wanted me to be posted to London for reasons I never learned. The last was in late 1975 when I was still in Bangkok, enjoying my second posting in Thailand. He instructed the Ministry that I be moved from Bangkok to London. However, fate intervened when a few weeks later news reached us in Bangkok that he had passed away in London. I was posted back to Kuala Lumpur instead, a plan which had been put forward earlier by Tan Sri Zakaria Ali, at the time sitting as Secretary-General. He and I had worked together in New York when he was Malaysia's Permanent Representative to the UN and I was his Deputy.

I was not disappointed by this change of destination. In London I would invariably have been involved in too much protocol work, for which I had neither the inclination nor the flair.

To be back in Kuala Lumpur handling Southeast Asian affairs was more appealing, and challenging. It was an interesting time for the region. The war in Vietnam had ended, the Americans had left, Vietnam was united, new governments had taken over in Phnom Penh and Vientiane, and the saga of the Vietnamese boat people was just beginning. These were demanding times and it was hugely rewarding for me to head the Southeast Asia and Oceania Division and handle these issues. In this capacity I would now be working under the Prime Ministership of Tun Hussein Onn, the third Prime Minister.

Tun Hussein Onn took over the premiership after the death of Tun Abdul Razak. Chandran Jeshurun stated, "He was never really 'groomed' to be Prime Minister and, consequently, it is usually believed that he was distantly aware of the goings on in the world of Wisma Putra... ."[209]

There were very few occasions when I was directly involved with him in any discussions. Sometimes I accompanied the Foreign Minister

Tengku Ahmad Rithauddeen, or the Secretary-General, for meetings with him. On the one occasion when I, on my own, represented Wisma Putra it was to discuss an issue sensitive enough for him to call in Tan Sri Ghazali Shafie, the Home Minister, and Dato' Malik Aziz, the Secretary of the National Security Council. It was an issue concerning a neighbouring country. We briefed him on what was happening and what we were doing in dealing with this issue. He was visibly angry and quick to reprimand us. "What you are doing is a bottomless pit. You cannot do to others what you do not want others to do to you." He called for an immediate halt to that particular piece of work. Tun Hussein was upright and righteous to a fault. I was thinking to myself that other leaders were not of the same mould and in furthering their country's strategic interests would not have thought twice of resorting to any kind of subterfuge.

He was also thorough to a fault and took time when vital issues were presented to him for quick decisions. Thus Wisma Putra was haltingly slow in reacting to issues that needed to be confronted quickly. I had great difficulty in connecting with him, and I am sure I was not the only one. However, after he left office and on the few occasions when I met him alone, he seemed to be in a different mode, friendly and approachable. He talked to me about some of his disappointments and regrets and expressed how fearful he was of where the country was heading.

The way foreign policy was handled changed when Dr. Mahathir became the Prime Minister and it was under his Prime Ministership that I was appointed Secretary-General. I worked under him for close to seven and a half years, and I would like to reflect at some length on that experience.

It is a well-known fact that Dr. Mahathir was deeply involved in foreign policy. Indeed, he was more involved than Tunku Abdul

Rahman, who was also the Foreign Minister, and Tun Abdul Razak who also held the portfolio of Foreign Minister until 1975 when he appointed Tengku Ahmad Rithauddeen to handle the job. Tun Abdul Razak was also deeply involved in the goings-on in Wisma Putra and would drop in from time to time to discuss matters with the Secretary-General Tan Sri Zaiton Ibrahim. Tun Abdul Razak was the architect of the shift in Malaysia's foreign policy from a pro-west to a more neutral and non-aligned stance, a policy change that was widely accepted by many. But it was Dr. Mahathir, even though he never concurrently held the Foreign Affairs portfolio, who took it a step further. He transformed the way foreign policy was handled.

It was within this changed situation, a situation new to us practitioners in Wisma Putra but refreshing all the same, that I began my stint as head of Wisma Putra. Stories abounded that Dr. Mahathir was strict, stern, that he was an unforgiving disciplinarian and perfectionist and could not stand fools. And, of course, having been Prime Minister for almost a decade, I knew how disciplined a man he was, personally and professionally. Despite warnings from some colleagues I actually looked forward to working under a Prime Minister whose aggressive and pro-active—even at times provocative—style had already carried the country to a new level of international standing. Having handled CHOGM and the G-15 Summit in Kuala Lumpur during my first year in office, I felt I had by then sufficiently won his confidence and trust. With the stress and tension of the two big events behind me I began in earnest to run the Ministry. I found that it was easier to handle my job with Dr. Mahathir as Prime Minister because decisions were taken on a personalised basis. What this meant was that when it came to foreign policy the Prime Minister was hands-on. Wisma Putra became, to all intents and purposes, an extension of the Prime Minister's Office.

I moved quite freely whenever there was need for me to consult the Prime Minister. The personality of the Foreign Minister Datuk Seri Abdullah Badawi, facilitated this. He gave me a free hand to run the Ministry and allowed it also to be *my* Ministry, so to speak. There were frequent consultations with the Prime Minister and the ever accommodating attitude of Tan Sri Aziz Ismail, the Prime Minister's Principal Private Secretary, facilitated my easy access to him. I never experienced difficulties when seeking an appointment, and at times he would call me on the phone either to seek my views or to give me instructions on some issue at hand.

I realised soon enough that his confidence in me grew in the wake of many issues I put on his desk, issues that were at times delicate but which needed to be presented to him as they were, warts and all. Somehow or other I seemed to be able to do this, and in the process put my head on the chopping block, as it were.

I have always wanted to be true to myself and in putting forward my views I was as frank and straightforward as I could be, quite often with more directness than subtlety. Having escaped with my head so many times I got a reputation for being someone who could get things across to him. Sometimes I would actually change his mind if reason convinced him. For example, in the privacy of his office, I managed to change decisions he had taken earlier, as at the meeting to discuss Pulau Layang-Layang where I managed to persuade him to accept the position I put forward (see Chapter 12). I took much personal satisfaction in this episode.

It was immensely rewarding to work with a Prime Minister who knew exactly what he wanted but who was also someone who responded to logic. I would not say that Dr. Mahathir listened to me but rather that he listened to reason.

There were also times when he was critical of the Ministry or some of our diplomats. This gave me the opportunity to tell him about the problems that I faced regarding the competency of some of our diplomats, in particular their lack of proficiency in English. I have always maintained that the only tool we have in the diplomatic service is language and this, invariably, meant the English language. I explained to the Prime Minister how worried I was for the future when these officers would be moving up the career ladder and handling important functions in the Ministry or as heads of mission abroad.

This was how the idea of the Institute of Diplomacy and Foreign Relations (IDFR) was born, an institute to train and mould young diplomats into astute diplomatic officials with fluency in English and adequate social skills, giving them confidence to hold their own in their interaction with foreign colleagues and to assertively promote the interests of the country.

I had a tough time negotiating the establishment of IDFR with the Public Services Department. Just when I thought that we had settled everything the Chief Secretary to the Government Tan Sri Ahmad Sarji, insisted that the head of the institute be someone senior from the home sector and that several senior administrative posts in the institute also be given to them. He even raised the possibility that a committee be formed, perhaps with him as head, although he did not say so, to manage Wisma Putra and the IDFR. I strongly rejected these preposterous attempts to take control of the Ministry. Dato' Albert Talalla, a former ambassador to the United States of America, became the first head of the institute. I doubt if I would have got my way without the support and intervention of the Prime Minister.

Following a cabinet decision the Institute was launched by the Prime Minister in August 1991 to coincide with the first ever Malaysian Heads of Mission Conference, an initiative that I had raised with him earlier and to which he readily gave his approval. I also managed, in due time, to obtain his agreement on the holding of a conference of Malaysian Honorary Consuls, arguing that they be invited to see the changes that had taken place in Malaysia. After all they were doing good work for the country at their own pleasure. This was not only to say thank you to them but to get them to be more connected to the country.

It was also a known fact that on several major issues Wisma Putra was not consulted by the Prime Minister but was told later of his decisions and instructed to carry them out. A case in point was his proposed EAEC (see Chapter 11), and also Malaysia's involvement in the war in Bosnia-Herzegovina and the civil war in Sudan. To be fair, in pointing out this flaw in the management of foreign policy, he did also give his approval, when I brought it up with him directly, to involve the country in helping to find a solution to the strife in Somalia and to assist the Kosovars in their struggle against the Serbian regime. But a glaring example of Wisma Putra being left out completely was when Finance Minister Tun Daim Zainuddin, on 27 November, 1990, signed what is known as Points of Agreement (POA) with Singapore Prime Minister Lee Kuan Yew. Wisma Putra got the first whiff of the POA through the *Singapore Straits Times*. It is a gross irony that the Ministry charged with all aspects of foreign relations was left completely in the dark on this all important agreement with a foreign country.

On one other occasion I found it difficult to accept Dr. Mahathir's decision to send Dato' Abu Hassan, the Foreign Minister, to Los Angeles to meet with James Baker, the American Secretary of State, with regard to the pending UN Security Council resolution on Iraq. Chandran Jeshurun has covered the whole episode of the Iraqi invasion of Kuwait and the subsequent Malaysian vote for the UN Resolution, which resulted in the invasion of Iraq.[210] I will not go over the grounds again but only say that it would have been sufficient if Razali Ismail, our Permanent Representative to the UN, informed the US Permanent Representative of our position, the telephone call by President George Bush to the Prime Minister notwithstanding. Malaysia has always adhered to the UN principle on the threat or use of force in international relations. When Iraq invaded Kuwait in 1991, it breached the UN Charter. For sure, this was an invasion by a Muslim country on a smaller and weaker Muslim country. Given the positions we had taken in the past in similar circumstances our position at the Security Council on Resolution 678 was clear to me and that was to support the resolution. If there was any *faux pas* in our supporting the resolution as some claimed, to send Dato' Abu Hassan to explain to James Baker was to me the *faux pas*.

Long after the dust of Desert Storm[211] had settled I was urgently summoned to the Prime Minister's office. I was told that he had received a call from British Prime Minister John Major, seeking his urgent help. Two Britons had been arrested for having wandered into Iraq without realising it and were now being held in prison. I was instructed to travel to Baghdad as the Prime Minister's special representative to seek an appointment with the Iraqi President. As the no-fly zone was still in force, I and my assistants travelled by air to Amman and then by road to Baghdad in a rented four-wheeler. I failed, however, to get to meet Saddam Hussein, and met instead Tariq Aziz, the Deputy Prime Minister, who, after I had explained to him the purpose of my visit, told me, "I will look into the matter and give it my full attention." In diplomatic parlance this could be regarded as giving hope to my mission.

About one and a half months later, back in Kuala Lumpur, I received a call from the Prime Minister himself to say that the two Britons had been released. John Major had called to thank him for his intervention. Soon after I received a letter from Prime Minister John Major to thank me for my efforts.

One of the more delicate moments in my dealings with Dr. Mahathir was when I had to raise with him the proposed visit of Australian Prime Minister Paul Keating to Malaysia. Since Keating's undiplomatic remarks about Mahathir's non-appearance at the APEC Summit two years earlier, the two men had not been on good terms. Mike Costello, my Australian counterpart, came to speak to me about the visit. I reasoned with the Prime Minister and he accepted my reasoning. Thus in early January, 1996 the Australian Prime Minister made his official visit to Malaysia.

In many ways for me at the Foreign Ministry what Dr. Mahathir had created was a fresh new way of pursuing foreign policy. It was a self-assured and assertive quest for a global centric goal that harnessed regional and Third World groupings and pivoted on the interests of the developing world, in which Malaysia was becoming one of the leading players.

At the epicentre of this was his push for a more substantial role for ASEAN; radiating outward from this was his drive, always in top gear, to propel Malaysia ever forward, whether leading the global fight against poverty, getting the Third World to play an affirmative role, encouraging South-South interaction, on berating and challenging US unilateralism and proposing instead an Asian brand of effective but not a bullying type of multilateralism. He questioned the monopoly of the west on issues of common concern to mankind, like the Antarctica Treaty, and decried the lack of transparency in international organisations, especially the UN Security Council.

Of course, this kind of tough and straightforward talk and with it the projection of Malaysia as a middle power caused some unease, not least from our neighbours and others who found themselves at the wrong end of his verbal lashing. Indonesia frowned at the inappropriate language sometimes used by Dr. Mahathir, the leader of a 'small' country and some media commentators condescendingly called him a 'little Sukarno'.[212] But Dr. Mahathir understood clearly that foreign policy is a nation's frontier to the world. It cannot be divorced from political, security and economic issues especially those of concern to the global well-being of humanity and the interests of smaller states and those in the region.

Malaysia's diplomatic strategies have always called for the adoption of principled positions, which are fully supportive of the accepted tenets of international relations, including support for the principles and purposes of the United Nations. The country's diplomatic strategies have always been crafted with these facts in mind, together with an awareness of ourselves as a small developing country caught inextricably in the web of international politics. Ours has been a delicate balancing act, the act of maintaining equilibrium between national and regional concerns on the one hand and political and economic requirements of the country on the other.

No one knew this better than Dr. Mahathir. His was a diplomacy that was both confrontational and effective although occasionally rash and, if I may add, impulsive. For me, having been brought up in the old style of doing business, this was a new approach. It was an ambitious and confident policy which fed off the confidence and self-assured leadership of the Prime Minister. Our confidence in our ability not only to do international relations but do them well grew—and I grew alongside it. Unlike some others, I did not find Dr. Mahathir intimidating, nor did I find working for him to be a roller-coaster ride. Knowing what he expected from us, we, in Wisma Putra, tried to live up to those expectations. I myself truly enjoyed this period of my career.

I was therefore pleased when I was asked to continue to work for him after my retirement, this time in the capacity of his special envoy. This became another chapter of my life where diplomacy took me further than I could have imagined into lands where suffering and war raged.[213] This was taking the battle for universal principles far from our own shores.

### Endnotes

209   Chandran Jeshurun, *op. cit.*, p. 369.
210   Chandran Jeshurun, *op. cit.*, p. 223.
211   Code name for the 1991 Invasion of Iraq by US and US-led Coalition forces.
212   See Barry Wain, *Malaysian Maverick: Mahathir Mohamad in Turbulent Times*, Singapore, Palgrave-Macmillan, 2009, p. 265.
213   As narrated in some earlier chapters.

# Postscript

Having been involved in the practice of diplomacy and the formulation and evolution of Malaysia's foreign policy for some 35 years, I have not proffered any theoretical or conceptual explanations. The reason for my having avoided such an approach is simple. I am not a theorist nor an academic, but a practitioner and as such, I know that international relations are innately unsettled, and complex, and cannot be reduced to an intellectual order because of its ever changing character. Some may claim foreign policy to be predictive, scientific and deductive but it is not. I therefore will have to leave it to the theorists to provide the theoretical explanations to the course of Malaysia's foreign relations.

It is foolhardy to assume that one can predict and manage the future of international relations. The best we can do is to evaluate and manage events that affect our national well-being.[214] As a small, developing country, Malaysia was never isolated from the external forces influencing its political, socio-economic and cultural configuration. Some may say that Malaysia is vulnerable to these forces which can influence its national make-up and daily existence but I like to think that Malaysia's strength lies in its ability to adopt, adapt and adjust to the external elements coursing through the national fabric and having significant impact on the nation.

Let me, as a start, explain the objectives of Malaysia's foreign policy. Like any sovereign state, Malaysia's policy is based on the need to protect, defend and promote its national interests. As Machiavelli said, "To understand foreign policy is to think in terms of public interest."[215] Malaysia has been fortunate that since its independence its policymakers have been persistent in ensuring that communitarian and normative values form part of that public interest. It is for this reason that Malaysia has been a strong proponent of issues, which have communitarian appeals. This is a natural course of action because it is a small and developing country and is not in a position to subscribe to cosmopolitan logic inherent among great powers. Being communitarian means being sensitive to the moral obligations expected of the members of the international community.

It is for this reason that one main thrust of its foreign policy has been to be at the forefront of participating and assisting in international humanitarian disaster reliefs and participating in international peace-keeping efforts in troubled areas across the globe.[216] And it has done so on the principle of impartiality and universality—which means that it does not discriminate against someone merely because they are far away from us or we from them.[217] Another conceptual lacuna is the emphasis on individual rights at the expense of the rights of the community. While western human rights concept puts greater emphasis on the rights of the individual, Malaysia emphasises the importance of community rights over the individual. We have seen how in the name of individual rights and freedom, racial prejudices and animosities are resurfacing to the extent that we are witnessing the rise of new forms of racism and xenophobia increasingly manifested in violence in many parts of the world.

Foreign policy also incorporates the economic interests of a country. In fact every foreign policy of every sovereign government will inevitably have an economic dimension. For some, economics may even provide the thrust of the government's foreign policy. This has currently gained significance in the international economic context where nations are persistently seeking entry into foreign markets. Of late there has been much talk about globalisation and its rather dreary outlook about what it holds for small developing countries. Globalisation as interpreted by the North means a borderless world where every country, big or small, rich or poor, would have unrestricted access to each other's markets. It means competing on equal footing in a world which is already unequal. The effects of economic globalisation would thus lead to the submergence of small companies in the developing countries as large international corporations based in the North take over. The little players from the small countries would be absorbed and disappear. It would leave weak economies exposed and unable to protect themselves as a globalised world would belong to the powerful dominant countries.[218] This is the implication of the cosmopolitan outlook, as I mentioned previously, against the developing countries' communitarian approach.

However, globalisation is a process that cannot be reversed. Thus, the country will be expected to be resilient in the wake of the new economic challenges and our foreign policy must serve both to protect and promote Malaysia's national economic interests. Only through such efforts can Malaysia meet the challenges of increasing globalisation.

Another challenge to the conduct of foreign policy is the question of global governance. Who in actual fact rules the world today? The concept of 'governance' has served to blur the distinction between what is governmental and what is not. The Commission on Global Governance defines 'governance' as 'the sum of the many ways individual institutions, public and private, manage their common affairs'.[219] It follows that 'a wide range of actors may be involved in any one area of governance', including that of international affairs.

There is increasing tendency that the central position of the state is now challenged by transnational organisations, which have an increasingly predominant role in the international arena, with some suggesting that *power* politics has been replaced by *issue* politics. Without getting into this debate, I can agree that these extra-state actors, whether or not they have effective power, certainly do have influence.[220]

The world media is one such actor with both power and influence. They play a critical role not just in *presenting* facts but in *interpreting* them, thereby not only *educating* the public but also *influencing* public opinion, which served in turn to change, in some cases, the attitudes of governments. Foreign policy practitioners need to be aware of these new forces which are not always cognizant of, let alone interested in, protecting the national interest of any particular country.[221]

I am not advocating that we subscribe to the view that the state should continue to be in full charge because these non-state actors at times do have a role to play in the international community. Instead, I believe it is within our interest to be aware of the prevailing forces around us and that while we interact with these forces, the protection of our national interest should always be at the back of our minds.

The basis of any foreign policy formulation is the national interest. This is the overriding edict for diplomats; it cannot be otherwise. Foreign policy must be based on national interests and this cannot be compromised. This in turn is derived from the national character, aspiration and values. The very character of Malaysia's existence is founded on cultural pluralism and social justice built upon communal tolerance and individual dignity. These broad principles and values are the core precepts by which the country has been governed through its more than 50 years of independence.

These are also universal values of the global community today. They *are also the core tenets and values of Islam.* Thus in pursuit of its foreign policy over the past 50 years Malaysia, while upholding strongly the universal values of human rights, individual dignity and freedom and support for national sovereignty and territorial integrity, generally found broad-based support for these policies from its diverse population and citizenry across all races and religions. These values, in fact, have parallels in every religion and civil society in the world. Thus to my mind by acting in accord with our national conscience we would indeed have embraced the core tenets and values of Islam.

But it is important to note that according to Tunku Abdul Rahman, our first Prime Minister, Malaysia is not a Muslim *state.* To quote, "All talk on Islamic States is just an empty dream. No man in his right sense would accept a nation which bases its political administration on religion, and in a country like Malaysia with its multiracial and multi-religious people, there is no room for an Islamic State." [222] Dr. Mahathir, as Prime Minister, at one point stated that Malaysia was a Muslim country. But this was for domestic consumption; he did not mean that Malaysia is an Islamic state. *Muslim country* and *Islamic state* convey distinctly different meanings. A Muslim country simply means a country in which Muslims are a majority, or where Muslims live. It does not denote an *Islamic theocracy*, an Islamic State.

By the Constitution 'Islam is the religion of the Federation; but other religions may be practised in peace and harmony in any part of the Federation.' [223] It is thus constitutionally embedded as a pluralistic state with a multi-ethnic and multi-religious population. Within this context it is, however, possible to discuss the incorporation of Islamic values and understanding into policy formulation, including Malaysia's foreign policy.

The current divisive internal political debate over the status and introduction of Islamic values and principles into foreign policy is inherently irrelevant and distracting. It is not in the national interest to compartmentalise our practice of diplomacy into being Islamic and non-Islamic. Even though the formulation of our foreign policy could be influenced, or even guided, by the core tenets of Islam, we are a pluralistic state and must act in the national interests of all citizens following universal principles. That these are in accord with Islam's own universal moral and ethical precepts would naturally deepen the support of our Muslim citizens and strengthen our national commitment.

There is, however, a notion in some quarters that Islam influences Malaysia's foreign policy only to the degree that it does not run counter to our interpretation of our national interests. I see nothing wrong in this profile. A nation state must necessarily project and protect its national interests but would inevitably be influenced by the inherent core values of its faith. While faith may not be a determinant of our action it certainly provides a guiding hand. If national interests are not treated as our foremost objective we could end up being stateless and subjugated. This is not what foreign policy management and diplomacy is all about.

At the other extreme of the pendulum, there are cynics, as there always will be, who maintain that our particular concern and involvement in Bosnia-Herzegovina in the 1990s was primarily driven by our rage and anxiety in witnessing an ethnic Muslim group being systematically exterminated in the heart of Europe. But, if that were the case, then how do we justify our active participation internationally in finding durable solutions to internal non-Islamic conflicts, for example, in the Congo, Angola, Cambodia and the Great Lakes region of Africa? And the Bosnian war effort was supported by the vast majority of Malaysians regardless of creed or race.

We were also very clear on the limits of any support we might give to any pressure or interest groups. We have never encouraged any group, Muslim or not, in a quest for self-determination within an established and *legitimate* state. There are large Muslim minorities in several ASEAN states. We have been invited to mediate in some, but we have never used the Muslim card to subvert another state. There are too many worms in that can. A minority in rebellion against an established government is doomed to backwardness at best, and extermination at worst, through such a seditious act.

As a successful pluralistic state, Malaysia has proven that it is possible for different ethnic groups to co-exist peacefully through tolerance, accommodation and compromise. This was the premise upon which we offered our good offices to mediate between the belligerent factions in Somalia and Sudan, and in neighbouring states who requested our involvement. A recent case in point was our mediatory role in the conflict between the Bangsamoro and the Philippine Government. In the case of Sudan we, in fact, leaned towards getting a fair deal for the south Sudanese who are Christians and animists.

Fundamentally, to be credible, we can only pursue and project our national interests if, in our own house, our actions are consistent with what we profess. But now, more than ever, Malaysia is faced with increasingly discordant religious and ethnic issues. The national image of unity in diversity and the integrity of the rule of law that we have so effectively projected as a pillar of our foreign policy seem under threat. Our standing as a harmonious, tolerant, pluralistic society that has transcended our differences and succeeded in nation building for five decades is showing signs of erosion.

This national image of unity and harmony has been a salient aspect of our foreign policy because it actually reflected a domestic reality. It was the product of a communally meaningful relationship between our different racial groups themselves. Mutual dependence creates a much valued sense of identity as well as a sense of security.[224] But at the moment of writing the ground on which we stand does not seem as steady and firm as it should be. This has to be looked into and worked on for it is the very foundation of our nationhood, indeed our very survival.

Turning to the subject of who I am and what I hold dear in my personal capacity as a diplomat, it is not everyone who can claim that carrying out one's professional duty also brought the fulfilment of one's beliefs and convictions. I was blessed that this was the case for me. I have always felt strongly that those who are less advantaged for reasons beyond their control cannot be asked to suffer the pains of inequality. I hold this dictum close to my heart. I do recognise that diplomacy, where the overriding dictum is pursuit of national interests, is an unlikely arena for the fulfilment of moral values. But I was gratified to be in a position to combine my moral quest with the practice of my profession. The work I was doing for the Balkan states and those in Somalia and Sudan and with the Vietnamese boat people and the Chams in Cambodia were carried out with moral conviction as well.

There are questions that might be asked about how and why we made some of the choices that we did. These are the postscript questions and thus, the answers I provide are subjective and may look like hindsight to critics. But to me they are honest truth. For example, during my time heading the Foreign Ministry, what was our involvement in Bosnia-Herzegovina, Somalia and Sudan all about? Was there any hidden agenda? Was our involvement really premised solely on the universal principles of fair play and justice, our sincere desire to support desperate nations in need of help to survive? Or could it be because it involved a nation with a Muslim population that was threatened with extinction? The fact that the victims were Muslims could have strengthened our commitment, but it was not the primary motivation for our involvement. The threat of extinction and helplessness in the face of aggression was the primary motivation.[225]

Or could the desire of getting a foothold in trade have been behind our actions? Or perhaps the prospect of oil exploration in Sudan and Somalia, noting that around that time our national oil company PETRONAS was prospecting for oil in the horn of Africa? Could this have influenced our decisions? I am not too sure how to answer these questions. All countries have economic interests and Malaysian businesses are just as quick to grab a chance as anyone else.

But I can honestly say that nothing of the kind was in my mind or in my brief. Our diplomacy was about finding solutions to the conflicts. If peace was established and that facilitated trade or oil prospecting then that was the next step. It was not why I was shivering in a hotel room in Kosovo or keeping my head down in a van in Somalia. I did it in the course of pursuing justice and providing help for the disadvantaged and those in desperate need of help.

## Endnotes

214 I can emphasise this by quoting Tun Abdul Razak's words to the ASEAN Foreign Ministers in Kuala Lumpur in May 1975, when he addressed the rest of the ASEAN 'family': "We are now at the threshold of exciting possibilities... This challenge brings new opportunities for peace, friendship and cooperation for us to grasp... Which path shall we follow? The path of unity or the path of division? The path of cooperation or of confrontation? It is a historic choice...". See Johan Saravanamuttu, *The Dilemma of Independence: Two Decades of Malaysia's Foreign Policy 1957–1977*, USM Press, 1983, p. 104.

215 Machiavelli, Niccolo (1513), *The Prince*, New York, Penguin, 1975.

216 Such as sending our peace-keepers to serve with the UN in the various trouble spots in Africa, Europe and Asia and also readily extending disaster reliefs to states affected by natural disasters like earthquakes, famine, floods, etc. who appeal for help.

217 Peter Singer, 'Famine, Affluence and Morality' in *International Ethics*, New Jersey, Princeton, 1990.

218  Martin Khor, 'Globalisation: Implications for development policy', *Third World Resurgence*, No.74, 1995.

219  See Peter Marshall, Diplomacy Beyond 2000, 'Are Diplomats Necessary?', The Diplomatic Academy of London, 2 April, 1996.

220  See Ann Hawkins, Karen Litfin in Lipschutz and Conca (Eds.), *The State and Social Power in Global Environmental Politics*, New York, Colombia University Press, 1993.

221  See Keith Hindell, 'The Influence of the Media on Foreign Policy', *International Relations*, Vol. XII, No. 4, April 1995.

222  Tunku Abdul Rahman, *Political Awakening*, Pelanduk Publications, 1986. p. 105.

223  Article 3 (1) of the Federation of Malaysia Constitution.

224  See Paul Taylor and A.J.R. Groom, *International Organisations*, London, Frances Pinter Ltd., 1978.

225  We acted in the same manner with regard to Cambodia in the 1980s and 1990s following the Vietnamese occupation. There was no Muslim factor in this; it was just a case of a helpless nation threatened with subjugation.

# Index

# C

# About the Author

Tan Sri Ahmad Kamil Jaafar is one of Malaysia's most distinguished diplomats, well known within the ASEAN region and Asian and Third World caucus for his diplomatic skills and role as negotiator and mediator. Having grown up in the throes of a budding nation fighting for independence, Tan Sri Kamil is very much a man committed to advancing the nation's interests and always striving for the betterment of his country, and for universal justice and fair play.

Tan Sri Kamil was born in Kulim, Kedah on 27 August, 1937. He studied at High School Bukit Mertajam before going on to further his studies at the prestigious Malay College Kuala Kangsar. He then obtained his degree in history from the University of Malaya, graduating in 1962.

He started his career in the diplomatic service upon graduation and retired as Secretary-General of the Malaysian Ministry of Foreign Affairs, the most senior office for a career diplomat, ending an illustrious career spanning 34-odd years. Following his retirement, he was appointed as Special Envoy of the Prime Minister, a post which he still holds today.